THE CZECHOSLOVAK
POLITICAL TRIALS
1950–1954

The Czechoslovak Political Trials 1950-1954

The Suppressed Report of
the Dubček Government's Commission
of Inquiry, 1968

EDITED WITH A PREFACE AND A
POSTSCRIPT BY JIŘÍ PELIKÁN

STANFORD UNIVERSITY PRESS

STANFORD, CALIFORNIA

1971

Stanford University Press
Stanford, California
© 1970 by Europa Verlag Wien
This translation © 1971 by Macdonald & Co.
(Publishers) Ltd
First published in Great Britain in 1971
Stanford edition printed in the U.S.A.
ISBN 0-8047-0769-3
LC 70-150328

CONTENTS

PUBLISHER'S NOTE

THIS edition of the Report has been prepared from the Czech original by a team of translators. The text is given in full, as is the Appendix containing a draft resolution 'on the completion of Party rehabilitation', for submission to the Central Committee. A second appendix (which contains a draft speech for the Commission's Chairman to make when introducing the Report at a plenary session of the Central Committee) has, however, been omitted from this edition, since to a very large extent it duplicates material contained in the body of the Report or in the draft resolution.

Since the Report is a historical document, its substance has been retained intact; in one case what appears to be an inaccurate or incomplete set of figures has been accompanied by a '[sic]'. For the same reason, the vocabulary and style, too, have in general been retained, even when – most notably in speeches quoted verbatim – there is clearly room for improvement. One term which has, however, been modified slightly in the interests of clarity is the Czech word *deformace*, which means literally 'deformations'. This expression, on the use of which Mr Pelikán comments in his Postscript, and which often means in effect little more than 'abuses', has usually been rendered as 'distortions' (with or without the implied 'of socialism') or by a phrase incorporating the word 'deformed'.

References in the text to documentary sources are given in the same form as the original, except that the abbreviation ACC CPC has been used throughout for 'Archives of the Central Committee, Communist Party of Czechoslovakia'. The vast majority, possibly all, of the references, are in fact to these archives, though the fact has not been consistently stated.

Mr Pelikán's Preface and Postscript have, with his full consent, been slightly abridged for this edition. Conversely, one or two new insertions have been made by him in order to

7

keep these contributions as up-to-date as the exigencies of publication schedules allow. A few small corrections to the supplementary material have also been made.

Footnotes in roman type form an integral part of the Report: *footnotes in italic represent the work of Mr Pelikán or of the translators*. [A few explanatory interpolations have also been made in the text of the Report; they are enclosed, like this sentence, in *square* brackets.] The biographical notes incorporated in the Index are the work of Mr Pelikán, as edited by the translators.

PREFACE

THE Report here submitted to the public, one of many documents from the famous 'Prague Spring' of 1968, contains the findings of a Commission set up in April of that year by the Central Committee of the Czechoslovak Communist Party with powers to make a final inquiry into the notorious political trials of the 1950s – especially the show trial of the Party's General Secretary, Rudolf Slánský. Another of the Commission's purposes was to examine why, when Antonín Novotný held power, every move to redress the wrongs was sidetracked long after the trials were known to have been rigged from beginning to end.

This resolve to right the wrongs of the past was an integral part of the new course initiated in Czechoslovakia in January 1968, when Novotný was replaced as First Secretary of the Party by Alexander Dubček. The meeting in April that appointed the Trials Commission also adopted the Party's Action Programme – the programme of that remarkable movement that was to acquire the title of 'socialism with a human face'.

High among the priorities of the reform movement was the demand for an investigation of the political trials with a view to rehabilitating their innocent victims (as had occurred in the other socialist countries, to a greater or lesser extent, after the Soviet Twentieth Party Congress), uncovering the sources of the evils, and installing safeguards against any repetition of such events. This demand was understandable, for the contrast between the ideals of socialism and the reality, disfigured as it was by the show trials, was among the mainsprings of the political crisis that had been maturing for years until it erupted with volcanic force in January 1968.

The documents contained in this Report – to this day unpublished and top secret in Czechoslovakia – and the proceedings of the Party's Fourteenth Congress throw light on the

9

country's development over the twenty years prior to 1968, including the reasons that impelled the five Warsaw Pact countries to make their armed intervention in those fateful August days. The Report is the work of a team of historians, lawyers, political scientists and economists – all of them Communists – who were requested by the Party Central Committee to assist the Commission.

The documents, it might be said, give a somewhat simplified view of international and national events, especially for the decade 1945–55, but an analysis of these events was not the main purpose of the Report. It should be noted that this exceptionally demanding examination was made wholly in the spirit of Marxism, contrary to one of the stock arguments of Soviet and Czechoslovak neo-Stalinist propaganda, namely that between January and August 1968 Czechoslovakia had backslid into a kind of Western-style political liberalism, and even plotted a restoration of capitalism. On the contrary, the scrutinizing of the political system that had generated the evils – a scrutiny made in order to identify their sources in that system and lay down safeguards against any repetition – represented, in essence, an effort to complete the job that the Soviet Twentieth Congress had left unfinished. That Congress, while frankly denouncing the horrors of the Stalin era, refrained from any thorough-going analysis of how these things could take place under socialism – an omission to which the Italian Communist leader Togliatti drew attention and which was seen as such by all who regarded socialism as a viable alternative to capitalism.

Nothing would have been easier for the Czechoslovak Communists than to have thrown all responsibility onto departed leaders, Klement Gottwald, for instance, or the politically discredited Novotný. But that would have been out of tune with the spirit and aims of the reform movement, its determination to restore the true image of socialism – to give it, in fact, a human face.

A study of these documents, and of other offshoots of the Prague Spring, will refute yet another accusation assiduously circulated – that the Czechoslovak experiment, while well-meant, was naïve, ill-considered and ill-planned. True, the

Programme that began to take shape in January 1968 could not be drafted until the spring months (for under the one-man rule that prevailed until then joint work on any such document was impossible); but its guiding ideas had been maturing for some years, struggling to the surface in the sway of the conflict between the opposition and the regime. Only when the really critical issues – economic decline, the clashes with the intellectuals and the youth, inefficient management, the generation gap, discrimination against Slovakia, and, above all, the shadow cast by the political trials – fused as they did in January, did the subsequent explosion clear the way for systematic work on a comprehensive programme. Its purpose was to strengthen socialism, for the Czechoslovak Communists regarded the economic base not as the goal, but as a means of ensuring an ever greater freedom for man.

It is my firm conviction that the present Report, with its proposals for radical changes in the political system of socialism, together with the Action Programme, the draft of the new Party Rules and the plans for economic reform, show that, far from being a naïve or improvised venture, we have here a really serious attempt to shape a new model for a socialist society suited to Czechoslovakia's needs in the modern world.

And here we see the difference between the new Czechoslovak Party leadership's approach to the rehabilitation of those unjustly convicted, and that of the other socialist countries. This is not meant in any carping spirit. In those countries, some at least of the victims were rehabilitated, whether posthumously or in their lifetime, and some of them could return to public life; their sentences were declared invalid, and the sorry tale of socialism travestied and perverted was apparently at an end. But experience has shown that neither the declarations nor the good intentions of politicians are of any avail so long as the machine that produced the trials remains. That is why we are witnessing in some socialist countries a return – in less drastic forms, admittedly – to the curtailment of civil liberties, to censorship, to the restriction of discussion, and to a renewed persecution of critics of the regime, who once again are accused of being in the service of foreign interests or even of intelligence services. It is precisely because the Commission succeeded in uncovering the *whole truth* about the trials, including the Soviet share, the truth so carefully concealed for a full twenty years by the old leadership, that its Report has been prevented from seeing the light of day. Indeed, this desire to suppress the truth was among the reasons for the military invasion of Czechoslovakia.

The Report was originally to have been submitted to the Central Committee of the Party by the end of 1968. The inquiry had been completed in time, but on various pretexts the matter was continually postponed. The Chairman of the Commission, Jan Piller (now Chairman of the Trade Unions and a member of the Party Presidium), informed the leadership in the summer of 1968 that the Report contained such alarming facts that publication might touch off an explosion likely to undermine the authority of the Party and of some of its top men. This led some Presidium members to agree to postponement – indeed not a few of them saw these documents as a threat to themselves. The experts who had been working on them were instructed to turn in all their notes, denied further access to the records and bound to complete silence. True, even after the August invasion Dubček tried to have the Report submitted to the Central Committee, but after the blow he had suffered he no longer had the political strength to get this done. The documents were marked top secret and deposited in the archives, in the hope that they would never see the light of day. Thus it seems that the new leadership under Dr Husák is haunted by the same fear of the truth as was its predecessor under Novotný.

As for the Commission members, since 1968 their ranks have been decimated. To mention a few – Marie Miková, formerly Vice-President of the National Assembly, was expelled from the Central Committee of the Party in September 1969, later deprived of her parliamentary seat and in March 1970 expelled from the Party; Jiří Rypel, once Deputy Minister of the Interior, was dismissed from that post, and expelled from the Party Control Commission; Leopold Hofman, a Spanish Civil War veteran and Chairman of the Security Committee of Parliament, was deprived of his parliamentary seat and expelled from the Presidium of the Federal Assembly; Karel

Kaplan, a historian concerned with investigating the trials, was dismissed from the Party Control Commission and subjected to disciplinary proceedings for 'misusing archives', his book on the trials was suppressed before publication, and he himself was later expelled from the Party.

In short, the truth is again locked up in the safes – its suppression designed to pave the way for renewed injustices, persecutions and crimes. That is why we Czechoslovak Communists who have remained faithful to the policy of socialism with a human face believe it to be our duty to our Party, to our people, to the international Communist movement and to democratically-minded people throughout the world to publish the truth in the hope that it may help to prevent another tragedy. We recall the lesson of the 1950s, when victims of despotism were isolated and alone, with no one to defend them, because many people at home and abroad believed the charges and confessions, or could say truthfully that they did not know what it was all about. The reader of these documents will no longer be able to plead ignorance; everyone will now be aware of what is at stake. Thus, if the tragedy of the 1950s should be repeated, anyone who remains silent will bear his share of guilt.

We Czechoslovak Communists who have worked for years in the Party are conscious of bearing a measure of responsibility for the wrongs recounted here – some by actively participating in the events, others by vindicating them, others merely by remaining silent. For us especially it is not enough to plead ignorance, or blind faith in our leaders. Certainly the Report is right in pointing out that the degree of each man's responsibility depends on his position and the opportunity he had to discover the truth; but we must never forget the admirable statement by the Nuremberg court that blind obedience to criminal commands is not an extenuating circumstance. Indeed, one of the terrifying lessons of the trials is precisely the discovery that a blind loyalty can cause fearful injury to socialism, and that it is therefore the revolutionary duty of a Communist to refuse to carry out decisions that conflict with the law, with justice, with his conscience and with his socialist ideals.

That is why we have refused to vote for resolutions approving the occupation of our country by foreign troops and spreading lies about the socialist revival of 1968; that is why we condemn those who, invoking socialism and the Communist Party, are taking the same road that led our country and the international Communist movement to such a tragic crisis. Publication of these documents is a part of our endeavour.

Publication of this document abroad has caused confusion in the Party leadership, and successive changes of tactics: silence, denunciation (by the Editor of the official *Rudé Právo*) as 'another invention by western propaganda', and, on 10 July 1970, a statement by the Government press agency CTK referring to the Report on the one hand as a 'political pamphlet' while on the other hand informing us that 'the Party leadership considered this version in February 1969'. This statement merely confirms beyond doubt the authenticity of the Report, and the contention that the leadership refused to submit it to the Central Committee.

But the truth cannot be suppressed for ever; the public, in Czechoslovakia and in other countries, has been able to learn something from such books as *On Trial* by Artur London (London, Macdonald; New York, Morrow, 1970), *Sentenced and Tried* by Eugene Löbl (London, Elek, 1969), *Report on my Husband* by Josefa Slánská (London, Hutchinson, 1969) and *Truth Will Prevail* by Marian Šlingová (London, Merlin Press, 1968). Moreover, in 1968–9 Karel Kaplan and other historians concerned with the trials were able to publish some of their findings in Czechoslovak journals. Should the publication of the present document impel the Party leaders to reconsider at least some aspects of the subject and take steps to prevent a relapse, it will have served its purpose.

It will be noted how the accusations made against Czechoslovak Communists were first voiced in neighbouring countries – most vociferously by the Party leaders in Hungary and Poland. The theory was already being propounded – evidently with Stalin's agreement – that Czechoslovakia was the weakest link in the socialist camp, and that consequently she must be 'the centre of a widespread international conspiracy'. Rákosi, for instance, wrote to Gottwald declaring his lack of confidence

in two Czechoslovak Ministers – Václav Nosek, Minister of
the Interior and a Communist of long standing, and Vladimír
Clementis, Minister of Foreign Affairs, one of the Party's
most gifted men. The Hungarians even supplied a list of
'suspects' for the Czechs to arrest. Finally, the Hungarian and
Polish leaders expressed fears about the country's internal
stability, because *there were no Soviet troops on her soil*!

At first glance such accusations seem absurd; for Czechoslovakia was at that time the country with the most favourable
conditions for socialism. The pre-war Communist Party had
been a major, fully legal political party in a liberal parliamentary democracy, enjoying considerable prestige among
both workers and intellectuals; and this prestige had been enhanced still further by its record in the wartime resistance.
Most of its top men had worked under Gottwald's leadership
ever since 1929. And there was no lack of experienced and
courageous men, for many Czechoslovak Communists had
fought in the International Brigade in Spain, on the eastern or
western front in World War II, and in the Resistance at home.
In the first post-war elections, the Communist Party emerged
as the strongest single party; from 1946 it had provided the
Prime Minister and its representatives had filled all key
positions in the Government, including both Defence and
Security. A large section of the public supported socialism
and saw the Soviet Union as their liberator.

The other Eastern European countries were much less
favourably situated. Their Communist parties emerged into
the open, after decades of illegal existence, decimated by
persecution, with a shortage of experienced men, with back-
ward and war-ravaged economies, and in the face of considerable political opposition, including remnants of the fascist
influences in their former regimes. Why, then, the fears about
Czechoslovakia of all countries?

After 1945 the Czechoslovak Communists sought new ways of
passing from the national and democratic revolution of the
immediate post-war period to the socialist revolution. They
envisaged the transition as peaceful and democratic, and in
this they were absolutely serious. For a time it seemed that they
even had Stalin's support; one recalls, for instance, an inter-

view with British Labour MPs in which he mentioned the possibility of a peaceful transition from capitalism to socialism. Progressives throughout the world followed with keen interest this experiment, in which the Czechoslovak Communists and the other parties on the National Front were partners. Had it succeeded, it could have been of international significance.

Yet the Czechoslovak Communist Party abandoned the opportunity of winning a real majority of the people for its socialist programme and adopted instead the Stalinist theory of intensified class struggle, which had as its logical consequence the labelling of all political adversaries as enemies, spies and traitors, fit only to be liquidated. To this day it remains unclear exactly how this switch in policy came about; all the documents tell us is that in September 1948 'Gottwald managed to get Stalin's agreement' to some divergences in Czechoslovakia's programme of socialist advance. The new policy seems to have been a response, partly to sectarian pressures inside the Czechoslovak Party, but primarily to the change in Soviet strategy and tactics after 1947, a change highlighted by the setting up of the Cominform. By insisting on the Soviet model as compulsory for all socialist countries, the Cominform – disregarding Lenin's view about the need for different roads to socialism – abandoned this idea and later expressly condemned it. The condemnation was manifested most dramatically in the Cominform resolution on Yugoslavia, which set the sights for the coming political trials: bourgeois nationalism, cosmopolitanism, underestimating the class struggle, stressing national considerations and slighting the role of the Soviet Army as the Liberator – all these sins are castigated in the resolution as 'treason' or 'conspiracy'.

One has the impression that what really worried Stalin, Rákosi, Bierut and the other dogmatists about Czechoslovakia was precisely the home-grown roots of her Communist Party, a national base from which it could have found its own way to socialism, one in keeping with the country's needs and the outlook of its people. They evidently feared that this example might evoke similar trends in their own countries.

The sole explanation for the exceptional pressure on Czechoslovakia and the scale of the political murders there seems to be that Stalin and his colleagues had no use for a Czechoslovak Communist Party deeply implanted among the people, able to rely on public confidence and possessing a team of skilled and experienced leaders. From the Stalinist standpoint, it was much better in those days – and today, too – to have an inward-looking Party, relying on a bureaucracy, lacking personalities in its leadership and wholly dependent on Soviet power, including the presence of Soviet troops. For the Soviet Party, evidently, troops are the sole reliable custodian of socialism.

Here, too, is the key to a question frequently asked. Why, after the invasion of August 1968, could Czechoslovakia not salvage at least part of the post-January reforms? Why was the country thrown back so sharply, not just to her pre-January state, but to that of a much earlier period? Why do we hear the same accusations today that were heard twenty years ago, this time emanating from East Germany, Poland, Bulgaria – and, of course, Moscow? Why these accusations against the Czechoslovakia of 1968 when the Communist Party had won tremendous popularity and prestige, when the people had spontaneously declared themselves for socialism, when not a single factory was handed over to capitalists, not a single collective farm dissolved, when a galaxy of genuinely popular and respected Communist leaders had emerged? The reason of course is that, as in 1948–50, the Soviet leaders, or perhaps we should say the dogmatists among them, refused to allow any departure from their model of socialism. To forestall any similar response in their own country or the other socialist states, they had to inflict an exemplary punishment. The tragic error of Czechoslovakia's post-January policy was that she adhered in 1968 to the Gottwald maxim of 1948 that 'Czechoslovakia shall not be a second Yugoslavia'; in short, she staked her all on the hope that after the Twentieth Congress of the Soviet Communist Party the case of Yugoslavia could never be repeated. All the greater, then, the penalty she has had to pay for daring to venture out on her own road.

Today the Soviet leadership has assumed the mantle of the Cominform. In imposing discipline it is concerned not with the Czechoslovak Party alone, but with all potential heretics – the Italian Party, for example, with its mass support, its position in Parliament, its able leaders and its own ideas about the transition to socialism. For the same reason the Soviet leaders have no scruples about letting the Austrian Communist Party fall apart, and have broken up the Greek Party at the very time its leaders are being jailed and tortured by the Colonels. They view with equal distrust the Left in the West, the national liberation movements in Africa, Asia and Latin America, and any country that has gained liberation by its own revolutionary struggle, countries such as Yugoslavia, China, Cuba and Vietnam. For, where a revolution has produced national leaders from its own ranks, obedience to a centre – the Soviet Party – is harder to command than it is where a government has come to power under the protection of the Soviet Army. One can say that at the heart of this Stalinist attitude is a lack of confidence in the strength of revolutionary movements and an overestimation of its own role – in other words, a determination to be the sole arbiter of what is or is not in the interests of socialism, which is not always identical with the interests of Soviet power politics.

As with countries, so it is with individuals: the harshest repression, now as twenty years ago, is reserved for Communists who took part in the Spanish Civil War and in resistance movements at home or abroad during World War II – men who are capable of thinking for themselves, who enjoy public respect and support, who have proved that they are ready to give their lives for their ideals.

For the selfsame reasons that sent Rudolf Slánský, Vlado Clementis, Ludvík Frejka and other prominent Czechoslovak Communists to the gallows in 1950–54, Alexander Dubček was seized and subjected to atrocious treatment on 21 August 1968 – Dubček, a dedicated Communist, educated in the Soviet Union, so linked with that country by bonds of outlook and feeling that between January and August 1968 he chose to suffer in silence the unjust attacks made on his Party by the Soviet leaders rather than allow their publication to stir up criticism of the Soviet Union in his country; Dubček, a man convinced to the very last that after the Twentieth

Congress of the Soviet Party the sovereignty of a socialist country could never again be trampled underfoot, a man of rare courage and rectitude, dedicated to his country and his people, the man who became a symbol for socialism in Czechoslovakia and throughout the world. Although his captors were forced to free him, they saw to it that in the end he was driven from public life. Josef Smrkovský, too, a man with a record of gallantry during the Nazi occupation, a man who had fought for his country and his Party, had to go. František Kriegel and Josef Pavel, veterans of the International Brigade in Spain, men who saw their public work as a service to their Party and to socialism and who could not compromise their consciences – they, too, were removed from office. And with them hundreds, thousands, of sincere Communists who had devoted their lives to the cause and who saw in the Prague Spring a new opportunity, perhaps the last, to redress the wrongs and correct the errors of the past twenty years, to restore the appeal of socialism and the meaning of their lives.

Thus the prelude to the Czechoslovak tragedy was the Stalinist idea of hegemony, the concept of a deformed internationalism presupposing a blind obedience to the Soviet leadership – a principle which could perhaps be justified up to 1945, when the Soviet Union was the only socialist country, but which clearly necessitated reconsideration from the moment other socialist countries appeared on the scene.

The socialist countries of Eastern Europe had two alternatives – to follow the path taken by Tito and the Communist Party of Yugoslavia, which saved socialism in that country, or to submit to *Diktat*. Gottwald opted for the second alternative, with consequences that are known. But what perhaps is even more tragic is that some twenty years later Dubček should have been confronted with a similar choice and have submitted to the same iron logic as Gottwald, although he must have known that he was signing his own political death sentence and that of socialism in Czechoslovakia. Such was the persistence, in the Czechoslovak Communist Party, of the dogmatic idea that socialism cannot be built without the Soviet Union (even though the result may be a deformed socialism), since any other road but the Soviet leads back to capitalism. And this despite the examples of Yugoslavia, China and Vietnam, which show that today the capitalist alternative is not the only one, and that in the very interests of socialism it may be necessary to resist the monopoly pressures of the Soviet Union, even at the price of temporary conflict.

This attitude of the Czechoslovak Communists to the Soviet Union could have been regarded as their own affair if they had not in the meantime become the ruling party, responsible for the fate of the Czech and Slovak peoples. In this respect we Communists bear a heavy burden of responsibility, for we have delegated decisions on grave matters of internal policy, and even of our sovereignty, to a foreign centre and to men who even with the best will in the world have often failed to understand our way of thinking, our traditions, the nuances of our political life and the structure of our society.

How, indeed, did it come about that we allowed Soviet politicians to express doubts about Czechoslovak Communists – men who have proved their devotion to socialism in the pre-war Republic, in prison, at the front and in the resistance movements of World War II? Significantly, we find in the Report a letter from the Soviet Party to Gottwald expressing lack of confidence in General Svoboda, then Minister of National Defence, now President of the Republic, a man decorated as a Hero of the Soviet Union. What kind of equality is it when one Party alone has the right to vote no confidence in the recognized leaders of other parties, men who enjoy the trust of their people? And the result? At the instigation of a foreign Party, men are dismissed from their posts, brought to trial and executed, as happened in Czechoslovakia in 1949–54. Even in 1968 the Soviet leaders arrogated the right to say who should or should not hold office in our country; again, poorly informed though they are, they have compiled lists of functionaries whose removal they have demanded as a condition of their goodwill – again, also, in remarkable agreement with the leaders of certain other socialist countries. From Dresden to Sofia, Moscow, Čierna nad Tisou, Bratislava, to the negotiations at gunpoint in August 1968 – ceaseless interference by the Soviet Party and its allies in the internal affairs of Czechoslovakia, all of it cynically lauded as 'proletarian internationalism'. True, Dubček fought harder than Gottwald, he defended his colleagues and himself from unjust accusations, he tried to convince his accusers. But again the Czechoslovak Communists were on the defensive, again they failed to pose the crucial questions: whence your right to pass judgement on us? What if we were to ask how socialism is benefited by the military bureaucratic regime in East Germany, the displays of anti-semitism in Poland, the silencing of writers and scholars and the grossly misguided nationalist policy practised in the USSR?

One aspect of the inquiries into the Czechoslovak trials that particularly alarmed the Soviet leaders was any suggestion that Soviet influence and the role of Soviet advisers might come under scrutiny. The 1968 Commission could not over-look this aspect, although – as we see from the documents – it tried to be strictly objective and fair, and was most careful not to give even the slightest encouragement to anti-Soviet sentiment. It is, indeed, tragic that the Soviet leadership, bound as it is by the decisions of the Twentieth and Twenty-Second congresses condemning the personality cult, and having rightly dissociated itself from the evils of the Stalin-Beria era, nevertheless, far from helping a brother Party to uncover the truth, regards any attempt in this direction as a provocation. Unfortunately, the Commission had no access to Soviet archives and could not hear the evidence of living Soviet witnesses who could have thrown light on those aspects of the trials in which, on the instructions of their Party, they were directly involved. In particular, no information was available on the Politburo meeting attended by Čepička in 1949, Stalin's correspondence with Gottwald, or Mikoyan's significant visit to Prague in November 1951, on the eve of Slánský's arrest.

Further inquiry will be necessary to show to what extent Stalin's advice to Gottwald was based on suggestions made by the Czechoslovak Party leadership itself or by the Soviet advisers in Prague and their colleagues in the Czechoslovak Security Service. Be that as it may, it is indisputable that Mos-cow had the main say in deciding the fate of Slánský and the other victims.

Of course, it is also true that the Soviet Party, which provided the initial impulse for the trials of 1950–54, was also responsible, after the Twentieth Congress, and especially in the first phase of Khrushchev's leadership, for the decision to re-examine the trials of the Stalin era and rehabilitate their victims in the Soviet Union and other countries. At Khrushchev's personal request, Ludvík Svoboda was one of the first men in Czechoslovakia to be rehabilitated, and, by all accounts, Khrushchev continued for some time to urge Novotný to proceed with rehabilitating other victims. Moreover, Beria and some of the Soviet advisers in the Slánský trial (for instance, Likhachev and Abakumov) were tried and executed in Moscow. Yet, as we have seen, in the absence of a thorough-going analysis it proved impossible to eradicate the evils. (Beria's hasty condemnation in a trial that has never been made public, and his subsequent execution without being forced to reveal many matters that bear directly on the Slánský trial, while they certainly attest to the severity of his punishment, suggest also an attempt by some Soviet circles to rid themselves of an awkward witness.)

While the causes of the Czechoslovak trials can undoubtedly be found in external agencies, these in themselves do not explain the magnitude and savagery of the operation – something utterly alien to the country's traditions. There were, as related in the Report, internal factors as well, not least among them being the resistance by some groups and individuals to Communist Party policy. While part of the resistance was, undoubtedly, a manifestation of the class struggle, much of it was a defensive reaction to the switch in policy already mentioned. After 1948 the Party isolated itself from the general public, driving entire groups into opposition, including many who had originally sympathized with its aims. Intoxication with power bred, undeniably, a sectarian intolerance in some Party members; yet even this is not in itself sufficient to explain the ruthless persecution of their non-Communist opponents, and later of Communists as well. This persecution was far more the logical consequence of Gottwald's decision to abandon the 'Czechoslovak road to socialism'. For Stalin was not satisfied with a verbal condemnation of this road; he wanted condemnation and execution of the people who, with Gottwald, had prepared, carried out, advocated and planned this heresy. And Gottwald, though with considerable misgivings, complied, sacrificing both his policy and his comrades. Perhaps he realized later how tragically he had erred. By then, however, there was no alternative but to go on, to banish the gnawing doubts and assuage the pangs of conscience with alcohol and withdrawal into himself.

All this could be taken as past history if almost exactly twenty years later another Czechoslovak Communist leader – Dr Gustav Husák – had not found himself in a like predicament. In April 1969 Husák took office as the First Secretary of the Party, pledging himself to preserve at least something of the policy of 1968. He himself had been imprisoned for years as a 'bourgeois nationalist'. Yet he in turn, pleading the interests of the Party and of the alliance with the Soviet Union, brought himself to accept the view that 'counter-revolution' was rampant in Czechoslovakia and that the invasion by five Warsaw Pact countries constituted a form of 'international aid'. And so Husák has sacrificed Dubček, Smrkovský, Kriegel and thousands of other dedicated Communists who had remained faithful to the policy of 1968 – a policy which he himself had supported, and which had returned him to active political life. And he has done so knowing in his heart of hearts that a million leagues divide these men from anything even faintly smelling of counter-revolution. History will judge Husák, too, not by what he intended, but by what he achieved.

A key factor in the trials was, as the Report shows in detail, the Party's role as the sole wielder of power in the State. Under this system power is concentrated in the hands of a select ruling group of ever fewer and fewer people, until ultimately we get one-man rule. This select group arrogates to itself the right to condemn as enemies not only individuals but entire social groups – often including the children, who are made to pay throughout their lives for the supposed sins of their fathers and for their 'class origin'. The Party decides on the verdicts – including death sentences – to be handed down by the courts; and this even before the opening of a trial.

In accordance with the Commission's terms of reference, the Report is predominantly concerned with the trials of Communists. Czechoslovak Communists who want the truth to be known, however, are equally indignant about the rigged trials of members of the other political parties, or of no party, for they were the first victims, and their trials – those, for instance, of Dr Milada Horáková and of various Catholic Church dignitaries – served as a rehearsal for the subsequent trials of Communists. It cannot be denied that during 1948–50 attempts at sabotage did take place in Czechoslovakia, there were isolated cases of assassination, spies were infiltrated and efforts were made to set the clock back. Some of those convicted were in fact offenders against the law. It was natural, moreover, that avowed enemies of the socialist course and of the Communist Party should not have been retained in sensitive positions. On the other hand, Communist support for the theory of intensified class struggle, and the seeking of hostile intent in all divergent or critical views, helped to widen the gulf between the Communists and the other parties in the National Front. In short these parties, together with the voluntary organizations, were relegated to the position of 'transmission belts', entirely governed by the dictates of the Communist Party.

The most drastic treatment was that meted out to the Social Democratic Party, which, despite some wavering, worked with the Communists before and after February 1948; in fact, it was this unity that made possible a parliamentary solution of the February crisis and so enabled the Communist Party to take power. Nonetheless, soon after the forced merger of the two parties, the Social Democratic leaders and members of their party became victims of concocted trials and other forms of persecution. Can one wonder that Socialists in the capitalist countries were sceptical about the sincerity of Communist invitations to cooperate in fighting imperialism, after witnessing such an example of 'cooperation'?

That this perversion of socialism is not just a thing of the past is proved by the outcry in 1968 from the Soviet Party and some of its allies, joined by dogmatists at home, when a group of former Social Democrats wanted to revive their party as an ally of the Communist Party on the National Front platform.

Towards the end of 1969 the Party press in Czechoslovakia was still printing articles about Social Democracy as 'an instrument of counter-revolution'. Yet the Soviet and other Communist parties in the socialist world do not hesitate to seek friendly contacts with the Socialist Party in West Germany, the Labour Party in Britain, or the Socialist Party in Italy. Is it compatible with Marxism to offer cooperation and unity of action between Communists and Socialists in the capitalist countries, while in the socialist countries the very existence of Socialist parties is regarded as counter-revolutionary and their members are thrown into jail?

Understandably, then, a leading feature of policy during the Prague Spring was an attempt to establish new relationships between the Communists and the other political parties, relationships based on equality, genuine partnership, and a common platform of socialism and democracy that would exclude anything like the past deformed versions of them. This, indeed, and especially for Communists and Socialists in the West, was the significance of socialism with a human face.

In view of all this, the present Czechoslovak Party leadership's assertion that any reassessment of the trials is an 'inner Party matter', to be kept secret from the public, can only be regarded as blatant hypocrisy.

From this standpoint the reader will undoubtedly question the Report's assessment of leading men such as Gottwald. Both historically and ethically it is difficult to accept the author's attempt to draw a line between the part of a man's career that is worthy of praise, and the years, however few, that ended in a series of political murders. We Czechoslovak Communists, especially, should remember how we have presumed to condemn the first President of our Republic, Thomas Masaryk, although during his term of office fewer Communists were killed than under the rule of the Communist leader Gottwald.

The Report contains an interesting portrayal of the way the political trials gained momentum. Leaving aside the external pressures, we can perhaps summarize the process as follows:

1. First the Party leadership enunciates a set of deviations (bourgeois nationalism, anti-Sovietism, revisionism, Zionism, Titoism, Social Democracy, Slánskýism and so on).

2. Next, a campaign against these deviations is launched on all fronts, their manifestations are sought everywhere, they are ideologically 'smashed and unmasked'.

3. Culprits allegedly holding these deviationist views are then sought; they are named as individuals and, as far as possible, linked in groups round a 'centre'.

4. Those so named are required to indulge in self-criticism, by means of which they will help the Party to rid itself of errors and will demonstrate their sincerity.

5. There follows – usually from 'below', that is from the branches, or through the 'voice of the workers' in the press – the demand that those who have at last admitted the error of their ways should be punished.

6. The victims are demoted, to the accompaniment of slander and allegations in the press, to which they have no opportunity to reply as long as they are unwilling to undertake 'sincere self-criticism' and thank the Party for helping them to comprehend their mistakes and crimes.

7. Further voices – carefully directed from behind the scenes – are heard demanding punishment, since the 'crimes' have caused incalculable harm.

8. Arrest follows – sometimes this occurs earlier, without public criticism – so that the accused shall be isolated and his misdeeds thoroughly investigated.

9. Arrest is the turning-point, for now the victim gets into the hands of the Security Service – after which he must, sooner or later, and with greater or less coercion, confess to his crimes. Security officials hold the view that an arrested man cannot be released, since that would shake public confidence in their organization. Some of the victims confess because they believe they are helping the Party, others because of promises that they will be spared if they do so; some just cannot stand the physical ordeal. Those who have the strength to resist are tried *in camera* and held longest in prison.

10. When the 'confessions' have been extracted, the scenario of the trial is composed, a 'group' or 'centre' is put together, the depositions are suitably adapted, and all – including the witnesses – learn their parts by rote.

11. The trial script is studied and endorsed by the Party

leadership, which also decides (before the trial) on the sentences – even, as in the Slánský trial, about the appeal procedure and the rejection of any plea for clemency.

12. Before and during the trial, mass hysteria is whipped up to a point where resolutions pour in demanding 'the supreme penalty'.

13. In the light of the 'confessions' by the victims, who accuse themselves of the most heinous crimes, and 'in the name of the people', sentence is passed and accepted by the accused as 'just punishment'.

This was the procedure of the trials in all the socialist countries, but in Czechoslovakia it was perfected and applied on an unprecedented scale. We learn from the Report that there was a time when the Ministry of Justice was forced to request a breathing-space because the accumulated death sentences could not technically be carried out. And this happened in a country with democratic traditions, an advanced industrial economy and a high level of culture.

Here, of course, is the reason why fifteen years later, during the Soviet invasion of 1968, there was a rush of collaborators to welcome the occupation. The world was amazed, for observers had been impressed in the spring and summer by the remarkable unity of the people and the Party. They could not know, however, that these collaborators, who held important posts in Security, the Army, the judiciary, the Party and the administration, and who had been involved in various ways with the political trials of the 1950s, were deeply disturbed by the democratic movement of 1968 and had done their utmost to halt it. Though they had been shown real humanity – some of them had to be dismissed from top posts, but most suffered no financial deprivation – these men feared the loss of positions gained by their zeal at the time of the show trials. Few of them had the courage to come out in open opposition to the new policy, and so they waited. The August invasion enabled them to take their revenge for the unwarranted freedom that has allowed the truth to be proclaimed, including the dreaded truth about the trials.

Perhaps the most dramatic part of the Report is the account of the rehabilitation of the trials' victims. We find that the leaders under Novotný did everything in their power to stave it off – although since at least 1955 they had known perfectly well that the trials had been a tissue of lies. Motivated primarily by fear, they tried to arrange things so that, while the innocent would sooner or later be released, there should be no meddling with the substance of the trials. They even justified their conduct by expressing fears that publication of the truth might undermine the authority of the Party and of socialism itself.

Nor could it be otherwise, for despite some relaxation the idea of Party leadership based on strong-arm methods was still in force, and the guilty men, the organizers of the trials, still sat in high places and shared in the process of 'rehabilitation'. It was natural, then, that all calls for more active measures to redress the wrongs of 1949–54 met with severe sanctions. The Report mentions as an example the 'Yugoslav group' of 1961. Since I was included in that 'group', it may be interesting to describe something of the background to the affair. In September 1961 a number of Party members were summoned, in groups of four or five, to the Party Central Office on the pretext of consultation. I myself was summoned to the office of the head of the International Department, Bohuslav Laštovička (now Chairman of the Foreign Affairs Committee of Parliament), who asked me to tell him what was taking place in the International Union of Students, of which I was then Chairman. Laštovička interrupted my account, however, to say that some comrades in the next room wished to speak to me. The said comrades proved to be Mamula, head of the Security Department at Head Office, Kudrna, Deputy Minister (later Minister), of the Interior, and some others. The interview opened with a bombshell: I was to 'confess' to having contact with a foreign embassy! On my replying that I had no idea what they were talking about, and therefore could not 'confess', they alleged that we, an anti-Party group, were in touch with the Yugoslavs, that we had praised the Yugoslav model of socialism, that we doubted the validity of the political trials (this in 1961!), and that one of our number, Klement Lukeš, had already confessed to being a spy in the pay of the Yugoslavs.

This was so unexpected and monstrous that I felt the world had collapsed around me. I had been a Party member for over twenty years; I had been imprisoned as a Communist by the Gestapo and in 1941 had gone into hiding from the Nazis; my mother had perished in a concentration camp after being arrested with my father as a hostage on my account; since the liberation I had carried out, often in an over-zealous and naïve manner, every task allotted to me – and here I was being accused of sabotage! How, I thought, could such a thing take place here in Prague, especially after the Twentieth Congress of the Soviet Communist Party?

I must admit that after my first heated denial I began to examine my conscience and wonder how it was I had failed to realize that my friend was a spy. I was detained in the Central Office all day, a guard even accompanied me to the toilet, and I had no idea if I would be sleeping that night at home or in Ruzyň Prison. Novotný later confirmed that there had indeed been a serious proposal from the Ministry of the Interior to the Presidium of the Party that we should be brought to trial. But while they were investigating us the Twenty-Second Congress of the Soviet Communist Party was diverting attention from Yugoslavia to Albania and thence to China. So the plan for bringing our 'group' to trial fell to the ground and we, its members, were subjected merely to Party discipline, several being expelled and sent 'into industry'. An interesting point is that again, as at the Slánský trial ten years earlier, the late Konni Zilliacus, MP, was to have been involved in the 'conspiracy': according to Laštovička, we were supposed to have sent a letter to Zilliacus asking him to exert pressure on the Party leadership to rehabilitate Slánský and reassess the trials. Later I had occasion to meet Zilliacus at an East-West round-table conference of parliamentarians, and I asked him if he had ever received such a letter. He replied that he had not.

For myself, I admitted at the time that I had been in touch with a Yugoslav journalist in Prague, whom I had known through the International Union of Students. I had seen nothing wrong in that, particularly since my duties as Chairman of the IUS included contact with the press. We had often discussed Yugoslavia and her relations with the Soviet Union and the other socialist countries; our talks had been frank and critical, but of course they had nothing to do with supplying information about internal matters. In the course of my interrogation, Mamula, replying to my contention that Yugoslavia was, after all, a socialist country, said: 'There are all kinds of socialism – why, even Nasser calls himself a socialist!'

Another point that emerges from the Report is that the Party leadership only began to think in terms of rehabilitation because of the pressure at home and abroad. This underlines the effectiveness of international solidarity in the fight against lawlessness, even though the results may not be immediately obvious. I remember how, when I first visited Algeria, in 1961, the then Minister of Foreign Affairs, Mohammed Khemisti, told me that after his arrest in 1957 his life had been saved by a solidarity campaign launched by the IUS and other student organizations – otherwise he would have vanished without trial. I mention this because Communists and Socialists in Czechoslovakia are urgently in need of solidarity today – not just for moral support, but for actual protection. Indeed, one can reasonably claim that progressive public opinion throughout the world has stayed the hands of those who at the end of 1969 and in 1970 sought to plunge Czechoslovakia once more into the tragedy of political trials, forcing them to put their designs in cold storage.

Significantly, the Party leaders who had so long delayed the rehabilitation of the innocent, and who continued to regard them as suspect, were very prompt indeed in their kid-glove handling of the interrogators and the murderers. Doubek, for example, the Security officer most actively involved as head of interrogation, was sentenced to eight years, but released after serving two. It is interesting to note that among the men who held up the rehabilitation for years, and denounced those who pressed for it, we find mention in 1956 of Vasil Bilak, now a Secretary of the Party Central Committee, a self-professed 'internationalist'. Bilak, of course, had his reasons for this behaviour – he was noted for his extreme harshness, notably towards the Greek Orthodox Church in Slovakia when he was a Party official there.

All in all, a notable feature of the political scene after August 1968, and especially after Dubček's dismissal in April 1969, has been the rise to eminence of men who were involved in one way or another with the trials or with blocking attempts to review them. Among these pillars of the occupation regime are Václav David, Ambassador in Bulgaria; Miloslav Růžek, Ambassador to London; Vladimír Koucký, Ambassador to Moscow; Václav Škoda, Vice-Chairman of the Czechoslovak group in the Interparliamentary Union; and Colonel Šalgovič, Chairman of the Control Commission of the Slovak Communist Party. Thanks to the Soviet occupation, moreover, most of the men who approved the trials, held up the rehabilitation programme, and rubber-stamped one conflicting policy after another, are still members of the Central Committee, firmly entrenched in their dogmatic attitudes. Faced with the choice between the truth and their privileged positions, they chose the latter.

The Report rightly emphasizes that declarations provide no guarantee against a repetition of the trials. It is enough to recall how, at the very time when the Bolshevik leaders were being annihilated by the thousand, Stalin could bring himself to say 'Man is the most precious of all capital,' and to promise a further blossoming of socialist democracy. We can find similar statements by Gottwald at the time of the Prague trials. Slánský is even accused of having placed the Party machine above everything, of suppressing criticism from below and stifling democracy in the Party. Yet the outcome of the trials was a far worse expression of these trends than anything attributed to the 'Anti-State Conspiratorial Centre' in the dock. And let us remember from more recent times the assurances that nothing would happen to Smrkovský, Dubček and others, that they would continue to hold responsible posts. Yet they have been stripped of their last positions, isolated and silenced.

The Commission, therefore, underlines the need for guarantees to be embedded in the political system, as demanded in the Communist Party's Action Programme of April 1968. The ideas contained in this Programme caused understandable horror in the upholders of 'socialism' of the bureaucratic police-state type. Hence the barrage of abuse in the Soviet press against Czechoslovak 'revisionism', 'nationalism' and the like. Of course, the authors of the attacks were well aware that the reforms would have enormously enhanced the popularity and strength of genuine socialism, and that the sole threat they offered was to the monopoly of power which had generated the trials and other forms of persecution. In Czechoslovakia, too, the threat is felt by the men whose careers are irrevocably linked with the political trials; they can have no interest in reforms that would allow the nation to breathe freely once more. They are not concerned with the vision of Liberty, Equality, Fraternity that has inspired men through the ages – ideals to which the victims of persecution held fast even under the gallows, believing that by their self-accusation they were serving their Party and the cause of socialism.

Jiří Pelikán

FINAL REPORT

INTRODUCTION

THE Commission[1] set up by the Central Committee of the Communist Party of Czechoslovakia to complete Party rehabilitation submits this Final Report, which contains three parts: I, The political trials; II, Reassessment and rehabilitation; III, Political responsibility for the trials.

The scope of the Report is limited by its terms of reference. Since it concentrates mainly on matters connected with the political trials and their reassessment, an overall picture of post-war developments in Czechoslovakia is lacking and in this respect the account may be considered incomplete. Moreover, the authors assume an acquaintance with the events and facts contained in the report of the Kolder Commission and with earlier published statements.[2] Consequently, some difference of treatment will be noticed between parts I and II of the Report. Since the present Commission was the first to examine the history of reassessment and rehabilitation, a substantial amount of purely factual matter has had to be included in Part II. It is also assumed that Central Committee members will have the Kolder Commission Report before them.

The present Report, the work of a group of historians, lawyers and economists, is based on the archive materials, primarily those of the Central Committee, and documents held personally by Antonín Novotný and Rudolf Slánský, which were made available. The Central Committee archivists with whom the group worked were most cooperative and understanding. It should be noted that the bulk of the archive

[1] *The members of the Commission responsible for the Report were: Jan Piller (chairman), Jaroslav Frýbert, Milan Hladký, Leopold Hofman, Štefan Infner, Karel Kaplan, František Krajčír, Marie Miková, Oldřich Rákosník, Jiří Rypel, Mária Sedláková and Jindřich Uher.*

[2] *Appointed in September 1962 to re-examine the political trials of 1949–54, the Kolder Commission presented its report in April 1963 (see below, pp. 220–39).*

documents were available also to the Barák and Kolder commissions; the work of our Commission differed in that the material was handled in keeping with the accepted principles of work with archives. Despite the quantity of documents available to the group, there were still some gaps. The materials on the trials from the Ministry of the Interior were incomplete, and some questions cannot be answered from Czechoslovak archives alone.[1]

The group's research covered over 1,500 pages of documentary material. Detailed accounts of all the main events have been written and the history of the political trials and of the rehabilitation has been evaluated from different aspects. In most cases comments were invited on the separate study documents from the people figuring in them, or from those in a position to correct or amend the information submitted. However, the group has not always met with understanding. These studies have provided the basis for the Final Report.

Parts I and II differ substantially from Part III. The sections on the political trials and their reassessment and on rehabilitation are attempts at historical and political studies; the authors, conscious that theirs is not the last word on the subject, feel that future research will throw more light on many points and suggest new inter-connections. These two parts cannot, therefore, be seen as material for a Resolution, for this would make further research impossible. The purpose of the third part – on political responsibility – is to assess the responsibility for the trials and for the tardiness in reviewing them and to draw the political conclusions therefrom, and this would presuppose grave decisions and resolutions.

The working group believes that much of importance for the present can be obtained from a study of the political trials of the 1950s and their reassessment, especially in shaping a future political system capable of averting such distortions of socialism as the trials represented. We therefore recommend that these findings be summarized for the use of the Party committees and members, to serve, one might say, as a historical lesson.

---

[1] *The suggestion is that access to Soviet archives would be needed.*

ONE

THE POLITICAL TRIALS

FROM 1945 onward the overwhelming majority of the Czech and Slovak working people were busily engaged in building socialism. This was a vital chapter in the history of the two nations, the key point being reached in February 1948 with the victory of the Communist Party. The post-war process of socialist revolution in Czechoslovakia – a part of the advance of the socialist forces throughout the world – was greatly influenced by the contribution of the Soviet Union to victory in World War II.

The changeover to socialism – the historical mission of the working class – is a manifold process, affecting all aspects of social life. In Czechoslovakia, an industrial country with a highly differentiated social structure, the process was especially complicated, not least because the first steps in the socialist revolution were taken in the days of the Cold War and international tension. Internal developments, especially the socialist measures and the way they were carried out, could not but be affected by this atmosphere. With a consciousness of common aims making membership of the socialist camp a natural thing, and having learnt from recent bitter experience, Czechoslovakia's policy was to seek security in the socialist community and in its defence. Thus, in the great global confrontation between socialism and imperialism, Czechoslovakia took an active stand on the side of socialism and fulfilled her international obligations, which were in accord with her fundamental national interests.

The socialist revolution brought profound changes, resulting in a new social structure in the country. One of the greatest successes of the measures carried out on the initiative and under the leadership of the Communist Party was the abolition of exploiting classes and, hence, of capitalist exploitation. This signified the realization of one of the fundamental aims

37

of the revolution. The capitalists were excluded from sharing in political power; there were changes in property relationships among the bourgeoisie and the petit-bourgeoisie. There followed radical alterations to the class composition and social structure of the population, accompanied by class conflicts and social discord, with resultant tensions in the community. These discords and tensions were aggravated by other factors, including the impact of the Cold War.

Every change in the social order is an historical process accompanied by difficulties, unsolved problems, shortcomings and, inevitably, mistakes. Thus, after winning power the working class of Czechoslovakia, allied with the other working people, experienced a phase in which, under the leadership of the Communist Party, it sought the best way to tackle the problems and to realize the fundamental principles of socialism. The search is protracted, indeed unceasing, and the contours of the new socialist society begin to take shape only when the social structure has been stabilized and the necessary experience has been gained. Consequently, blunders and shortcomings – the inevitable concomitants of this historical process – are not peculiar to Czechoslovakia. They are inevitable also because the working class and its allies are learning how to rule, with the members of these groups sharing for the first time in a big way in the exercise of power; moreover, in a small country like Czechoslovakia the quest is greatly influenced by external factors.

The socialist reconstruction of Czechoslovak society resulted in considerable gains for the working people. Let us note those that are significant for the further growth of socialism. In addition to ending capitalist exploitation, the reconstruction did away with the social insecurity that had marked the capitalist regime. The poverty of people well below the subsistence level was ended. In the economic field, a production base was built up in industry and agriculture which, with structural changes, can generate further rapid advances in output. In the world of culture, the new democracy was reflected in the keen interest in the arts displayed by all sections of the population. Abroad, too, Czechoslovak culture recorded notable successes and won international recognition. In the political arena, the working people gained enough experience in administration at local, district and national levels – experience, it should be noted, both good and bad – to enable them to extend socialist democracy and exert their power. This very brief enumeration shows that the reconstruction provided, among other things, a solid foundation for the continued advance of socialism.

Socialism owes its success primarily to the industry of working people in many fields – the industrial workers, farmers, intellectuals, Communists and non-Party people, rank-and-file and officials in political, local-government and other organizations – the great majority of whom spared no effort and willingly made sacrifices for their ideals. In these early days the young people, especially, dedicated themselves to these ideals – and the sacrifices and labours were the greater because of the repercussions of the Cold War, which affected the life of every citizen. A sincere belief in the future of socialism helped people to surmount all the obstacles. Without this remarkable activity, without the sacrifices and hardships, without faith in the socialist cause, the results could never have been achieved.

Grave defects, however, darkened the image of the socialist reconstruction, and chief among these were the political trials. The trials were not just errors or aberrations; but neither were they the sole or even the leading feature of the social process, although their impact was everywhere felt. The political trials have detracted from the success of socialism in Czechoslovakia, damaging it in the eyes of its convinced upholders at home and abroad and, in the outcome, have discredited the endeavours of the people. The tardy and reluctant reassessment and rehabilitation have had the same effect. All who bear responsibility for these trials and for the pretence at reassessing them in 1955–7 have, objectively, harmed the interests of socialism. From the start these things were alien to the bulk of the working population, who believed in the socialism they were trying to build, and in time this incompatibility between their ideals and everything to do with the trials turned into a source of social crisis, a crisis that had to be tackled and solved.

That is why the Party has considered it necessary, following the rehabilitation of 1963, to make a new inquiry and to draw from the findings conclusions for the future. Moreover, this is essential in order to show how the distortions represented by the trials run counter to the true nature of socialism, how the trials and those who staged them are in conflict with the socialist interests of the majority in the country, and how what was done by a handful of men at the top – the men who staged the trials – had nothing in common with the mass of the Party members and officials, whose trust in the leadership was abused and who, since they bear no direct responsibility for these things, should be relieved of an unjustified sense of guilt. These circumstances and contrasts serve to underline the burden of responsibility and guilt resting with the men and institutions that shared in staging and 'reassessing' the trials, be they top politicians, Security officials or those concerned with the administration of justice.

In sum, we repeat: we are concerned solely with matters directly connected with the trials, that is solely with one particular aspect of the social process, and that not the main one. In this sense our view may be called one-sided. Nevertheless, we are dealing with a deformation of socialism, and so it may seem that the negative predominates in our account. This stems from the subject-matter and from the nature of the trials, not from research methods or the presentation of the material.

The political trials derived from external and internal factors. The weight of the two was not constant, their intensity varying from time to time. While the external influences were the stronger in providing the immediate impulses when action was first taken against leading Communists, internal factors – the precedent of the legal abuses of 1948–9 when non-Communist politicians were put on trial – created the right climate for the impulses to fall on fertile soil. Later the internal factors operated as it were automatically, playing an increasingly independent role. Ultimately they in their turn were to act as external agents with respect to other socialist countries.

From 1953 to 1956 the external factors worked in a positive direction – as impulses for the halting of the trials and for the righting of wrongs. However, internal agencies, represented notably by the top political leadership, ignored these impulses.

THE INTERNATIONAL SCENE

Soon after the end of World War II the anti-Hitler alliance began to disintegrate: once Germany and Japan had been defeated, the common interest in opposing fascism was no longer strong enough to keep the Allies together. Conflicts grew, the arena of dissension being Europe, particularly that area where the two worlds then taking shape had common frontiers.

As time went on the USA came to base its policy towards the Soviet Union on the doctrine of 'containing Communism'. This policy, systematically formulated during 1947, rested on the theory that Soviet influence was growing, that the USSR had expansionist aims, and that adequate force had to be present wherever that power might wish to attack. A consequence of this was that the Soviet Union was not to be allowed to share in decision-making concerning the key issues in the world; its spheres of interest were not to expand, and should if possible be reduced. This policy underlay a number of moves and trends in Washington's European policy in the early post-war period – notably the Truman Doctrine and the Marshall Plan, later the handling of the German question and the emergence of Nato. In the economic sphere the USA, followed by other capitalist countries, pursued the policy of discrimination and embargo vis-à-vis the socialist countries. And the Czechoslovak economy was especially hard hit.

This deterioration in international relations was accompanied on the American side by reactionary legislation on the home front, for example, the ill-famed loyalty oath introduced by Truman in 1947. This measure, which exposed democratically-minded people to all manner of persecution and bred an atmosphere of suspicion, was a powerful weapon in the mounting wave of anti-Communism.

The era of peaceful cooperation had ended, the Cold War had taken its place. The world was now divided into two camps – the socialist and the capitalist. Both sought to rally and consolidate their ranks. Tension was growing. The Cold War erupted into the war in Korea and another outbreak was awaited, this time in Europe. The leaders of both camps envisaged the possibility of a major conflict in the mid-1950s. Armaments were stepped up on both sides of the divided world. The cold war atmosphere bred a war psychosis, bringing tension not only between countries on either side of the divide, but also within the camps headed by the two great powers – the Soviet Union and the United States. The source of rising tension lay not only in the capitalist world, notably the USA, it lay also in the foreign policy pursued by the socialist countries. In 1956, at the Twentieth Congress of the Communist Party of the Soviet Union, Anastas Mikoyan declared: 'We, too, made some mistakes in our foreign policy, and it was sometimes our fault that relations deteriorated.'

In consequence of American policy, the Soviet Union found itself to some extent on the defensive and in isolation. By degrees it was deprived of the opportunity to share in decisions about West Germany, and the same applied to Japan, another area close to its frontiers. In the four-power institutions, insofar as they survived, it met with a united front of the Western representatives.

The socialist countries reacted to the Cold War by closing their ranks and looking to their defences. Among the instruments for uniting the socialist community, the Information Bureau of nine Communist parties (Cominform), the Council of Mutual Economic Aid (Comecon) and overall coordination of foreign policies played a notable part. Unification was carried out by applying the Soviet method of government and organization throughout the People's Democracies. This practice was in contradiction to the earlier theory about different roads to socialism, now condemned as a hostile idea by the Cominform and by the leaders of the Communist parties in the socialist countries. In the course of building up the socialist camp there were tendencies to put relations among member countries on a footing that overstepped the bounds of prole tarian internationalism; these tendencies were subsequently condemned by the Central Committee of the Soviet Communist Party in a resolution dated 30 August 1956.

The leaders of the socialist camp held the view that war might soon break out. Consequently, these countries expended large resources and efforts on defence, including modern weapons. They commanded powerful ground forces equipped with conventional weapons and deployed in part in Europe, where at the time there was no equivalent counter-force. In 1949 the USSR tested its atom bomb, thus breaking the US monopoly. However, the Soviet leaders were aware that in the economic field the United States was far ahead and that in a relatively short space of time this could radically alter the military balance, especially if, as was assumed, the reconstituted West German Army were to be included in the armed forces of the West. The Soviet response was to counter US military preparations by prompt and determined measures, drawing on its own internal resources and concentrating the potential of the other socialist countries as well.

The socialist camp, confronted with moves to debar it from any participation in solving European and world problems, and seeing little prospect of any immediate revolutionary situation in Western Europe, responded by compensating for these disadvantages by general preparedness and a reinforcement of Soviet influence in the community.

The renewed international tension revived the theory and practice of Stalinism, which during the war and the immediate post-war period had to some extent been relegated to the background, but had never been forgotten.

The main feature as far as the political trials were concerned was a groundless suspicion, expressed in ideological terms by the theory asserting that the class struggle was growing in intensity. With the advent of tension in international relations, this theory gained plausibility and was buttressed by interacting elements deriving from the new situation. And so, as the final break-up of the anti-fascist coalition saw the United States adopting anti-Soviet and anti-Communist policies, the socialist countries, in their turn, gradually developed an attitude of suspicion towards anyone who had in the past,

under totally different circumstances, been in touch with
political, administrative or military institutions in the capitalist
countries. Indeed, to have lived for some time in the West or
to have relatives there was to come under suspicion. Some
of the suspects occupied leading positions in one or other
socialist country – a fact which seemed to confirm the theory
that the most dangerous enemy was the one who held a Party
card and occupied a high post.

Hostile activity came to be seen as a ramified, complex
affair. The idea was plugged of a widespread conspiracy by
the imperialists against all the socialist countries, with the
recruitment of agents and planting of spies playing an important part. Moreover, the more advanced and influential the
People's Democracy concerned, the more relentless would be
the pressure exerted on it and the higher the posts the foreign
agents would try to occupy. According to this theory, then,
it was impossible that saboteurs and spies should be in leading
positions in Hungary and Poland but not in Czechoslovakia,
the most industrially advanced country, and the one with the
closest past contacts with the West.

There were many ways in which the Cold War contributed
to creating the atmosphere for the political trials directed
principally against the Communist parties, but neither the
atmosphere nor the trials themselves can be explained solely
by the deterioration in international relations. The impact
of the Cold War as an external factor was so strong precisely
because the soil had been well prepared by the warped methods
used in building the socialist order and by the increasing
distortion of the political system. And the distortions were
aggravated by the theories revived and adapted during the
Cold War. By the early 1950s both the key factors, the external
and the internal, were operating simultaneously.

Engaged in putting these policies and theories into practice
were several agencies, with the Cominform, founded in 1947,
well to the fore. Centralist and sectarian tendencies were
increasingly evident in this organization, together with a lack
of discrimination between the various non-Communist political
groupings and a growing suspiciousness, even within the
Communist movement.

These trends reached a high point in 1948, when the break with Yugoslavia came to a head in the Cominform. The resolutions on the Yugoslav question in 1948, and again in 1949, were aimed against the earlier ideas about different roads to socialism. They had strong repercussions in political life, the greatest damage being done by the theory of intensified class struggle. With the adoption of the resolution on the Communist Party of Yugoslavia, leading members in the Cominform parties who had shown, or were alleged to have shown, even the slightest sympathy with the Yugoslav attitudes were named and pilloried.

As a further product of these theories came the political trials in neighbouring countries. At first they were aimed at eliminating former political adversaries – the leaders of bourgeois parties that had shared in the Government up to 1947. These men were seen, not as opponents, but as enemies, instruments of imperialism, engaged in military conspiracies and espionage.

Later, in accordance with the theory that the most dangerous enemy was now the one with a Party card, the punitive measures were extended to the Communist parties. It was now the turn of those officials whose views on any points could be labelled as 'Titoist'. In June 1948 L. Patrascanu was dismissed from his ministerial post in Romania, having previously lost his place in the leadership at the founding congress of the Romanian Workers Party; Patrascanu's arrest and condemnation to death were delayed until 1954. In Poland, the first serious denunciation of Gomulka, General Secretary of the Party, came also in June 1948; the attacks reached their peak at a Central Committee meeting in August of the same year, when he was removed from his post. About a year later – in November 1949 – he was expelled from the Party. In September 1948 the Albanian Dzodze Koci was demoted, and at the First Congress of the Albanian Party of Labour he was denounced for trying to attach Albania to Yugoslavia. His trial, which lasted from 12 May to 6 June 1949, ended in a sentence of death. January 1949 saw the first attacks on Traicho Kostov in Bulgaria; a Central Committee meeting in March of that year deprived him of his posts in the Party and in the Government; by June he had been expelled from the Central Committee and from the Party. A month later he was arrested, along with others, mainly top men in the economy. In Hungary, meanwhile, László Rajk was coming under grave suspicion; he had been denounced as early as August 1948 and transferred from the post of Minister of the Interior to Minister of Foreign Affairs. On 30 May 1949 he was arrested, together with other Party personalities. The Rajk trial, later held up as the 'model' trial, took place in September 1949 and resulted in three death sentences. Kostov's trial in December was staged along the lines of the Rajk trial, with the difference that Kostov refused to plead guilty, whereupon the summary of evidence was simply read out. He, too, received sentence of death and was executed. We may note that after 1956 Rajk, Kostov and others were fully rehabilitated, just as Gomulka, and later Patrascanu, were cleared of all charges.

The area of suspicion now began to spread, with war-time émigrés to the West, veterans of the Spanish Civil War and similar groups bearing the brunt. Soon attention came to be centred on people of Jewish extraction. From the anti-Titoist line there was a shift to an anti-Zionist line, which reached its peak in Czechoslovakia.

This country, because of its geographical position and its high level of economic development, occupied a foremost place in considerations of military strategy. Czechoslovakia was intended to be the engineering centre and in part the armoury of the socialist camp; and the political, economic, military, security and other possibilities were assessed from this angle.

The Communist leaders had years of experience as members of a legal party in a parliamentary democracy. They had therefore known some contacts with other parties, in addition to disputes. Many Czechoslovak Communists had fought in Spain – where, conceivably, they might have been recruited by various intelligence services – and many of them now held key positions in various organizations, including the Security Service. During World War II there had been a fairly large contingent of Communist refugees in the West, mainly in

Britain, where they were in touch with the Czechoslovak Government in exile. After the war, too, many leading men maintained their contacts with people abroad. Now they were all seen as potential spies.

Czechoslovakia's post-war economy had a strong initial Western orientation, and the re-alignment with the socialist countries seemed from the outside to be proceeding slowly. Moreover, there was an impression that she was tardy in opening up and exploiting her own resources in raw materials.

Some of the Soviet leaders of the day lacked confidence in the staffing of the Czechoslovak Army Command – including its General Staff. This mistrust was not confined to members of the 'western units', but extended also to former commanders of the Czechoslovak forces in the USSR. In a letter addressed to Klement Gottwald on 8 April 1950, the Soviet Party leadership rejected a request for advisers made by the then Minister of National Defence, Ludvík Svoboda.[1] 'Our military staff,' they wrote, 'consider that General Svoboda is not deserving of confidence and that it will be impossible to talk openly with him about military secrets of the USSR.' Even changes in personnel, the attachment of Soviet advisers to the Army and the detailed copying (introduced in 1950) of methods used in the Soviet Armed Forces brought little change in this attitude, as became evident at a summit meeting of the socialist countries held in Moscow in 1951.

At this meeting, indeed, the Soviet view was reinforced by Rudolf Slánský when he said that the big changes since February 1948 had not been reflected in the Armed Forces. The cause lay in Svoboda's occupying the post of Minister of Defence.

Essentially Svoboda was a man, who, although he joined the Party, was alien to it. He surrounded himself with officers such as Drgač, Drnec, Klapálek, Novák, Bulander, ex-Legionaries who had been trained in Western military doctrines and were not favourably disposed to Soviet military doctrine; some of them, as we now see from the case of General Bulander, were actual agents of the Anglo-Americans. Our mistake has been that we left Svoboda and his

---

[1] *Elected President of the Czechoslovak Socialist Republic in April 1968.*

protégés so long in key positions and that only on the urgent advice of Comrade Stalin have we removed them.

Starting in 1949, it became inevitable that not least among the weaknesses was counted the number of people of Jewish extraction who held top posts in the Party, the Government and the economy – the more so since Czechoslovakia, having shown energy and initiative in implementing the common policy of the socialist countries towards Israel, had failed to respond as promptly as she should to the policy switch of 1949. The concluding phase of Czechoslovak-Israeli relations overlapped with the time when the other socialist countries had broken off relations and were adopting a tougher attitude to their Jewish citizens. At the time when the anti-Yugoslav line began to be turned into the anti-Zionist line, relics of the early policy on Israel were still to be found in Czechoslovakia. The evolution of the political attitude to Israel is important for an understanding of the ideological trend and the nature of the trial of the 'Centre'.[1]

The Near East, notably Palestine, was among the places where the interests of the powers met and clashed. While, at the time we refer to, this clash was not yet in the forefront of the international scene, it later carried serious implications in relation to the political trials, especially their antisemitic aspects.

With the active support of the USSR and the other socialist countries, the United Nations General Assembly decided in November 1949 that Palestine be divided into two states – Jewish and Arab. So far from solving the problems, this decision merely exacerbated them, its announcement being followed by an immediate flare-up of the 'unofficial' Arab-Jewish war. Some of the Arab countries responded to the ceremonial declaration of the State of Israel, on 14 May 1948,

---

[1] *The reference is to the trial of the 'Anti-State Conspiratorial Centre headed by Rudolf Slánský', also termed in the Report the 'Slánský trial' or the 'main trial'. Held in November 1951, it resulted in sentences of death for Vladimír Clementis, Otto Fischl, Josef Frank, Ludvík Frejka, Bedřich Geminder, Rudolf Margolius, Bedřich Reicin, André Simone, Rudolf Slánský, Otto Šling and Karel Šváb; Hajdů, Löbl and London were sentenced to life imprisonment. The majority of the victims were of Jewish extraction.*

by sending troops into Palestinian territory. With brief intervals, hostilities continued into 1949. The Arab countries at that time enjoyed substantial support from Great Britain, while the United States backed Israel. The issue was tied up with Anglo-American disputes then current, and on both sides it reflected the strategic interests of the two powers in the highly sensitive area of the Near East. In determining the American point of view, fear of Soviet influence spreading to Palestine evidently played its part. In Israel, the attitude taken by the Soviet Union and its allies aroused much sympathy, especially in democratic circles, and to some extent at governmental level also. By degrees, however, the United States gained the predominant, indeed exclusive, influence in the country, thus filling the political vacuum left by the British withdrawal.

The deterioration in Soviet-Israeli relations set in when American influence gained the upper hand in Israel, where the progressive movements had failed to achieve any notable successes. This change in one aspect of Soviet foreign policy and strategy had its reflection now in home policies, with a growing mood of suspicion and outright repression directed against certain Jews. The political and security implications of the Jewish question began to receive more attention. Theories emerged about the big part played by Jews in a world imperialist plot, and in ideological and political subversion throughout the socialist countries. As the trials were prepared and conducted, the emphasis on Zionism, and on the Jews as a whole, became more pronounced, although the whole thing was a fabrication, with Communists and other progressives as the main victims.

The role of the Jewish question in the fabrication of the trials came to the fore during 1949 in the guise of a campaign against 'cosmopolitanism'. It was to reach its height, however, at a later date, primarily in connection with preparations for the trial of the 'Anti-State Conspiratorial Centre' in Czechoslovakia, and with the 'Doctors' Case' in the USSR, which was later found to have been rigged by Beria and his agents.

In January 1951 Czechoslovakia was named by some of the top men in the socialist world as the weakest link in the community of People's Democracies. Simultaneously they stressed her special position as an industrially advanced and strategically important country. And so, seeing her both as a key member of the community and as its weakest link, and possessed as they were by a belief in imminent war, they were, inevitably, obsessed by the aim of raising Czechoslovakia to a level that would really safeguard her key role.

Moreover, in the views outlined above we have one of the basic reasons why the search for the 'leader of the conspiracy' was pursued at ever higher levels and why the 'Centre' came to involve more and more people.

The Czechoslovak Party leaders did not comply passively with these external pressures; at all international meetings they reported on their success in unmasking the enemy, and offered self-critical assurances that future successes would be even greater. For example, at a meeting of the Cominform in November 1949, Rudolf Slánský stated:

It is still a weakness in our Party that the mass of the membership underestimates the resistance of the class enemy, his unceasing effort to plant agents in the Party and to carry out subversive and disruptive activity against the people's democratic regime. In underestimating the class enemy they show insufficient Bolshevik vigilance. It is not enough to call for increased vigilance merely in words. We have to exercise increased vigilance in our day-to-day cadre policy, by knowing and verifying cadres thoroughly, by prompt measures to remove all who are alien and hostile to the Party and the working class, and by subjecting those who neglect the principles of Bolshevik vigilance to strict and exemplary punishment. . . . It is purely because of our inadequacy in advancing cadres from below and our inadequate verification of people's activities that we are still tardy in ridding our economic machine of saboteurs and spies. We are still unmasking many enemy agents among Army officers. Experience teaches us that, with a few exceptions, we need new men to replace the entire officer corps.

These declarations about success in unmasking agents, and the various self-critical speeches about lack of vigilance, merely helped to instil a belief in an extensive and powerful conspiracy.

Along with the general and external circumstances and pressures, there were also direct pressures for going ahead with political trials in Czechoslovakia. A glance at the trials both of non-Communists and Communists in the neighbouring People's Democracies shows that Czechoslovakia lagged somewhat behind in this respect.

The course of events in the immediate post-war years, the original ideas about different roads to socialism, the manner and also the period in which the decisive class conflict took place – all these factors led the Czechoslovak Party leaders to be far more concerned in 1948 with reshaping the political system and introducing social and economic changes than with using security methods in the Party. Not that these were lacking. But on the whole they still played no great part. True, several illegal trials of non-Communist politicians, of members of the Armed Forces, and of others, had taken place. It is clear that, sooner or later, the Party would have proceeded, of its own accord and without any external pressure, to unmasking the enemies in its midst. The external pressures were calculated to accelerate developments, since the delay was causing certain leaders in the other socialist countries to feel anxious about Czechoslovakia's weakness (especially as no Soviet troops were stationed there); and they derived from trials in preparation, taking place or already completed in neighbouring countries, with the Hungarians and Poles, together with the Soviet advisers in their security services, to the fore in pressing for action.

In connection with 'unmasking hostile agencies' in the Hungarian Workers Party, the case of Noel Field, and of his brother Herman, was concocted. The projected trial of Rajk then became an instrument whereby Rákosi in Hungary and Bierut in Poland exerted pressure on Gottwald. After the phase when the Czechoslovak Party leaders maintained a sober attitude in facing the mounting accusations from abroad against Party officials, there came a break in the autumn of 1949. The Party began to move into step with the other countries and, as a result, Czechoslovakia became the scene of the biggest post-war trials of top-ranking Communists to be held in Europe; the timing meant that the intensive preliminary investigations coincided with a cooling off in the drive against

Tito, while the anti-Zionist course had not yet gained momentum.

THE HOME FRONT

The years from 1948 to 1953 were marked by events, processes and changes that imparted some characteristic features to Czechoslovakia's internal development; many were connected with the political trials.

The events of February 1948 were followed by social and political tensions that varied in intensity and at times exploded into bitter clashes. These tensions arose from a number of causes and assumed different forms.

Western intelligence services, anxious to exploit the post-February situation, stepped up their activities. In this they were helped by inadequate frontier controls and the wave of émigrés leaving the country after February. In blocking most of these attempts, the Czechoslovak Security Service performed a valuable service. Naturally, interest in Czechoslovakia on the part of Western intelligence services was not confined to the brief period immediately after February, and it continued in later years.

Moreover, many members of the classes and groups that had been excluded from any share in political power and deprived of the means of production came out in opposition to the regime of people's democracy. Isolated cases of resistance and attacks on Party and Government officials were not lacking. There were several illegal groups, some of which maintained contact with émigrés.

These forms of class struggle provided one of the sources of tension in the community. Another source was the situation of the lower middle class and the way in which it was integrated with the socialist economy. By mid-1948 unmistakable signs of social uncertainty and fear for the future were evident among farmers and the urban middle classes. There were expressions of disagreement with the post-February policies of the Party and the Government, particularly from tradespeople and intellectuals, who utilized the Eleventh Sokol Meeting and the funeral of President Beneš to demonstrate their hostility.[1] The Party leadership, influenced by the theory of intensified class struggle, saw in these events an open move towards a putsch and responded with a change in policy, including harsh measures against the capitalists and the above-mentioned sections of the population. Outstanding were the practice of rationing according to social class, and the institution of forced labour camps (TNP)[2]

Yet the tension among the middle classes was not reduced; rather the reverse. It was accentuated, for instance, by collectivization, which encountered resistance from the rural bourgeoisie and lack of sympathy among many farmers with small or middle-sized holdings.[3] The transfer of the smaller urban industrial enterprises to nationalized, cooperative or municipal ones produced similar results. There were cases when punitive measures originally aimed at capitalists were used against lower-middle-class opponents of these moves. The tensions grew year by year, reaching a climax in 1953 when a mass exodus of farmers from the cooperative farms took place.

Another source of tension was the shortage of consumer goods in 1948. While dissatisfaction on this score was evinced by all social groups, it was most pronounced among the

[1] *The Sokol physical training organization, a national institution with strong patriotic roots, held massive displays (slet) every few years; the Eleventh Slet focussed national feelings at this critical time. Beneš died on 3 September 1948.*

[2] *Food rationing was still in force at the time; working-class people received bigger rations than those regarded as survivors from the 'exploiting classes'. Forced labour camps, instituted by special decree in 1948–9, were scattered up and down the country, the most notorious being those attached to the uranium mines. People were committed, without trial, to these camps by commissions which on paper were directed by local government authorities, but in practice consisted of Security 'threes' or 'fives' appointed by the Party (see p. 85). Detention could be ordered for limited or unlimited periods, and for some years it was the practice to draft the sons of 'capitalist and middle-class families' to this forced labour, usually in the mines, in place of military service. Ultimately some 10 per cent of each age group met this fate, especially during the first years of collectivization of farming. The camps were run by officials of the Ministry of the Interior.*

[3] *Collectivized farming was introduced on the Soviet model and without due regard to the specific conditions of the country's agriculture.*

working class. Nevertheless, the difficulties were overcome, and the first two years of the Five Year Plan brought a rise in the standard of living, while many of the social injustices inherited from capitalism were removed. In 1951–2, however, came stagnation, followed in 1953 by a fall in the standard of living. Sections of the working class reacted by localized strikes, and in May 1953, at the time of the currency reform, by demonstrations as well.

Economic and social measures were not the sole sources of tension; there were political causes, too. In addition to the manifestations of class struggle noted above, a prime factor was the handling of conflicts between the Catholic Church and the State. The opposition of the Church hierarchy, under Vatican direction, to the changes made in February 1948 and to subsequent developments, and its unwillingness to affirm loyalty to the State, led to new governmental measures; to these the Church reacted with still greater resistance. Despite negotiations between Church and State, the rift widened; dissatisfaction spread among believers whom the Church tried to rally in its defence – that is, against the State. These dissensions produced, on the one hand, some instances of subversion by Catholic clergy, and, on the other, show trials of ecclesiastics.

The Communist victory in February 1948 was accompanied by an upsurge of popular effort, both politically and at work, especially among Party members. But many functionaries and rank-and-file members suffered from the 'intoxication of victory and power' – the normal reaction after success. It was manifested in a sectarian attitude to non-Communists and by a tendency to override democratic procedures and disregard the law. The Party leaders, aware of the dangers involved in these attitudes, criticized them and warned against them. They looked for ways to prevent the abuse of power. Yet, coming as they did at a time when such ideas were out of step with the Cominform resolutions, both Gottwald's and Zápotocký's suggestions proved unrealistic. The intensification of class-struggle theory actually encouraged sectarian trends and reinforced the strong-arm elements in the Party.

We have confined our account to the social and political

tensions that set in between 1948 and 1953, involving both the class struggle between the working class and the defeated capitalist class, and the expressions of uncertainty, unrest and dissatisfaction among the middle strata, as well as processes taking place in the working class. These socio-political movements were influenced by international events and proceeded in their turn to influence the growth of the people's democracy and the shaping of the political system.

The regime of people's democracy that emerged after February 1948 operated increasingly as a dictatorship of the proletariat. The external factors shaping this process, notably the intensified class struggle and the assumption that the dictatorship of the proletariat could take one form only, were reinforced by social conflicts and tensions. The class-struggle theory gained ground among Party officials up and down the country and among the public, resulting in an increasingly distorted view of society and its problems. Exaggerating the danger from class enemies, the theory placed in this category entire groups of the middle strata and even the working class. Many actions, including, for instance, penal offences, were attributed to the hand of the class enemy; and unmasking this enemy was often regarded as the best way to overcome obstacles and shortcomings. The theory of one single model for a socialist regime led to the error of taking over the Soviet model, including all the distortions that were later criticized and condemned at the Twentieth Congress of the Soviet Party and in subsequent resolutions.

In the administration of the people's democracy the element of repression came gradually to the fore. It was aimed, justifiably, against the resistance by capitalists and their supporters, and against the efforts of the foreign intelligence services, but, with growing severity, it hit the middle and working classes as well. Political and legislative actions began to reflect class aims; examples are the policy of 'a stern course against reaction' adopted after President Beneš's funeral, the Law for the Protection of the Republic, the criminal law, a number of agricultural measures, etc. The class approach was evident also in the way the law was interpreted and applied against individuals. The consequent growth in illegal procedures, with arbitrary infringements of the law, represented the very opposite of the class aims that had been intended.

By 1 November 1949, of the prison population of Bohemia and Moravia alone, 6,136, out of a total of 23,141, were serving sentences for offences against the State. By 1 March 1950 the figures were 8,491 out of 26,748; by 1 May 1950, 9,765 out of 28,281.

Classification by social group (which for each prisoner was recorded for 1938, 1945 and the time of arrest) showed that, in the middle of 1950, of the 11,026 people in prison throughout the country for alleged anti-State crimes the largest groups consisted of industrial workers – 3,488, i.e. 31·6 per cent – and office workers. Lower-grade office workers numbered 3,082, i.e. 28 per cent, and higher-grade 961, or 8·7 per cent. By job classification, the figure for workers rose to 4,307, or 39·1 per cent.

If we take the number of people arrested by State Security, the figures for 1951 were 2,977 arrested individually and 3,112 in groups; for 1952, 3,365 individuals and 1,089 group members, i.e. a total of 16,010 [sic; the figures appear to be incomplete].

The largest groups under arrest at the time consisted of industrial workers, 5,962 in all, and office workers, totalling 3,162. Other social groups included 1,080 farmers and 544 kulaks,[1] 32 big landowners and aristocrats.

The figure for death sentences was also high: between October 1948 and the end of 1952 the State Court imposed 233 sentences of death, of which 178 were carried out.

The number of death sentences pending was so great that early in 1951 the Ministry of Justice gave the following reason for a delay in bringing cases to court: 'Earlier convictions in all these cases are impossible, because we should have death sentences accumulating in too short a space of time.' (Archives of the Ministry of Justice, Security Commission, No. T 4474/56, Vol. 3.)

The decisions on all death sentences were made by the appropriate Party committees – the Security Commission of

[1] *The Soviet term for farmers with medium-sized holdings; in Czechoslovakia this pejorative label was attached—with all its grave consequences—to farmers owning over ten hectares (twenty-five acres).*

the Central Committee, later the Political Secretariat of the Central Committee. Between 1951 and 1954 the Political Secretariat approved 148 death sentences.

Thus, alongside justifiable measures against adversaries, illegal practices were spreading.

During 1948 and 1949 the most pronounced cases of illegality and injustice occurred in the Armed Forces – in the Army and in the Security Service. Following dismissals of high-ranking officers (some Slovak generals for example) who had come, often quite unjustifiably, under suspicion, attention was turned to organizing provocations and arresting military personnel. In the notorious 'Cottage'[1] people wrongfully arrested were assaulted and tortured until they made the 'confessions' that served to convict them. Provocation and, in some cases, brute force were used also by some officers of State Security, although as yet only occasionally. Here were the origins of the political trials – which began, in the main, with non-Communists. Some of the interrogators really believed they were acting in the interests of the working class, for the socialist cause, and that the ends justified the means. It can be demonstrated that some high-placed Party men – Rudolf Slánský, Bedřich Reicin, Karel Šváb – knew about the illegal methods used by Security and the Army. Evidence that high-ranking Security officers were aware of the physical force being used is provided, for example, by the minutes of a meeting with the Deputy Minister of National Security on 12 May 1952:

Comrade Deputy Minister emphasized that the interrogators responsible to the Ministry are now acting in quite a different manner; up to the middle of last year it was common practice for interrogators to exert pressure and use physical force during investigations. Comrade Baudyš concluded from this that it would not be in place to lay charges against those whose resort to violence – insofar as it was used during the above-mentioned period – becomes known, because such action was permitted also by senior officers, who were well aware of this. At present the staff of the Ministry use force during interrogations only in exceptional and justified

[1] *The name used in Security circles for a place of detention maintained by the Ministry of National Defence. It was closed in 1951 (see p. 118).*

cases, and even then only after previous approval. (VHA – HSS – Secret. 21.1/10.6.1952.)

Inevitably, members of the Communist Party, too, began to fall victim to illegal procedures. As early as 1949 there were cases of Communists being arrested, and penalized in other ways, for views openly expressed at Party meetings.

It was in the years following February 1948, years replete with conflicts and social tensions, that the new political system had its genesis. It evolved from February, notably from the fact that the Communist Party had become the sole ruling force in the country with the power of decision-making; and the political system was a new way of implementing the Party's leading role. The structure and operation of that system are exceptionally important from the standpoint of the trials. Some features are of special significance, and we shall deal mainly with these.

A feature of the political system was the unprecedented concentration of power. The structure of the institutions of government and the mechanism of governing were such that all power in the political, economic and cultural spheres was concentrated in a small group of Party officials – the political leadership. The Communist Party monopolized all decision-making; from its committees there went out all the directives or proposals for legislative action and orders or directives for the exercise of executive power. Through its committees at all levels the Party assumed virtually the sole responsibility for policy and its implementation down to the minutest detail, thereby precluding any effective system of checks and balances.

This exceptional concentration of power in the hands of a few individuals meant that the former *division* of power was abandoned, while the mechanism for the *control* of power and the barriers to the *abuse* of power were bypassed. Nor was any new control mechanism established. These changes contravened the Constitution and the law, contravened even the measures introduced by the Party itself. Moreover, the natural chain of political responsibility for the actions of constitutional office-holders and political leaders was no longer operative, because the men involved were responsible neither to the appropriate departments of State nor to the institutions and the public that elected them, but to Party institutions – in the final analysis, to the top political leadership.

This monopoly of power undermined the authority of Government and Parliament and restricted the independence of the courts, since many of their functions were taken over by the ruling group or delegated to other departments. This, too, helped to erode the system of power control, because the departments and institutions that should properly have participated in framing, implementing and controlling Government policy had become mere 'transmission belts', that is, they executed the orders of the handful of men at the top.

The National Front,[1] no longer the platform for shaping the nation's policy through debate among its members, became a mere instrument for implementing that policy, without any chance of exerting effective influence or control.

While Parliament remained, *de jure*, the supreme legislative assembly, its political structure and the mechanism for preparing and handling measures were such that its role was confined to the mere endorsement of legislation submitted by the Government. Its powers of control were limited accordingly. True, Parliament expressed its views on Government programmes and on statements by Ministers, but, conscious of its limitations in respect of initiating and framing measures, it abstained from criticism and resorted to the theory of the unity of Government and Parliament under the leadership of the Communist Party. While the Government was still formally responsible to Parliament, in practice it answered to the Party. The result was that Parliament lost much of its weight in political life, playing little more than a passive part in policy-making, that of endorsing what had already been decided.

A symptom of Parliament's decline in the political system and in public life as a whole was the practice of recalling and nominating Members without the knowledge of the electorate. During 1948–52 dozens of Members were recalled or appointed in this manner.

The Government's share in policy-making was degraded to an executive function. Its area of decision was restricted;

[1] *An umbrella organization of all political parties and public bodies.*

security, the Armed Forces, foreign affairs and most economic matters were now reserved to Party committees which, quite unconstitutionally, assumed governmental powers. The move towards centralization, however, strengthened the hand of the Government vis-à-vis lower levels of administration, and within the Government the status of the Premier was enhanced. All in all, the Government was primarily concerned with realizing the main lines of policy laid down by the Party leadership and in carrying out the instructions of its top officials.

The process of eroding the legal code and legal security was accelerated. While the worst sufferer was public administration, the sphere of personal freedom was also greatly affected. The Constitutional Court was abolished; the Administrative Court was placed in abeyance, before being abolished in 1952. Numerous new laws and political measures were passed in complete disregard of the principles embodied in the Constitution of 9 May.[1] The mounting legal nihilism began by spreading the idea that the existing law and regulations need not be respected because they were outdated. But even the new laws, which substantially weakened the safeguards of civil rights and freedoms, were not respected.

By controlling all sources and media of information, the political leadership had a vital instrument for moulding 'public opinion' and 'direct expression of the people's will'.

A special place in the ideological armoury was occupied by the system of Party education, which played its part in paving the way to the political trials by preparing the membership and, later, in acquainting them with the proceedings in court. The daily press carried articles full of hatred for the accused even before they were convicted, and after conviction their 'evil deeds' were recalled again and again. During the big trials the press campaign was stepped up, subjecting people to even greater pressure, confusing them with false information and urging redoubled efforts to find the still lurking 'enemies'. This propaganda yielded its fruits in a universal psychosis of

[1] *The Constitution drawn up by the Communist Party after February 1948 and adopted by the National Assembly on 9 May 1948. Superseded by the present Constitution, adopted in 1960.*

mistrust, and in calls for the severest punishment. Thousands of resolutions on these lines were received by the courts, the Party and the Government leaders, especially during the trials of Dr Horáková and others, of Church dignitaries and, later and above all, of the 'Anti-State Conspiratorial Centre'.

On the other hand, the public was not informed about the appeals made by well-known personalities (Einstein, Bertrand Russell, J. D. Bernal and others) for mercy in the cases of Horáková, Kalandra and others.

The new status of the Communist Party after February 1948 affected its internal life, too. Centralism increased at the expense of the democratic elements; branches and members had less and less say in policy-making. Party life became highly centralized, with the emphasis on small, select committees, while commissions and other auxiliary bodies were kept in check by the importation of a large paid staff, which also restricted the rights of members at lower levels. All this made nonsense of the Party Rules, with their principle of democratic centralism. By degrees an unquestioning performance of set tasks came to be the rule for Party members. Efforts to win the confidence of the public and work among the masses were largely replaced by organizational jobs. Consequently, passivity spread and interest flagged.

With a considerable body of members assumed to be ideologically and politically unreliable, the secret ballot was abolished in elections for Party committees, and from 1949 the nominees for committees at lower levels had to be approved at higher levels before voting could take place; this system was really a cloak for the practice of appointing committee members. A growing atmosphere of mutual suspicion poisoned relationships among Party members, and from this it was only a step to a systematic hunt for the enemy within.

With its dominant position in the system of government, the Party could freely extend and concentrate its power. Government departments and public bodies were often replaced by Party institutions and, as power grew, it came into the hands of smaller and smaller groups of officials or of individuals. These people exercised their power regardless of accepted legal standards, and they violated all the principles of internal Party life. As the Party steadily extended the range of matters within its jurisdiction, it often spent time on the trivia of everyday life, while serious policy-making was neglected. This way of exercising the leading role inevitably made for the use of an elaborate machine which tended to replace the elected committees and to decide for them. In the end the power wielded by this machine grew out of all proportion.

Such an interpretation of the Party's leading role, and the undemocratic way it conducted its affairs, when combined with the unquestioning faith of the members in the socialist ideals proclaimed by the Party, gave practically unlimited power to the top committees. Yet this same process went still further, concentrating power in ever smaller units, until it was held by the Presidium or even smaller groupings (threes, fours, fives and so on) and ultimately rested with a few individuals.

The Central Committee lacked the influence proper to its status as the supreme elected leadership. Gradually its Presidium, or smaller groups, took over, while Central Committee meetings did little more than passively endorse the resolutions and measures put before them. The Committee never even tried to assert its function; indeed, with the theory about intensified class struggle operating in the Party system of the day, this would have been a highly risky undertaking. Yet not even all the members of the Presidium of the Central Committee could really share in making and implementing policy. Some of the vital questions – security, the Armed Forces, foreign affairs – were never on the agenda. The Chairman, Klement Gottwald, handled them in the select circle of his colleagues (Slánský, Zápotocký, Široký). In any case, Gottwald usually came with ready-made proposals, which he enumerated in his summing-up; and they were usually adopted.

On 28 June 1948 an 'inner Presidium' was set up to handle current political, economic and personnel matters. Later, on 29 January 1951, the Presidium elected a Political Secretariat. Complementary to these centralized institutions were groups for which there was no provision in the Party Rules (threes, fours, fives); these groups were attached to the different committees and often took independent decisions on vital matters. In time their functions were taken over by the Party machine, which began to be firmly organized in the autumn of 1948. Sections that had been fairly independent were fully integrated in the main departments, which acquired 'secretariats' at departmental and sectional levels. A substantial reorganization took place in September 1951, affecting the leading committees and commissions; the departments took over most of the business of commissions that had been abolished.

There were other factors, too, affecting the Party's status in society and the political system and also impinging on its inner life. Foremost among them was the relationship between the leadership of the Czechoslovak Communist Party and the international Communist movement. The roots of this relationship went back before the war, when the Party was a disciplined section of the Comintern. During the war the Comintern was dissolved, its role as leader of the international movement being assumed by the leadership of the Soviet Party, that is, by Stalin. After the war this function was performed by the Cominform. From this state of affairs, which up to 1956 was regarded throughout the movement as a matter of course, stemmed the uncritical faith in Stalin common to all the leaders of the Czechoslovak Party, including Gottwald. Another notable feature in the early 1950s was the Cold War, which caused an element of militarism to penetrate public administration, while it also encouraged the centralistic trends inside the Party. Among the more obvious results was that the relationship between members and higher Party committees became a matter of absolute obedience to orders. The implications were serious when it came to the trials, because members and committees were obliged to carry out decisions that directly contravened the Party's programme. That most members were quite unaware of the contradiction can in no way alter this fact.

Understandably, the theory that the class struggle was bound to gain in intensity, and the atmosphere produced by the break with Yugoslavia, played their part in all this. The exchange of letters between the Soviet and Yugoslav parties and the subsequent Cominform resolution on the Communist

Party of Yugoslavia engaged all the attention of the top men in the Czechoslovak Party, including the Presidium and the Secretariat.

The first warning signs came when this resolution was debated at a Presidium meeting on 28 June 1948, at which, Václav Kopecký was to the fore in advancing an extreme attitude on the Yugoslav question. His contribution, and that of Július Ďuriš, also contained the first attempt to apply the Cominform standpoint to the situation in the Communist Party of Slovakia. Tension between the Party leaders and some of the top men in the Slovak Party was reflected in a speech by Široký at a meeting of the Slovak Central Committee in September, when without advancing any factual evidence he spoke about the problem of 'petit-bourgeois nationalism' in Slovakia.

In September, too, more serious events began to divert the Czechoslovak Party onto an unhealthy course. The Gomulka case in Poland, and other circumstances, indicated that criticism was to be expected, and on 11 September Gottwald left for talks with Stalin. The outcome of this visit seemed uncertain at the time, but a number of documents suggest that it was not too unfavourable. Gottwald did at least obtain Stalin's agreement to Czechoslovakia's taking her own course in some matters. Nevertheless, it was in connection with these talks that the first serious case of disregard for the standards of Party conduct and for the law occurred. This was the Kolman case; the Commission feels that a further reason for explaining this case in more detail is that Kolman's rehabilitation was carried out by the Soviet authorities, whereas the matter still awaits full discussion and a decision by the Czechoslovak Party.[1]

Professor Kolman, a leading figure in the Czechoslovak Party after 1945, had considerable standing as a philosopher; for many years before and during the war he had worked with the Soviet Communist Party and he was a Soviet citizen. His views on some matters were radical, differing from those of the Czechoslovak leadership. Immediately after Gottwald had set

[1] For a fuller account of the case see the report by Karel Jech, prepared for the Rehabilitation Commission.

out for his talks with Stalin in September 1948, Kolman wrote an article entitled 'For Bolshevik Self-Criticism in our Party', dated 12 September and intended for the weekly *Tvorba*; twice – at branch meetings in the Party Central Office on 15 and 16 September – he waded in with severe criticism of a section of the leadership (Slánský, Švermová, Bareš). Kolman's purpose was to raise within the Czechoslovak Party the conclusions of the Cominform resolution on Yugoslavia and the denunciation of Gomulka at a Polish Central Committee meeting. His statement – an unusual one for those days – was discussed by a group of Party leaders, which included Slánský, Zápotocký, Dolanský, Kopecký, Švermová and Bareš. They condemned Kolman's views as 'incorrect', and 'factional activity', and sent a message to Gottwald in Moscow informing him of their attitude.

In all probability the matter was among the points discussed by Gottwald with the Soviet leaders, but we have no record of these talks. On 24 September Gottwald informed Slánský in writing about his disagreement with Kolman's statement. On the same day, it appears, an undated message from the USSR was delivered at the Czechoslovak Party Central Office; it demanded that Kolman be detained and delivered to the Soviet authorities, who had serious reasons for bringing charges against him. This was done: Kolman was taken to the USSR, where he remained in prison until 1952.

The Kolman affair cannot be regarded as a mere episode. If their implications had been realized, his statements could have had incalculable consequences for the Czechoslovak Party. Indeed, Slánský was probably influenced by them when he spoke at a meeting of Party secretaries on 21 September about the need to draw conclusions from a certain Cominform resolution, about the danger of underestimating reactionary forces in Czechoslovakia, and about the need for determined application of the theory of intensified class struggle. Slánský's conclusions, which were translated into practical work in the Party Central Office and elsewhere – instructions being sent out for a critical review of policy in all sectors – were only slightly modified after Gottwald's return from the USSR, and more particularly his address to the Central Committee in

November. On the other hand, Kolman's case was the first flagrant example of a leading Party official being subjected to illegal procedure. Many of his colleagues, employees at Party headquarters and personal friends suffered varying degrees of discrimination for expressing agreement with his statements. For some years the case poisoned intellectual life, prevented any debate or exchange of views in the Party and bred an atmosphere of mistrust, fear and sterile unanimity. It formed, in fact, a prologue to the political cases and the trials that were to shake the country in later years.

If we are to judge further developments correctly, we should bear in mind that they did not follow solely from the search for members of an international conspiracy against the socialist countries; even before that, the atmosphere created by the Cominform resolutions on Yugoslavia, the series of 'political cases' and trials in other countries – all accepted by the Czechoslovak Communist leaders as genuine – had prepared the ground, without outside intervention, for redoubled efforts in hunting the enemy and for the existence of hostile activities to be taken as proven. There is evidence for this in statements made by Party leaders in those days, notably by Slánský at a meeting of regional Party secretaries on 10 March 1949, where he stressed the need for vigilance in the Party and warned: 'We have many agents here.' The Party introduced a system of strict secrecy and security measures; vigilance became the yardstick in making appointments; while unmasking potential enemies occupied more and more time in the Records and Personnel departments at Central Office and in the Party Control Commission (established at a Central Committee meeting in November 1948).

Reference to the circumstances and situation prevailing in the Party in late 1948 and early 1949 is necessary, since they formed the background to methods and practices that violated the most elementary standards of Party life. The door was thus opened to subjective and pragmatic judgements on events of the day, and so to an ever-increasing persecution of Party members and the use of penal sanctions against them.

We will mention two of many cases: the Karlový Vary case of 1949 and the Olomouc case of 1949–50. Both originated inside the Communist Party and both were accorded tremendous publicity.

The Karlový Vary case, which was brought to public attention in May 1949, originated with information and complaints received by leading Party officials and the Control Commission.[1] The Commission, which had been investigating the matter since mid-February, confirmed cases where undemocratic methods had been used in the Party, criticism suppressed, people browbeaten and so on; but its conclusions were marked by the atmosphere of hunting the class enemy. On 19 April Josef Kapoun submitted to the Central Committee Secretariat a full report on the investigation carried out in the Karlový Vary region and recommended a check-up. Among other arguments in support of his proposal he said: 'There are grounds for suspecting that an enemy of the Party and the State is in a leading position in the regional secretariat in Karlový Vary.' The suspicion centred on A. Tannenbaum, who was in charge of security for the region. On 20 April the Secretariat decided to send a five-member commission (Kopřiva, Taussigová, Homola, Bína and Šváb) to Karlový Vary. Early in the morning of 23 April the doors of the regional office were locked, the telephones disconnected, and the entire personnel confined in the building and interrogated one by one. A search was made of the offices and of Tannenbaum's home. After hearing the report on the investigation from Kopřiva, the Secretariat decided on 26 April to remove the Secretary of the Regional Party Committee, Škrlant, and the Security chief Tannenbaum from their posts. Other extensive personnel changes were made. In line with a decision of the Presidium of the Regional Committee on 28 September 1948, amended on 18 November, several former officials were expelled from the Party or subjected to other Party penalties. Slánský, acting on the proposals of Taussigová and Šváb, decided in June 1949 that Tannenbaum should be taken into custody; the idea was he would admit to having aided the class enemy. Although a Security investigation failed to reveal conclusive evidence of his working with an enemy,

[1] For a fuller account of the Karlový Vary case see the study by V. Brichta, prepared for the Rehabilitation Commission.

Tannenbaum, after two years in detention, received a nine-year sentence, of which he served some four and a half years.[1]

The Olomouc case bore similar features. This time it was disagreements among the leading members of the regional organization that provided the reason for an investigation. On 30 June 1949 Taussigová recommended to the Central Committee Secretariat that the Party Secretary in Olomouc, Stavinoha, and two senior regional staff members, Ryšánek and Gába, be dismissed. The Secretariat rejected this proposal, based on accusations of shortcomings and blunders in Party work. Taussigová, however, contacted Security in Olomouc and suggested they investigate; the materials they helped her to collect, plus Stavinoha's criticisms of the Secretariat, provided a pretext late in 1949 for another Party enquiry. On 4 January 1950 the Secretariat resolved to send a commission to Olomouc, its members being Švermová, Kopřiva and Taussigová. This Commission was to submit its findings to the Party Control Commission and to draft a resolution on Stavinoha's dismissal for the Presidium, which on 9 January decided to remove him immediately and have him charged. Arrest followed in the early hours of 10 January. The reasons given for these measures were corruption and – an unfounded accusation – wartime collaboration with the Gestapo. There was also talk of neglect of the 'class approach' in Party work. Penal and Party sanctions were likewise applied to others in the region. Stavinoha was interrogated by Security at Ruzyň,[2] where illegal means were used to make him confess to hostile activity. He was brought to trial in May 1950 with other accused and sentenced to imprisonment.

In the light of facts objectively ascertained it is possible to say that in both cases – Karlový Vary and Olomouc – there were defects and errors that should have been handled along Party lines. In the conditions that prevailed at the time, however, they were made into exemplary cases by means grossly

---

[1] For a fuller account see the study by J. Biebrle, prepared for the Rehabilitation Commission.

[2] *A notorious prison used mainly for political cases, and situated not far from Prague Airport.*

at variance with Party and legal procedures. The two cases demonstrate the degree to which by 1949 the search for class enemies was influencing the Party's life. Moreover, because of the tremendous publicity they received, these cases helped to distort the thinking of Party members and the work of their organizations.

THE EVOLUTION OF THE TRIALS

The main build-up of the major political trials started in our country early in 1949. Yet the situation at home, the distortion of Party work and violations of the law such as we have described above could not in themselves have given cause for the fabricating of such large-scale political trials as those in which the Czechoslovak Party became involved in the early 1950s. Throughout 1949 the Party leadership still adhered to the view expressed by Gottwald that they had all known each other over many years of joint work, and that in a legal Party, as the Czechoslovak Communist Party had been before the war, there were no grounds for such conspiracies as were supposed at that time to exist in Hungary, Poland and Bulgaria. A big part in the concocting of cases against top men in the Party and Government of Czechoslovakia was played by international factors – the Cominform policies that assumed the existence of an international imperialist conspiracy against the socialist countries, the specific political and ideological pressures exerted from without, notably Hungarian, Polish and Soviet insistence that an extensive conspiracy, or even the centre of an international plot, was located in Czechoslovakia. In the course of time these ideas came to be accepted by the Czechoslovak Party leaders, and in other quarters, especially Security. We cannot judge the conduct of the men and institutions in our Party's drama – unless, of course, we wish to exonerate them from responsibility, politically and otherwise – without taking cognizance of the distortions that had set in in political life; and in this we include the political attitudes and ideology that these men. and institutions had helped to create, and of which they, too, were, in a sense, victims.

In the end, a band of 'potential enemies' emerged, embracing certain groups of the population and, later, mainly Communists, who came under suspicion where even a shadow of doubt was cast. Their numbers grew. The first people involved had been members of the former non-Communist parties, officials of various organisations; subsequently Resistance fighters and members of the International Brigade[1] were included, besides Slovak politicians, officials of Jewish extraction, ex-Trotskyists and others. Then there were those suspected by the Soviet authorities, or whose reliability had been put in doubt by Soviet politicians, such as Vladimír Clementis, Evžen Löbl and André Simone. While the range of potential 'enemies' was fairly well defined, an often incomprehensible element of chance was also at work. In Czechoslovakia, with its wide Western contacts, a considerable number of International Brigaders who had later joined the wartime Resistance, and a sizable body of political workers, the band of 'enemies' was numerically quite considerable.

Linked up with the external circumstances leading to the search for members of an international imperialist plot, and for a 'Yugoslav agency' in the Party and in the administration of our country, were the investigation of the Rajk case in Hungary and the previously mentioned affair of the Field brothers. The relevant events were: visits by Hungarian Security officers to Prague and of their Czechoslovak opposite numbers to Budapest and Warsaw; the talks held on various occasions; letters from Rákosi and messages from Polish leaders to Gottwald.

The starting-point for the events leading up to the trials of members and officials of the Czechoslovak Party is usually said to have been a demand made in January 1949 by Hungarian Security for cooperation in investigating the case of Noel Field, and Field's abduction to Hungary in May. But there is a background to this case.

On 13 August 1948 two Security officers – Štěpán Plaček (head of internal intelligence, political counter-intelligence and economic defence) and Karel Černý (head of the organization

[1] *A volunteer force that fought on the Republican side in the Spanish Civil War.*

and personnel sector) – sent a detailed letter to Gottwald, Zápotocký and Slánský, saying that Czechoslovakia was,

especially since February, more than ever a hunting-ground for foreign agents. . . . We consider that many British nationals advertising themselves as Lefts, or even as Communists, are trained agents of the Intelligence Service. . . . It seems that in the Slav countries in general the Intelligence Service is fond of using ostensible Communists or Left intellectuals. We have no means of combating them other than infiltration of their ranks by agents.

The following quotation from the letter is typical of the psychosis then prevailing in this particular department of Security:

We point out that such a small staff of intelligence officers cannot safeguard the Republic. We fear that serious attacks on individuals may happen at any moment, we suspect that treason of a most grave nature is already rife, that the most secret documents are known to the enemy, or may become known to him at any moment. (ACC CPC,[1] File 100/24, Section 919.)

The measures advocated were intended primarily to serve the interests of national security, but they also provided an opportunity for seriously restricting unofficial information from the other side, with the result that any dialogue or exchange of views was stopped by administrative means;[2] in this the governmental machine, chiefly Security, worked hand in hand with the Party.

The department at the Ministry of the Interior headed by Jindřich Veselý (with whose knowledge the letter from the Security officers was written), and known as the State Security Service, worked closely with the Records Department of the Party Central Committee. It took part in the surveillance over Noel Field, who towards the end of 1947 and early in 1948 had expressed an interest in doing journalistic work in the People's Democracies. From the documents at present available, it is not clear whether this action was undertaken

[1] *Archives of the Central Committee, Communist Party of Czechoslovakia. This abbreviation will recur frequently.*
[2] *In other words, barriers were erected to personal contacts with the West – by restrictions on Czechoslovaks travelling abroad, by granting fewer visas for visitors to Czechoslovakia, and by keeping a strict watch on any contacts that did occur.*

on the initiative of Security or at the instigation of someone else.

Security investigation of Noel Field started in October-November 1948, when he applied for permission to stay in Czechoslovakia. At that time information about Field was conveyed to Šváb's department at the Party Central Committee by people – Alice Kohnová, Dr Gejza Pavlík and Dr Karel Markus – who were later accused of working with Field.

From the Czechoslovak side no great importance was attached to Field's case in the winter months of 1948. He was probably regarded as merely a potential spy and no wider implications were sought. (ACC CPC, File MV [i.e. Ministry of the Interior] 372 – Z – 842 – MV.)

This was the time when preparations for political trials had begun in some other countries, and a suitable link was needed to show a connection between the imperialists and a definite group of Communists in all the new democracies, including Yugoslavia. In this respect, Noel Field, as we have already mentioned, was seen as the most suitable candidate. It seems that up to February 1949 Party and Security officials in Czechoslovakia had not been let into the secret of what was going on. Things must have changed greatly when they were asked to help in inducing Field to travel from Switzerland to Czechoslovakia. They were told that an unnamed married couple from Slovakia was working with him.

On 28 February the Regional Command of Security in Prague, Department 2, gave orders to Department 4 to initiate a preliminary investigation of Dr Gejza Pavlík, Director of Čedok [Czechoslovak Travel Bureau]. Dr Pavlík had worked before the war with the Communist Party as a lawyer; as refugees from Nazism, he and his wife had spent the war years in Switzerland. There they had met Noel Field, who had assisted them from the funds of the Unitarian Service Committee (USC). Field had invited the Pavlíks (also Rudolf Feigl and his common-law wife Dr Veselá) to work with the USC in Czechoslovakia after the war. A condition of qualifying for USC aid was that the recipient should send reports on the social and economic situation in countries or areas needing help. Immediately on his return to Czechoslovakia, Dr Pavlík had given full information about the USC project to top Party officials (Dolanský, Široký, Hodinová), who did not reject it. He had worked with the USC until 1946, having by then sent Field about four reports.

Field's arrest (after being inveigled into leaving Switzerland for Prague) and that of the Pavlíks in May 1949 was made at the request of the Hungarians. From Jindřich Veselý's deposition and from other documents it seems that the Hungarian action was not particularly welcome. Veselý stated that he had been reluctant to yield to the request made by the representative of Hungarian Security for Field to be arrested on his arrival in Prague at the beginning of May. Only after personal intervention by General Belkin, and with Gottwald's agreement, was the request met. Gottwald is alleged to have said: 'If General Belkin, too, has verified it and supports it, then do as they want.' (ACC CPC, Commission II, Section 88.)

On the Czechoslovak side it was probably expected that with Field's arrest the cooperation between our Security and the Hungarians in this matter would end. On 28 May 1949, we read, 'Comrade Szücs (Colonel in the Hungarian Security Service) unexpectedly returned to Prague and recommended that Pavlík be arrested.' (ACC CPC, File MV 37 – Z – 842 – MV.) According to Szücs, Szönyi (who was condemned to death during the Rajk trial as an imperialist agent and collaborator of Field's) and others had stated that Pavlík belonged to a Hungarian Trotskyist group and was by way of being a link man between this group and Field. After preliminary interrogation in Czechoslovakia, the Pavlíks were taken to Hungary; several reminders had to be sent before they were returned to Czechoslovak Security on 30 June. Brutal physical force was used during their interrogations in Hungary, where they were questioned also by Soviet advisers.

The depositions which Dr Pavlík was forced to make were apparently designed to set the pattern for subsequent investigation in Czechoslovakia. According to these statements, the Trotskyists were planning to insinuate themselves into the top echelons of the Czechoslovak Party, as agreed at meetings with Field, and to influence policy in all areas; they were to support the Jewish bourgeoisie, incite nationalist strife – there was mention of Gustav Husák's nationalist attitude – and so on. The summaries of evidence on the Pavlík case made in Budapest are examples of the 'art' of writing such reports, an art which at that time our Security had not yet mastered.

Before the Pavlíks had been returned from Hungary, Feigl and his wife Vlasta Veselá had been arrested on 'evidence' extracted from the Pavlíks and Field. On 7 July came the arrest of Dr Alice Kohnová, who in the autumn of 1948 had helped people in the Party Central Office to keep a watch on Field.

A commission, in which Kopřiva, Veselý and Šváb had the main voice, was set up to investigate the case of Field, Pavlík and others. As a guideline, the interrogators in the case were given reports of the Trotskyist trials [in the Soviet Union] (MV 39/2, Vol. 7, p. 216), as well as notes and questions prepared by Kopřiva on 28 July 1949. (MV 39/1, Vol. 4, p. 161.) Gottwald and Slánský were kept regularly informed about the commission's findings.

The depositions made by Field, Pavlík and others in Hungary provided names for a list of sixty officials of the Czechoslovak Party suspected of various kinds of anti-Party activity, and at the end of July this list was used in working out a 'solar system' for the case that would suggest a link with a 'Trotskyist' named Ungar. Then, as the investigation proceeded, the number of suspects grew. People named in connection with the case included, for example: Clementis, Frejka, Fuchs, Goldmann, Goldstücker, Hajdů, Bedřich Hájek, Mrs Hodinová, Laštovička, Löbl, Moško, Nosek, Nový, Polák, Richard Slánský, Spurný, Šling, Való, Zmrhal, Rais, London, Falťan, Bráník, Friš, Zupka. Many of those named were later arrested, tried and condemned. The commission decided which of the suspects should be summoned for interrogation by State Security, or arrested, and who should undergo Party interrogation. The net of investigation was spread wide, but despite the brutal treatment to which the prisoners were subjected their interrogators failed to obtain evidence of any organized subversive group.

The Pavlíks withdrew their Budapest depositions on the

grounds that they had been extorted by physical coercion. Dr Pavlík protested that, as Czechoslovak nationals, they had been questioned by Hungarian officers, and on matters concerning Czechoslovakia. He also gave the names of the Czechoslovaks about whom he had been questioned.

Nor did other Security and Party investigations reveal any hostile network in the Czechoslovak Party. In those days the interrogators were not practised in pinning guilt on the innocent; they were looking for real enemies. In this situation Szücs [of the Hungarian Security Service] suggested in a talk with Šváb early in August 1949 that the whole case should be coordinated 'under the direction of the Soviet authorities'. (MV 39/1, Vol. 5, p. 338.)

At the beginning of September 1949 'only' five people were in prison in connection with the Pavlík case. Consequently the Czechoslovak handling – by Party and Security – of the job of unmasking the enemy in the Party came under fire from the top men in some of the neighbouring countries.

From then on the case proceeded under strong pressure from abroad. Proof of this is provided by a letter from Rákosi to Gottwald, dated 3 September 1949. Rákosi was highly dissatisfied with the state of affairs in Czechoslovakia. 'You have the names of the people whom the prisoners here have identified as Czechoslovak spies for Western imperialism, or who have given information to Western espionage services.' He suggested that neither the Minister of the Interior (Nosek) nor the Minister of Foreign Affairs (Clementis) could be trusted. He named as outright suspects Ludvík Frejka, Josef Goldmann and Vilém Nový.

The conclusion of this letter is interesting:

In two weeks we shall begin the case of the first group of accused in the Rajk trial. The indictment will be published in a week. In this connection we come up against the difficulty that, if we include in this group spies who were sent from England to Hungary, then Czechoslovak names will appear by the dozen at the hearing, names which you also know. All these people are at liberty. This part of the hearing would come as a surprise to the Czechoslovak public. One should realize beforehand that in such an eventuality the hard core of the people named would protest vehemently about the things said in court, and this would link them with the Titoists, who of course will not spare any effort to undermine the credibility of the charges levelled against them. (ACC CPC, File 02/2, Section 201.)

From this one can learn a lot. On the one hand, the Czechoslovak Communists were expected to regard it as their international duty to prevent suspects – people not proved guilty – from protesting against accusations, because that might create doubts about the validity of the trial; and so, to stop them protesting, it was better to shut them up. On the other hand, there is the veiled threat that Czechoslovak Communists might be labelled as allies of the Titoists.

Party and Government officials in Hungary and Poland, pleading the common interest, urged our people to arrest suspects without delay – which, it was alleged, would be dangerous not only for Czechoslovakia, but also for Poland and Hungary. There was no time, they insisted, for long preliminary investigations; it was necessary to reach the goal quickly by means of arrests, interrogations and confrontations. This was the trend of the talks Šváb had with Rákosi and with General Belkin in Budapest on 7–8 September 1949, and Veselý on 12–13 September in Warsaw with Security officers Colonels Roczanski and Swiatlo, Minister of the Interior Radkiewicz, President Bierut, Party General Secretary Zambrowski, and Berman. (MV 39/1, Vol. 4, p. 122.)

Further steps by the Czechoslovak authorities were taken in an atmosphere of psychosis about an imminent threat to the Republic and the entire socialist camp – an atmosphere further poisoned, probably, by fear that they might be labelled as allies of the Titoists for preventing a final 'unmasking' of these 'enemies'. On 16 September Gottwald and Slánský requested Malenkov to send to Czechoslovakia, as advisers, men acquainted with the handling of the Rajk case. The request was granted and on 23 September two Soviet experts, Likhachev and Makarov, arrived in Prague.

In the second half of September 1949, and after the arrival of the Soviet advisers, the hunt for a 'Czechoslovak Rajk' proceeded vigorously. The number of arrests was stepped up; altogether seventeen were made in direct connection with the case of Field, Pavlík and others. By 7 July Pavlík and his wife, Feigl, Veselá and Kohnová had been taken into custody; after 21 September they were joined by Melan, Kosta, Žaludová, Král, Brieger, Markus, Klinger, Löbl, Löblová, Milan Reiman, Nový and Nová. By 21 October, however, Šváb had reached the conclusion that the people arrested in connection with Field and Pavlík would not make possible 'any great progress in unmasking the more dangerous wreckers'. (MV 39/2, Vol. 6, p. 299.) Veterans of the International Brigade in Spain, Yugoslav partisans, 'Londoners'[1] and other potential anti-Party 'elements' had already, on the basis of information received from representatives of fraternal parties, become objects of inquiry and arrest by the end of September. Early in October a special department of the Ministry of the Interior, headed by Šváb, was set up to handle the cases in the Party.

It is clear from the documents that attempts were made to include the Field-Pavlík group in some bigger political trial. But no link with other anti-State and anti-Party groups could be proved. Ultimately the Pavlíks were tried *in camera* by the State Court in Prague, on 29 June 1950, together with Feigl and Markus. They were convicted of espionage; Markus for negligence in protecting State secrets. Unlike others whose names appeared in connection with 'Fieldism', they were not labelled as members of a conspiratorial centre. Some of the seventeen arrested in the Field case were tried on totally different 'charges'. Dr Vlasta Veselá and Milan Reiman both committed suicide before the Pavlíks came to trial.

Thus the first phase in the search for an imperialist plot at top levels in the Party and Government was unsuccessful. True, a group of suspects was defined, and interrogations, investigations and arrests took place, but the main purpose was not achieved. There followed a retreat from the earlier idea about how to seek out the enemy inside the Party, though this was merely part of an attempt to cast the net at still higher levels. The trials held in Czechoslovakia (of Pavlík *et al.*, etc.) did not seem, compared with those in the other countries, to be

[1] *People who had been refugees in Britain during the war were often referred to as 'Londoners'.*

sufficiently representative, and they failed to support the theory that our country was the scene of the most widespread subversion; but there was no question of a renunciation of the political and other motives that had set things in motion. A useful link between the investigations carried out up to this point and the subsequent trials was provided by people under arrest, through whom enquiries were directed into higher official circles.

One cannot omit to mention the consequences of these developments for public life. The trials in the neighbouring countries, especially the Rajk trial, greatly affected the atmosphere in the Czechoslovak Party. The Rajk trial was still in progress when, on 20 September 1949, the Central Committee Secretariat decided to launch a large-scale campaign within the Party. Mention of Czechoslovakia, during the Budapest proceedings, as a country where a powerful foreign agency was operating undoubtedly made an impression. The Party was seized by a craze for hunting the 'Czechoslovak Rajk', and a Cominform meeting in November of that year reinforced this atmosphere. The failure to achieve visible results merely produced a still greater tension, together with a steady widening of the range of potential suspects, and reorganization and expansion of Security.

The state in which the Party found itself is best illustrated by a speech made by Slánský at a meeting of Prague activists in the Lucerna Hall on 7 December. Referring to the experience gained from the trials in the other countries, he said:

Nor will our Party escape having the enemy place his people among us and recruiting his agents among our members. . . . Aware of this, we must be all the more vigilant, so that we can unmask the enemies in our own ranks, for they are the most dangerous enemies.

At this gathering Slánský also outlined ways of seeking and finding the enemies. The first thing was to take a good hard look at those who voiced incorrect views, because that was the way that 'the true bourgeois-nationalist face' of a spy revealed itself. Secondly, it was necessary to examine how political tasks were carried out, because difficulties, irregularities and muddles could be signs of deliberate sabotage. Lastly, a daily check on Party functionaries was needed, with special attention to their past, because 'dark spots' in their lives could be misused by enemy agencies.

Slánský's speech provided a complete justification for extensive security work inside the Communist Party, and for the general attitude of suspicion; it could not but have the gravest consequences. By the end of 1949 the course of events abroad and the trend of Party policy had produced a state of affairs where it was no longer possible to halt the process of distortion in the Party and in State Security. Lack of success in the investigations led, not to any reassessment of the original assumptions, but, on the contrary, to a compounding of the blunders. Under these conditions the preparation of the political trials entered upon a new and more dangerous phase.

The second half of 1949 and the beginning of 1950 saw the emergence of circumstances which were to have a far-reaching effect on the political 'cases' and trials. Impulses from the outside found the soil already prepared by previous developments, and on this soil they assumed their Czechoslovak form. The significant factors were, on the one hand, the Rajk trial in Hungary and the November 1949 Cominform meeting, and, on the other hand, a number of internal decisions and moves directed towards a more intensive search for 'class enemies', whether presumed to come from the classes that had been overthrown, from the crushed Opposition, from 'imperialist agents' or – the favoured candidates – from 'enemies inside the Communist Party'.

In the implementation of the Cominform's second resolution on the Communist Party of Yugoslavia (certain measures actually anticipated this resolution), the emphasis was on rapidly 'improving' the mechanism designed to hunt out political offenders.

In consequence of the Rajk case, however, both Budapest and Warsaw began to insist more and more that the centre of an internationally linked plot existed in the Czechoslovak Republic; and responsible circles in that country – the Party leaders and State Security – were blamed for their failure to uncover it. Evidently it was these charges that impelled Gottwald and Slánský to write in September 1949 to the Party leadership in Moscow asking them to send security advisers, although it seems that initially they had been reluctant to take this step, having heard from Veselý and Šváb about the harsh treatment of Czechoslovak nationals during the preparations for the Rajk trial.

The Czechoslovak request was granted, and the Soviet advisers Makarov and Likhachev, who had handled the Rajk trial in Budapest, arrived in October; soon afterwards, however, they were replaced by a second group headed by Boyarsky.

Almost from the outset these advisers wielded extraordinary powers; they were not controlled in any way by the Czechoslovak authorities and felt themselves responsible solely to the Soviet Ministry of State Security, then headed by Beria. They kept the top political and security people in Moscow informed about the progress and trends of the investigations in Czechoslovakia, and about people who might be suspected of political deviations or subversive actions, especially about leading personalities in the Party and the Government, and about people employed in the political, military, security, economic and diplomatic fields.

With the arrival of the Soviet advisers, changes took place in the work done by Czechoslovak Security. Preparations for political trials now assumed massive proportions. An entirely new *modus operandi* was introduced; the investigation of genuine offences in the light of verified evidence was replaced by the search for enemies, primarily inside the Communist Party. Political views expressed not only in deeds, but also in words or intentions, fulfilled or otherwise, and also confessions of imaginary 'hostile acts', now served as evidence. By variously combining such testimony from prisoners, the Security officers were able to fabricate hostile groups and treasonable offences. Once a man was detained, therefore, his confessions could provide the starting-point for further investigations and convictions. Hence everything was done to extract 'confessions' and depositions. The inhuman methods used, involving a carefully worked out system of physical and mental coercion, have been described in numerous books and newspaper articles.

Often a sincerely self-critical admission of error, or a single obscure point in a *curriculum vitae*, was enough for a man to be denounced and arrested; or the cause could be mere tittle-tattle or slander, a fabrication or provocation. Special attention was paid to anybody even remotely suspected of holding Trotskyist or nationalist views (the latter being automatically taken to be anti-Soviet), to people of Jewish extraction (denounced as Zionists), and to anyone who had spent some time in the Western countries or lived in a 'bourgeois environment'. In a word, an arrested man was assumed to be guilty, and the interrogators had merely to 'make' a case out of him and secure his conviction. The purpose of the interrogation was to break the victim at all costs, to extract a confession irrespective of whether he had committed an offence or not. To achieve this, all kinds of mental and physical coercion and brute force were permissible. The usual method was an endless interrogation of the victim, with the officers working in shifts so that he or she received only a minimum of rest; to this was added beatings, torture by hunger and thirst, confinement in the dark chamber, the inculcation of fear about the fate of the prisoner's family, subtly staged confrontations, the use of stool pigeons, the bugging of cells, and many other refinements.

In our archives we have confirmation of the kind of activities carried out by Soviet Security men in the socialist countries – activities condemned by the Central Committee of the Soviet Communist Party in June 1955. In addressing this meeting, Khrushchev said:

To have agencies in the fraternal parties, to spy on these parties, and especially to spy on their leaders, that is the worst violation of the standards of conduct in the relations between parties and states. A situation of this kind can, in the end, lead only to conflict.

The leadership of the Soviet Party criticized the conduct of the advisers and some of them were brought to trial as 'Beria's agents' and executed.

From the moment they arrived in Prague the advisers Likhachev and Makarov were critical of Czechoslovak Security for being weak and indecisive, for allowing itself to be sidetracked, for not pressing its views and demands with sufficient energy, and for being 'soft' with the class enemy. On these grounds they urged that the reorganization of State Security, started just before their arrival, be speeded up. This project involved a whole set of changes in approach, organization and staffing, a notable feature being that a section of the Party machine became interlocked with the State Security mechanism as never before.

The entire concept[1] can be taken to date from mid-1949, when the General Secretary of the Party, Rudolf Slánský, was exerting an increased influence – for which he had no legal justification – on the direction of State Security. This took place, in effect, without the knowledge of the Minister of the Interior, Nosek, who, though a member of the Central Committee and the Presidium, was under suspicion in connection with the Rajk case (and because he had spent the war years in Britain), and was by now kept in almost complete ignorance of what was happening in the department of his Ministry involved. In 1950 Gottwald himself assumed responsibility for security.

At the end of September or beginning of October 1949 Slánský informed Nosek, Veselý and Pavel that

it has been decided to set up a special department for investigating Party and political offences. . . . It will be headed by Šváb, who will remain an employee of the Party and will not in any way be answerable to the Ministry of the Interior. The Party will provide him with the staff and the Ministry will give him office space, transport and everything he needs for the job. Formally he will be named as second in command of State Security.

Šváb was joined at the Ministry of the Interior by three other employees of the Party Central Office: Synková, Doubek and Pimpara.

His first move at the Ministry was to divide his staff into two groups, one concerned with evaluation, the other with investigation. The first group, headed by Synková, evaluated the summaries of evidence obtained from people already under detention: the second, headed by Doubek, worked under the

[1] See M. Mnichovský: 'State Security and the Records Department of the CC CPC, and the Party Control Commission, 1946–51'.

personal supervision of Šváb and supplied him with daily reports on the investigations. Towards the end of 1949 and early in 1950 Šváb's department, its staff reinforced by State Security men and Party officials – early in 1950 there were 28 to 30 working there – was reorganized on a more sophisticated basis and named Sector IIa. It was divided into the following sections: an anti-Trotskyist section, a section for enemies inside the Party, one for members of the International Brigade and one for bourgeois nationalists.

Towards the end of 1949 Šváb decided that a Commission of Inquiry that had been working in Hradec Králové should be wound up and some of its members (Dr Smola, Arazin, Šubrt, Linhart and others) transferred to Sector IIa, where they formed a section, headed by Dr Smola, which was to check up on the police intelligence network operating in the Party and to unmask class enemies.

In Slovakia, too, a department for seeking the enemy inside the Party was established at a meeting held on 10 October 1949 and attended by Šváb, Široký and Kopřiva. One of the first tasks of Baláž, the head of the new department, was to keep tabs on Karol Šmidke, then in charge of the personnel department of the Slovak Party. Soon there was another assignment when the Soviet adviser Likhachev gave instructions that compromising material should immediately be collected concerning Koloman Moškovič and other leading Slovak Communists.

The reorganization produced a new Security machine for hunting the enemy inside the Party. A feature of this institution was that it was supervised by the General Secretary, and later by the Chairman of the Party, while the actual work was controlled by employees of the Party Secretariat. In Slovakia, Party Chairman Široký and General Secretary Baštovanský held similar powers.

On a national scale this apparatus soon became a key part of the newly-established (May 1950) Ministry of National Security, headed by Kopřiva (from January 1952 by Bacílek).

Our picture of the mechanism for hunting 'enemies' and initiating political trials would be incomplete without some mention of various other factors that developed from 1950

onwards. First, a section of the staff working for the Party
Control Commission switched from its original job – checking
on members' performance of Government and Party work,
countering bureaucracy and so on – to the search for 'enemies'
among Communists in the most varied spheres of Party and
public life. Thanks to the screening campaigns of 1948 and
1950 and to a wide network of informers, the Control Commission's section for Party institutions had at its disposal a
growing body of damaging reports about functionaries, and
about the situation in various branches and at places of work;
and these reports were used with increasing frequency as the
basis for a witch-hunt against supposed saboteurs. Security
methods were introduced in some sectors of the Commission's
work, with encouragement from Köhler and Kopřiva. Some
of the staff, indeed, had from 1949 onwards been indulging in
such practices as tapping telephones, opening mail and making
combined Party and Security interrogations of Party suspects.
In short, the Control Commission was losing its image of a
political instrument and turning into a kind of Security arm
engaged in a massive search for the enemy inside the Party.

The situation was complicated by growing rivalry and mistrust in the relations between the Control Commission and State
Security. Some of the Commission's staff (Taussigová, Hora,
Bína, Klicha and others) gradually became convinced that
quite a number of top people in State Security lacked the
necessary ability and determination to discover the Czechoslovak Rajk, that they were even covering up political sabotage
(in the Brno case, for example), and that they wanted to
break free from Party control – indeed, to impose their own
control on the Party. Towards the end of 1950 suspicion turned
against Šváb, the man whom the Party leadership had appointed
to a top post in State Security. Two of the Control Commission
staff (Hora and Klicha) were installed in the central Security
office to collect information about leading people there.

These facts indicate that in the second half of 1949 a truly
paradoxical situation was taking shape. On the initiative of the
top men in the Party, a section had been established for hunting
enemies in the Party; while operating in parallel with this, in
the shape of the Party Control Commission, was a Party

section that included Security methods in its repertoire of techniques used for unmasking enemies among the Communists employed in State Security. It is easy to understand how in the early 1950s, when both organizations took a hand in preparing and carrying through the political cases and the trials, there were often sudden switches, with the hunter becoming the hunted, the prosecutor the accused, and the interrogator the interrogated.

Not least among the links in the mechanism of hunting enemies and staging trials was the establishment of a Security Commission in the Party Central Office and of the 'fives' (or in districts 'threes') which from 1949 to 1951 were attached to the Regional Committees. Here, too, there was a close inter-locking of Party and Security work. As a rule the 'fives' consisted of the Security Secretary of the Party's regional secretariat, the regional Chief of State Security, the regional Chief of Police,[1] plus the regional Prosecutor or other officials according to need; they were directed by the Party Secretary for the given region. These 'fives' coordinated all the Security work in the various regions. Gradually it became common practice (especially in 1950 and 1951) for them to assume quite un-warranted powers, operating as centres of repression in their respective areas. They issued the directives and orders for security 'cover' in connection with such political and economic measures as the selection of people to be sent to forced labour camps, the handling of Church matters, the removal to remote districts of political undesirables, and punitive action against opponents of collectivization or against farmers who failed to fulfil the harsh delivery quotas. They intervened drastically in legal matters, pre-judging, for instance, the outcome of all major criminal and political cases in their regions; the political trials, indeed, they managed from beginning to end, vetting the case for the prosecution, deciding the sentences to be handed down, expressing opinions on pleas for clemency, and directing how cases should be exploited politically.

Thus by the end of 1949 and the beginning of 1950 (after the

[1] *The word Police is used here for the National Security Corps (SNB), comprising all police departments (transport, public order, crime), excluding State Security (STB), but working in close contact with the latter.*

Rajk trial, the second Cominform resolution and the subsequent meetings of top Party committees) the method of dealing with anti-socialist forces had been established in broad outline and the necessary mechanism prepared. Moreover, people detained earlier were now 'exploited' for the set purpose of discovering suspects and hostile groupings at every step and in the most varied walks of life; fresh large-scale arrests also served these ends.

One of the areas of search (not, as it shortly appeared, the main one) was among the classes that had been deposed by the post-war revolution, that is among the one-time political partners and, later, adversaries of the Party in the days before February 1948. The idea was that in the endeavour to put the finishing touch to the 1948 victory, and provide additional evidence that the takeover was justified, while also hitting back at the sporadic attempts at post-February opposition, it should be demonstrated that there really was an organized underground of former capitalists and members of the pre-February political parties; this underground should be shown as having links with imperialist intelligence services and anti-Communist organizations abroad. By November 1949, over 600 arrests had been made, mainly among members of the Czech Socialist, Catholic and Social Democratic parties, and some alleged Trotskyists. The outcome was a monster trial with 'the leaders of a terrorist conspiracy headed by Dr Horáková' in the dock. The hearing from 31 May to 8 June 1950 ended with four death sentences and nine long terms of imprisonment. A number of subsidiary trials followed. There was a similar background to the arrests and trials of numerous Church dignitaries. The first of these trials was held in the spring of 1950. One of the more spectacular, the 'Trial of Vatican Agents in Czechoslovakia' (December 1950), clearly demonstrated that the men who staged them had thoroughly assimilated the techniques and the professional know-how needed for the purpose. The accused replied to questions precisely according to a prepared script, confessing to sabotage at home and to contacts abroad. The fanfare which accompanied this trial (and that of Dr Horáková and others) played its part in whipping up spy mania, convincing the public that the accused were guilty, and encouraging the idea that there must be still more plots waiting to be discovered. In this respect the trials were a rehearsal for the still bigger events to come.

From the time of the Cominform's second resolution, attention had been centred on uncovering the Czechoslovak Rajk, his collaborators at home and his confidently assumed links with the imperialist intelligence services and with the 'Titoist agency'.

The impulse for the first arrests of individuals, and later of Party officials by the dozen, came from the list of people named during the Rajk trial, and also from testimonies made under compulsion by those arrested earlier. The net of suspicion was spread wider as prisoners 'confessed' to their errors and were forced to name colleagues and friends. For example, two of the first to be arrested – Evžen Löbl and Vilém Nový – while not admitting to sabotage themselves, were soon reduced to a state in which they testified about others and developed the theme placed before them, according to the wishes of the interrogators and advisers. Then, when the moment was ripe, the appropriate ideological campaign was launched, providing the public with plausible arguments designed to secure their cooperation.

This was the case, for instance, with the first of the big trials in Slovakia, that of 'the Slovak bourgeois nationalists'.[1]

It should be stated that the first serious public reference to 'the influence of petit-bourgeois nationalism' in the Slovak Party came in a speech by Široký to the Central Committee in Slovakia in September 1948, evidently in connection with the first Cominform resolution and with the attacks on Gomulka in Poland. At the time, however, an assurance was given that the Slovak leadership showed no particular trend away from the policy of the Party as a whole.

The subject was revived early in 1950. On 13 March, in a speech to the Presidium of the Czechoslovak Central Committee, Kopřiva voiced criticism of Foreign Minister Clementis, who was accused of bourgeois nationalism, of a hostile attitude to the USSR in the past (Clementis had disapproved of the Soviet-German Pact in 1939) and of an 'intellectualist' approach to the Party. The meeting resolved (a) to recall

[1] See J. Měchýř and L. Niklíček: 'The Case of the Bourgeois Nationalists'.

Clementis from his post as Minister of Foreign Affairs, and (b) to require him to submit to the Presidium a detailed statement criticizing his own work over the years.

At a joint meeting of the Presidia of the Czechoslovak and Slovak Central Committees the attacks on Clementis were repeated. (Slánský referred to such criticism as the first step in implementing the Cominform resolution of November 1949.) The really bitter denunciations of Clementis came from Kopřiva, Šafránek, Ďuriš and Slánský. Other speakers, too, were critical, differing only in the sharpness of their attacks. No one supported Clementis, who found himself completely isolated.

On 16 March regional Party committees were informed of the criticism, and a fresh campaign was launched throughout the Party; and this before the victim could say a word in his defence.

For Clementis this whole business was a crushing blow. 'I was stupefied', he wrote, 'by the suddenness of the attack and by the way it was carried out . . . because for a full five years I have not had any reprimand or criticism.' It was perfectly easy, he went on, to check on the things with which he was charged; in 1945, for instance, he had submitted in writing a self-criticism at the time his Party membership had been restored. In short, he advanced logical arguments. But this was a fundamental error, since it assumed his accusers were really anxious to establish the truth.

Eventually, it seems, he realized that a defence based on factual, logical argument was hopeless, and he finally complied with the Presidium's demand by submitting a self-critical document in which he admitted, in effect, the errors attributed to him, while trying to explain them. It was rejected by the Presidium. A commission composed of Kopecký, Bareš and Köhler wrote a reply, which was sent to Clementis, and in which his rebuttal was described as 'legalistic' and a new statement was demanded. Even his self-critical speech at the Party's Ninth Congress was rejected, and in due course Clementis took the next step along his path of no return. In yet another statement, dated 27 June 1950, he abandoned his resistance, admitting without any reservation all the charges.

But even this was not enough, even abject humiliation was unacceptable.

Meanwhile the case had acquired new dimensions. The list of alleged bourgeois nationalists was extended in April 1950 to include Ladislav Novomeský, Gustav Husák, Karol Šmidke, Eduard Friš and, in the course of time, others. At the Ninth Congress of the Slovak Party held in May it was claimed that the accused had been guilty of a bourgeois-nationalist attitude from the 1930s (the *DAV* Group),[1] that they had injured the struggle for national liberation, especially the national uprising in Slovakia,[2] that they had allied themselves with the Slovak capitalists against the Czech nation and the Czech working class, that they had wavered in their attitude to the Soviet Union (particularly Clementis over the Soviet–German Pact), and so on. After the Congress, Husák, Novomeský and Šmidke were also removed from their posts.

Subsequent revelations have shown that the ideological and political drive against the 'bourgeois nationalists' was merely the outward expression of Security's drive for a monster trial at which a group of leading Communists would be pilloried as traitors to the working class, men who had allied themselves with the capitalists on an anti-Soviet and anti-Czech platform. This fitted in with the pattern of the Cominform's second resolution, insisting as it did that any attempt to stress national features and any deviation from the Soviet model of socialism were tantamount to a betrayal of socialism.

Security's preparations for 'rounding up' a group of Slovak 'bourgeois nationalists' went ahead from the autumn of 1949. Šváb and the Soviet advisers, who displayed much initiative, were responsible for assembling the 'incriminating information', and with the aid of Löbl and Nový, then in custody, they at last managed to concoct a more or less coherent case. Using this

[1] *DAV was a periodical published in the 1930s by a group of Communist intellectuals in Slovakia. The name, which means 'crowd', was composed of the initials of three moving spirits in the group, two of whom, Okáli and Clementis, are mentioned in this Report.*

[2] *In August 1944 Slovakia rose in revolt against the Nazis. The uprising was crushed, but it provided an inspiring example to the liberation movement. In the 1950s the whole affair became the subject of political recrimination.*

material, they prepared a document on the bourgeois-nationalist deviation in the Slovak Party, basing themselves on the assumption that in the person of Clementis they had discovered the Czechoslovak Rajk. Their document was submitted to Gottwald, and many passages from it were incorporated verbatim in a speech by Široký at the Ninth Congress. In fact, the ideological onslaught on bourgeois nationalism launched in March 1950 was a brain-washing operation intended to prepare the accused and the public for the 'liquidation' to come. So that no matter how Clementis and others might try to respond by self-criticism, the Party was no longer in a mood to listen to them.

We know from many testimonies that Gottwald, Slánský, Široký, Baštovanský and Zápotocký were kept in the picture by Šváb about all Security's projects. Široký, especially, was active in cooperating with Security and in providing ideological leadership to the campaign.

It was only a matter of time – given the principle that every deviation must conceal hostile intent – before the ideological attacks would, with the duly prepared agreement of the Party membership and the public, be translated into charges of sabotage. This happened early in 1951, in connection with the parallel 'case' of Otto Šling and Marie Švermová. At a meeting of the Czechoslovak Central Committee held on 21 February, Baštovanský officially announced in a speech on 'the unmasking of espionage and sabotage by Clementis, and on the anti-Party factional group of bourgeois nationalists in the Slovak Communist Party' that the affair of Clementis and his associates was no longer a political issue; it was now a criminal case to be handled by Security and the courts. Dismissals, arrests, expulsions from Parliament and Party, were now the order of the day. In addition to Clementis, Gustav Husák, Ladislav Novomeský, Daniel Okáli, Ivan Horváth and Ladislav Holdoš were among those taken into custody. Orders for the arrests were issued by the Minister of National Security, Kopřiva, acting on decisions made by Gottwald, Zápotocký, Slánský and Široký.

Later the fabricators of the trials transferred Clementis to the 'Conspiratorial Centre of Rudolf Slánský', because by then the more highly placed Slánský had been picked for the part of the Czechoslovak Rajk.

The 'Brno case', initiated in 1950, resembled in many respects the initiation of the previously mentioned Karlový Vary and Olomouc cases. But the Brno case developed in an atmosphere of greater tension, with all the threads acquiring greater substance and the circumstances being treated more seriously.

Reports on the Brno region reaching the Party's Central Office from various quarters focussed attention on Party work, on the critical situation in the Brno engineering plants, on the coercion used to make farmers pool their resources during the 1950 harvest, and so on. While there were some complaints by individuals, the bulk of the information came from numerous Security reports referring to such internal concerns of industry as plan fulfilment, deliveries and absenteeism. Security interest in Otto Šling (the Regional Party Secretary) dated from late 1949, but the personal element did not appear in the Party investigation of the Brno case until July 1950, and even in October it was still not pronounced. Šling undoubtedly represented a certain concept of Party policy which had yielded visible results – indeed, it had been held up as an example to other regions – but it had its opponents and its critics who, taken together, formed a fairly well-defined opposition to Šling, both in the region and in the Prague Central Office. Thus his leadership was attacked from somewhat contradictory standpoints. He was criticized, for example, for not appointing pre-war Communists to top posts, for slackness in applying Soviet experience, for insufficient attention to the specific features of the region, for introducing Security practices and dictatorial methods into Party work, for failing to appreciate the outlook of the working class and not living their life, and so on. As a man Šling was full of initiative, energetic, but ambitious, rather intolerant and apt to go to extremes. While he could hit back hard at his opponents, he was not in a position to defeat criticism, which was now turning against Communist Party policy; and in this context he, too, was a target, both as an active and often over-zealous practitioner of Stalinism, and also as a politician of 1945–8, unable entirely to forget the less rigid methods of those days.

For about six weeks in 1950 a Party enquiry examined the growing complaints (here the Control Commission was active); but Security, too, was taking an interest in more and more questions – indeed, on some points it was the first in the field and it did not hesitate to resort to outright acts of provocation in the endeavour to arouse opposition to Šling. A Party check-up, however, attended by Dolanský and Köhler on behalf of the Central Committee, ended favourably, and the Secretariat even considered whether Šling might not be appointed Secretary of the Prague region in place of Antonín Novotný, whose work was meeting with considerable disapproval among the top leadership. Šling's position was still strong enough for him to silence some of the opponents of his regional policy. He accused, for example, Zavazalová of Titoism and handed her 'case' to State Security for 'implementation'; he also made a political case, handled by a special commission, out of criticisms voiced by a Member of Parliament, Marie Syrovátková-Palečková.

Soon, however, some of Šling's ill-considered campaigns – a theatrically staged check-up on district officials in Znojmo and plans for a similar step in the regional Presidium – led the Control Commission and the central Secretariat to suspect some infringement of rules in the Brno region. Accordingly, in June 1950 enquiries were started, the Control Commission being assisted by groups of Communist industrial workers. Some matters were under investigation simultaneously, or even earlier, by State Security.

When the Secretariat heard the report of the Party inquiry on 15 July, it unanimously rejected the conclusions, and the Control Commission's procedure came under heavy fire. It was generally felt that the Commission had not verified its information and had included in its report tittle-tattle and petty reactionary matters (Bareš). The debate ended in arguments about how to interpret the Party's leading role in relation to other parts of the social organism and about the method of handling cases submitted by the Control Commission.

Examination of Brno affairs continued under a Commission headed by Josef Frank, which within a few weeks produced a draft resolution 'on errors and methods of work in the conduct of cadre policy by the Brno Regional Committee of the Party', the author being Bruno Köhler. The faults recorded were depicted as shortcomings shared by the entire regional organization, and no disciplinary measures were suggested. Plans for Šling's transfer to another post were not connected with this. However, the draft resolution was never discussed, for quite unexpectedly, on 6 October, Šling was arrested.

The arrest followed the production by Security of a letter allegedly sent by Šling to a Czechoslovak intelligence officer, Emanuel Voska, on 17 April 1939. Since there was no conclusive proof of Šling's authorship, the document was of doubtful validity (it could have been a plant by Security), and in any case it provided no real evidence of spying or of commitment to a foreign espionage centre. Nevertheless, this letter was passed by Šváb and Kopřiva to Gottwald and the Presidium; after hearing their opinion, Kopřiva gave a verbal order for Šling's arrest to Prchal [a Security officer]. The letter then served as the starting-point in building up the entire case, which rested on a theory advanced by Kopřiva and the Soviet adviser Boyarsky that the background to the letter was a commitment to cooperate in spying and that it proved this cooperation had continued. All the errors and shortcomings in Šling's work, previously examined by the Party, were now seen in a new light. Security and Party officials were convinced that thorough investigation would reveal a broadly based conspiracy inside the Communist Party.

For several days Šling's arrest was kept secret from his colleagues and the public, but security measures were taken (telephone-tapping, shadowing, surveillance of people's homes, etc.) and the ground was prepared among Party members and the public for organized mass agreement with the arrest. From the moment when Party activists in Brno were told the news, the information was so falsified and exaggerated that the outcome could only be hysterical revulsion against Šling. Even at this stage the public was being manipulated into believing him guilty of dreadful crimes against the Party, the State and the people, and demanding drastic punishment. The green light was given in the Party branches and in the factories to declarations of no confidence in Šling's colleagues; an inspired campaign, highly dogmatic in tone, insisted on 'Bolshevik' methods being introduced in the Party and the Stalinist idea of the way to socialism being enforced in all sectors. More than a few voices were heard suggesting that in punishing Šling and his associates the experience of the Soviet trials of the 1930s and the recent trials of Rajk and Kostov should be borne in mind.

This campaign reflected the new attitude in Party and Security circles to the whole affair. The Party Secretariat instructed Köhler to rewrite his resolution on the Brno region; accordingly, Köhler now attributed to Šling evil intent and espionage, although, apart from the dubious letter taken from the Voska file, there was no new evidence. Ail that was available was Šling's confession of espionage, extorted at grilling inter-rogations and immediately retracted.

Then, on 10–11 November, the case came up for discussion at the Regional Party Committee in Brno; a Central Committee delegation consisting of Frank, Bareš and Köhler, accompanied by Karla Pfeiferová, Taussigová and Kapoun, took an active part in the meeting and submitted the final draft of Köhler's resolution, in which Šling was described as an 'enemy agent' instead of a spy (the amendment was made by Gottwald and Slánský). In his summing-up, however, Bareš made an open accusation of espionage.

Both in the resolution and in Frank's speech, Šling was accused of introducing incorrect methods into Party work, of suppressing criticism and self-criticism, and of ingenious sabotage in personnel policy. Lack of proper attention to opposition from the class enemy in Czechoslovakia was acknowledged as a grave error. The remedies suggested in a programmatic statement by the leadership foreshadowed events to come; they were to be sought in the experience of the Soviet Party, in the Soviet political trials, in the Cominform resolutions on Yugoslavia, in the trials in Bulgaria and Hungary – that is, in foreign sources and not primarily in an analysis of the political issues at home.

Having voiced no doubts about the procedure in Šling's case, the Brno meeting approved the measures taken. Šling was expelled from the Party and drastic changes were made in the regional leadership. On the evening of 11 November 1950, when the meeting was over, State Security proceeded to make arrests – the victims including employees of the Party Regional Committee and of the National Committee in Brno, dismissed only a few hours previously from their posts.

After the meeting the entire region was swept by a renewed wave of suspicion against anyone in any way connected with Šling's work; as the hunt for his potential allies and for a 'reserve Šling leadership' proceeded, the mood of apprehension grew. The term 'Šlingism', coined in those days, was applied to anyone who strayed even an inch from the straight and narrow; it was also a useful weapon in settling personal accounts.

The atmosphere of mistrust and intolerance spread in all directions, sweeping into other regions, into the branches and even into the Central Office. At the Brno meeting, for instance, Rudolf Barák (soon to become Chairman of the Regional National Committee), speaking for his District Committee, called for a search for Šling's protectors in the top Party committees and demanded self-critical statements from Central Committee members Švermová, Dolanský, Kapoun and Sova. Soon voices demanding severe punishment for Šling's accomplices, regardless of their positions, spread far beyond the Brno region.

Few places where Šling had had official or personal contacts escaped this feverish search. The chief target was State Security, alleged to have been his main support. On 14 December 1950 the Ministry of National Security received information about a group of Brno Security officers then working in Prague (including Procházka, of the Security Department of the Party Central Committee, and Zahajský, Regional Commander of State Security in Prague), while the reports also referred to Šling's contacts with Josef Pavel, Ivo Milén, Dr Karel Černý and others. Taussigová doubted whether the top men in Security really intended to pursue the investigation to its conclusion and suggested more than once to Slánský that they should be screened.

Šling's contacts before February 1948 with generals in the Brno area, the activities of the 'Brno Trotskyists', the situation on the State Farms, for which Smrkovský was responsible nationally; these and other matters came in for attention. From all this there emerged a tangled skein that could easily be seen as a deep-laid plot involving all the top echelons in the Administration, Security, the Armed Forces and the Party. On 6 November 1950 a special Security group headed by Captain Kroupa was set up to unravel the threads; as part of 'Action B' it was to keep under surveillance, interrogate and check up on anyone who had had anything to do with Šling. On 13 November the Secretariat of the Central Committee was instructed by the Presidium to make a detailed investigation along Party lines and to examine all functionaries who had been appointed to Party or Government posts on Šling's recommendation. The investigation was carried out by Köhler, Baramová, Papež, Synková, Vecker, Bína, Moravec and Pechník of the Personnel Department at Party Central Office. (In the records that have been preserved this group is referred to as the 'Special Commission' for the Brno case.) Smaller groups dealt separately with the Party, Government and economic apparatus, the International Brigaders, wartime émigrés in the West, illegal groups in the Brno region, and Trotskyists. Baramová, via Papež, was responsible for keeping the Minister of National Security, Kopřiva, posted about the most important findings.

By the beginning of 1951 some twenty arrests had been made in connection with the investigation of the Šling affair, mainly in the Brno region. They included members of the 'Generals' Group' (General Bulander and Army General Novák, Commander of the Third Military Area). On 29 January they were joined by Bedřich Kopold (formerly a political officer with the Third Military Area), while suspicion spread to other military personnel, and similarly to people holding governmental and economic posts. Baramová reported to Gottwald on 3 January that her Commission had examined over 600 personal dossiers and managed to find a number of Šling's friends in leading positions. At the time of the Central Committee meeting in February 1951, some fifty people were under interrogation in prison, including a group from Slovakia and three regional Party officials (Ervín Polák, Hanuš Lomský and Vítězslav

Fuchs) who, like Šling, were of Jewish extraction and were regarded as his accomplices.

In the first big group of Communists under arrest, the Command of Czechoslovak Security occupied a special position; indeed, there was almost a clean sweep of the top men (Josef Pavel, Osvald Závodský, Ivo Milén and others). This was a necessary step in preparing the political trials, for most of these experienced Communists and Resistance fighters knew the men due for arrest and had raised spasmodic objections to certain moves. They were under suspicion, both from the Soviet advisers and from some members of the Party Control Commission, because they came within the circle of potential enemies – International Brigaders, 'Londoners' and others.

The persistent probing among Šling's colleagues and friends proved fatal for Marie Švermová, a member of the Presidium and a Secretary at the Party Central Office. Her involvement in the Brno affair promised to give the case the character of a conspiracy extending into the highest levels of the Party and of Security (she was Šváb's sister) and directed against leading politicans, notably Gottwald and Slánský. Speculation about a possible anti-Party relationship between Šling and Švermová started shortly after the former's arrest, and Gottwald referred to the Brno case at a meeting of the Presidium on 14 December 1950. In view of certain statements extorted from Šling, Švermová was recommended to take a holiday and to hold no office until the next meeting of the Central Committee, when a final decision about her would be made. From the end of January 1951 she was kept under house arrest. On 22 January the Presidium appointed a Commission, composed of Kopecký, Köhler and Bareš, to examine the relationship between Šling and Švermová and to estimate the extent of all Šling's activities. By mid-February the Commission had held several interviews with Švermová; two Security officers (Doubek and Roček) attended, and the results of Šling's interrogation were used to bring pressure to bear on her. The presence of the Security officers at these interviews was not the only evidence of the merging of the Party and Security investigations, for Köhler, in his turn, took an active hand in influencing the investigation of Šling, sending through Kopřiva his suggestions for a system of questions that could build up the Šling and Švermová cases into something of Party and nation-wide significance. Both the Investigating Commission and the highest Party authority ignored Švermová's letters to Gottwald which, in addition to the self-critical statements that she was manœuvred into making, expressed a most urgent appeal for recognition of her innocence and for an objective assessment of the false charges against her. In a long talk Gottwald personally urged her to help the Party 'unmask the agent'. In this way the Brno case was put in a new light and turned into the case of Šling-Švermová, with Švermová accused of knowing about Šling's sabotage and, instead of helping to expose it, concealing it.

It was on these lines that Kopecký in February 1951 reported to the Central Committee, speaking for the Commission of Inquiry and the Presidium. He cited as proof a number of 'confessions' invented by Šling and he also attempted to link the case with that of Clementis, which was the subject of a report by Baštovanský at the same meeting. Kopecký categorically denounced Šling as 'a spy, brute, cynic and murderer', who was now revealed as 'a criminal monster, a vicious pervert, a wicked adventurer'. He accused him of plotting a major conspiracy in all sectors of Party and governmental machinery, the alleged aim being to depose Slánský, kill Gottwald and change the leadership. With the approval of this report by the Central Committee and its acceptance throughout the Party, the green light had been given at the highest level to the fabricated Šling case and to the course the inquiry was to take.

In Kopecký's speech Švermová was charged with aiding and abetting Šling, and highly distasteful allegations were made against her. She was dubbed a nationalist intent on forging a special Czechoslovak road to socialism, a Trotskyist of violently anti-Soviet views, and a Titoist. Other speakers suggested that Šling and Švermová had wanted to oust Novotný from his post as Party Secretary in Prague. Švermová denied having been involved in any conspiracy or having known about one. The Central Committee, however, refused to accept her statement, and removed her from her post and expelled her from the Party. Upon leaving the hall she was arrested. Not until a month later did she confess, under extreme pressure, to joining with Šling in 'enemy activity' – a confession which she later retracted completely. For the trial that condemned her to life imprisonment she had to wait until January 1954 [by which time Novotný had come to power], under detention all the time. She was tried as the leader of a fabricated group that included former regional Party secretaries Lomský, Fuchs, Polák and Landa, together with Taussigová and Bedřich Hájek. She resolutely denied before the court all accusations of subversive activity, admitting only political errors.

Further interrogation of Šling failed to yield the results expected, although the Minister of National Security and the Soviet advisers all took a hand. The prisoner offered imaginary confessions, only to retract them. Later he showed signs of resignation, seeing the political meaning of the projected trial in the fact that 'the international situation demands it and it is being organized at the direct wish of Moscow'. He spoke of being 'sacrificed by the Party, which on the instructions of the Soviet Party wants to use this trial as an example of vigilance'.

Until the summer of 1951 the evident intention was to stage a trial featuring Šling and Švermová as the ringleaders of a conspiracy. Later, however, statements obtained during the interrogation of other prisoners began to point in Slánský's direction, and in Šling's case also the trend of the questioning was readjusted. Šling realized that he was no longer to be the main figure in the coming trial and in the interests of the Party he considered it his duty to help provide evidence about Slánský. The moment the theory of an 'anti-State conspiratorial centre headed by Rudolf Slánský' emerged, the Šling case seemed to offer a convenient starting-point for staging an even more spectacular trial in Czechoslovakia than had originally been envisaged. Consequently, the idea of trying Šling, Švermová and their 'accomplices' together was abandoned. Šling was chosen as one of the fourteen accused in the trial of the 'Anti-State Conspiratorial Centre', in which constellation he was assigned the role both of 'spy' and of the instrument of the 'Centre' in the Brno region. He believed that by compliance at the trial he would be fulfilling his duty to the Party and that this would be taken into consideration in the verdict. When visited in his cell by Minister of National Security Bacílek, he declared that he took a political view of the case and would not cause difficulties. On 27 November 1952 Šling was condemned to death and on 3 December he was executed. His last words were: 'Mr President [of the Court], I wish every success to the Communist Party, the Czechoslovak people and the President of the Republic. I have never been a spy.'

In 1950–51 Czechoslovakia was sinking deeper and deeper into a crisis. In the international arena tension was rising, with fears of a new world conflict and a switch to an intensive armaments programme making severe demands on the economy. Difficulties multiplied in industry, in the supply of consumer goods and in the sphere of management. The targets of the first Five Year Plan were raised in an unbalanced and unrealistic way in 1950, and still more after the February 1951 meeting of the Central Committee; and this happened simultaneously with the intensified attack on 'saboteurs and enemies'. The centralized economic model was tightened up, steps to eliminate private enterprise in small industry, the crafts and agriculture were accelerated, while still harsher methods were used against large sections of the community. Circumstances connected with the fabrication of further trials were driving the Communist Party and the entire country into a profound moral crisis.

The events recounted above took place, in some respects, behind closed doors, in the strictest secrecy (for instance, the public knew nothing about the background to the particular cases, about the number of arrests or the illegal treatment of prisoners); while in other respects they were staged in full view of the public. The responsible leaders did grave injury to the Party members and to the public at large by completely misrepresenting the facts and thus spreading confusion. The devotion of a large section of the population to the socialism in which they believed was openly exploited to further the distortion of that socialism. Step by step society became divorced from its cherished traditions and the values inherited from the past, while moving away from the ideals of a humane socialism. The will to resist the illegality weakened as more and more people were drawn into the hunt for imaginary enemies.

Changes of structure and quality also took place at the top levels of Government and in the Administration. At the apex of the power pyramid a still smaller group held the monopoly of decision-making and management. Towards the end of January 1951 the Presidium set up a 'Political Secretariat' of the Central Committee (Gottwald, Slánský, Zápotocký and Široký) endowed with extraordinarily wide powers of decision, extending to the spheres of Security and the political trials. Arrests and reorganization in Security and the Armed Forces involved a considerable turnover of personnel, as occurred increasingly, also, in Party work at all levels.

The large-scale arrests of Communists late in 1950 and early in 1951 were a sure sign that yet another wave of political repression was on the way. Top men in the Party, in Security and in military and industrial posts suddenly found themselves in prison, and a similar fate befell many people at lower levels. A selected group of prisoners was held for some weeks in a hurriedly improvised prison at Koloděj House near Prague. Many witnesses have confirmed that the brutality of the interrogations at this place was the worst known up to that time. On the recommendation of the Soviet advisers, and with their most active participation, people were subjected to non-stop questioning, beaten, and tormented by hunger and thirst. Prisoners were kept in damp cellars with earthen floors where they suffered frostbite on their hands and feet.

In these conditions the interrogators managed to get most of their victims to 'confess' to sabotage, or to make statements about other people. But, while they extracted a lot of 'damaging findings', the interrogators and their advisers had to admit that the 'evidence' was not very conclusive and that it failed to confirm their view of Šling and Švermová as the leaders of a conspiracy. Anxious lest the scheme publicly announced at the Central Committee meeting in February should come to nothing, and impatient at the slow progress, some of the staff suggested to Gottwald and Slánský that the ringleader must be someone in a higher position than Šling.

At this point the name of Rudolf Šlanský began to appear with increasing frequency in statements by prisoners. Some mentioned him in self-defence, saying truthfully that they had been posted to responsible positions at his suggestion or that they had acted with his knowledge or consent, or even on his orders. Others named him because – rightly or wrongly – they thought him responsible for agreeing to their arrest.[1]

Slánský's name had been mentioned during the February interrogations at Koloděj, but, since the inquiries were still directed against Šling, these remarks attracted little attention and, in obedience to a political ruling about the names of prominent people, were not recorded. Nevertheless, the Minister of National Security and the Soviet advisers were informed, either by word of mouth or in written reports.

Before long, however these anti-Slánský statements began to attract greater attention as offering a possible way out of the impasse reached by the investigation. Moreover, by the spring of 1951 several statements accusing Slánský of definite offences had been made by detainees in the Ruzyň Prison (by Löbl, Šváb, Kopold, Vondráček, Závodský and later by Artur London). For the most part they had been obtained by interrogators Smola, Holvek, Arazin, Čermák and some others who were so dissatisfied with the restrictions on direct questions about Slánský that they went so far as to go behind the backs of the Ministry of National Security and the Soviet advisers and state their views at the Embassy of the USSR.

The idea of turning the inquiry against Slánský was also encouraged by the fact that at this time Zionism was regarded as a major weapon in the imperialist conspiracy against the socialist camp. Moreover, after Šváb's arrest his place at the head of the department handling the search for enemies in the Party was taken by Keppert, a man described in a report made in 1963 as notorious for his 'rabid antisemitism'.

The danger of Jewish bourgeois nationalism and Zionism was underlined by the Soviet advisers at meetings with Doubek and Košťál in June 1951; it was agreed that attention should be called to this in the 'proper' quarters. Doubek and Košťál then drafted the first comprehensive report summarizing the findings on 'Jewish bourgeois nationalism' and naming Slánský and Geminder. After editing by the Soviet advisers,

[1] See the study document by V. Brichta, 'The Origin of the "Centre" Case'.

this document was handed to Kopřiva and Gottwald, whose response was a decision to allow the investigation to continue in this direction so that 'all the facts about the projected conspiracy' could be discovered, though the ban on direct questions about Slánský was maintained.

On 20 July Stalin sent a coded message to Gottwald acknowledging the receipt of evidence against Slánský and Geminder, but describing the information as insufficient to justify a charge because it was based on 'denunciations by known criminals'. Stalin also announced the recall to Moscow of Boyarsky on the grounds that his approach to this matter was not serious enough. In his reply of the same date Gottwald said that from the outset he, too, had had doubts about statements by 'convicted criminals'; he asked, however, that Boyarsky be allowed to remain, as his help was valuable and his recall would create difficulties in security work.

On 23 July Alexej Čepička, Gottwald's confidential aide, attended a meeting of the Politburo of the Soviet Party. After Čepička had spoken, the meeting spent much time in discussing the cases of Slánský and Geminder. In a letter to Gottwald on the following day Stalin declared that the Soviet Party leadership still regarded the evidence of convicted criminals as untrustworthy. They concluded, however, from reports by the Soviet advisers in Czechoslovakia, that Slánský had made many mistakes in cadre policies and therefore could not retain the post of General Secretary of the Czechoslovak Communist Party. Stalin also confirmed that Boyarsky was being recalled and offered 'a stronger, more experienced man' in his place. The letter concluded by saying that an adviser should in all circumstances be guided and strictly controlled by the Czechoslovak Party leadership and should never be allowed to assume the powers of the Minister of Security. The coming weeks were to show that this was simply a paper declaration and that the reality was very different.

On 26 July Gottwald replied to Stalin agreeing to his recommendations and saying that he and Zápotocký were considering transferring Slánský to a Government post, as part of a reorganization planned for September. He also asked Stalin to send a security adviser to replace Boyarsky. (The post of Chief

Security Adviser was occupied from the begining of November by Beschasnov.)

A remarkable point is that the letter actually sent did not include the following self-critical note contained in the draft: 'After all, even I do not feel myself free from blame and responsibility for the mistakes that have been made.' In line with his correspondence with Stalin, Gottwald gave orders for interrogation about Slánský to be stopped; nevertheless, the questioning continued, with neither the Czechoslovak Security officers nor the Soviet advisers paying any heed to the orders from Stalin and Gottwald.

On his fiftieth birthday, 31 July, Slánský was awarded the highest Czechoslovak decoration (the Order of Klement Gottwald for the Building of Socialism) and a letter of congratulation from the Party's Central Committee; at the last moment Gottwald deleted some of the superlatives contained in the draft, and the words that Slánský was among Gottwald's most faithful colleagues. No birthday greetings came from Moscow, however, although that was the message he seemed most concerned to receive.

At the very time when the press was carrying laudatory articles about Slánský (including articles by Kopecký and Bareš) and when the letters and telegrams of congratulation were pouring in, Artur London and Karel Šváb were writing their statements in the Ruzyň Prison 'convicting' Slánský of espionage and subversion. The advisers Galkin and Yesikov then got Doubek and Košťál to write a second report on the whole affair. Early in August the four of them used this document in order to persuade Minister Kopřiva to agree that direct questioning about Slánský should proceed. Kopřiva consulted Gottwald at his residence in Lány and returned with the news that the President had received the reports in all seriousness, and considered that all possible means should be used to discover the head of the conspiracy. This indirect answer was enough; orders were immediately issued for renewed interrogation of certain prisoners.

At a Central Committee meeting in September Slánský was subjected to searching criticism: his misjudgements in making appointments had given an opening to the enemy, he had elevated the Party apparatus above governmental bodies (the theory of the second centre of power), and he had failed to appreciate the fundamental question, 'where is the actual seat of government?' Gottwald clearly took his speech largely from material received via Kopřiva from the interrogators and the Soviet advisers. Slánský made a self-critical statement, which was sent with a confidential letter from the Central Committee to all Party branches. He was appointed a Deputy Prime Minister and Zápotocký was supposed to pay special attention to him. At about the same time one of the Soviet advisers was arranging for all the material against Slánský, Frank, Geminder, Frejka and others to be assembled; after which he left with it for Moscow.

The criticism and demotion of Slánský evoked a powerful response. The general feeling expressed at meetings and in resolutions was that Gottwald had opened the door to the correction of errors in Party work; there was appreciation for the fact that he had not hesitated to criticize even his closest associate of many years' standing. Gottwald's prestige grew, and Communists, especially, pinned their hopes on him as the wave of universal suspicion mounted once more. Slánský's self-criticism was received with approval in some quarters, in others with mistrust; not a few voices declared that he had been treated too lightly, that he had not told the Party everything and that he might well be the hidden enemy in the top Party leadership.

The results of interrogations about Slánský, Geminder and others conducted in the autumn of 1951 proved disappointing to the Security men. Insofar as new facts were gleaned, they added little to the charges and self-criticism made at the September Central Committee meeting; they could be taken as pointing to the mistakes that had earned the penalty of dismissal from the post of General Secretary of the Party, but they provided no grounds for arrest and criminal charges.

Again the Soviet advisers came up with a suggestion. On their advice a fairly rapid 'reorientation' was made in the interrogation and in the testimonies obtained from a number of prisoners who had previously been accused of sabotage on their own account and even of plotting against Slánský. For instance, interrogator Košťál suggested to Šling that he and his associates had carried out their subversive activities with Slánský's approval. Šling and others greeted this change with some relief, for it offered hope of lighter sentences. In the records of the interrogation, Slánský now figured as the central figure of the conspiracy. Earlier statements by prisoners were said to have been crafty attempts to divert attention from their carefully masked leader who at all costs had to be saved, both for the success of the conspiracy and to save its remaining members.

The Slánský case took a new and decisive turn when Mikoyan made a sudden visit to Prague on 11 November in his capacity as a member of the Soviet Politburo. He brought with him a personal message from Stalin to Gottwald, differing substantially from the standpoint of July. Stalin now insisted on Slánský's immediate arrest, because, it seemed, he might escape at any moment to the West.

According to Čepička's testimony, Gottwald hesitated – which merely confirms that the investigation following the July talks and the decision to demote Slánský had yielded no fresh evidence justifying arrest – whereupon Mikoyan broke off the interview in order to contact Stalin, which he did from the Soviet Embassy. When the meeting was resumed, with Čepička present, Mikoyan said that Stalin had insisted on his view and reminded Gottwald of his grave responsibility. Although he had no facts, Gottwald ultimately drew the conclusion that Stalin, as usual, had reliable information and that his advice was sound. He sent back a message through Mikoyan agreeing to Slánský's arrest.

However, there was a delay, as yet unexplained, of thirteen days. A pretext for the arrest was found in a letter addressed to 'the Great Crossing-Sweeper' and sent to Czechoslovakia on 9 November by an agent of a foreign service who was also working with the Czechoslovak State Security. This message warned the recipient that he was in danger of meeting the same fate as Gomulka, and offered help in crossing the frontier, a safe refuge and, at a later date, opportunities to earn a living, though not a political career. Despite the thorough enquiries made by the 1962-3 Commission and our own, we have still not succeeded in discovering the true background to this affair. The letter, clearly, was a provocation, but there is no reliable evidence to tell us whether it was the work of a foreign intelligence service, a brain-child of Beria's men, a scheme emanating from home sources, or perhaps a combination of several elements.[1] Nor is it clear who actually suggested that Slánský should be taken as the man to whom this letter was addressed. We have, however, reliable evidence that a group of Security officers and the Soviet advisers shared in making this inference. On 23 November Gottwald expressed agreement with the idea at a meeting with Zápotocký, Kopřiva and the adviser Beschasnov, and the decision was taken that Slánský would be arrested the following night (although he had no inkling about the 'Great Crossing-Sweeper' letter and had never received it). After the event, on 24 November, the Political Secretariat and the Presidium approved what had been done; on 6 December the Central Committee followed suit. Gottwald misinformed this meeting by stating that important new evidence had made the arrest essential. He blocked any attempts by members to ask for details by the plausible excuse that their publication would hamper the inquiry. The decision about 'Rudolf Slánský's treachery' and his leading role in 'the anti-Party and anti-State conspiracy' adopted by the Central Committee provided a strong political lead for the further handling of the case. Neither Slánský's insistent declaration of his innocence addressed to the Presidium on 26 November, nor any facts speaking in his favour, were of any avail – his fate, and that of others, had to all intents and purposes been decided; all that remained was to act out the performance to the climax of trial and execution.

The response of Central Committee members to the sensational news of their General Secretary's arrest was a combination of approval and undisguised relief. No one voiced any doubts, no one expressed a willingness to hear what Slánský had to say on the matter; on the contrary, speakers in the discussion promptly labelled him an agent, an enemy and a traitor. Moreover, the Committee invited anyone who could help uncover the plot to send their information to the Party. It is a sad fact that many letters arrived in response to this

[1] See special study on the 'Great Crossing-Sweeper' affair.

appeal; rank-and-file Party members, officials and men in high places volunteered 'new findings' about the prisoners and denounced other people into the bargain. 'Self-critical' speeches and an abundance of written confessions by leading people (Bareš, Hendrych, Reiman, Dolanský, Frank and others) provided more ammunition for interrogating Slánský and his 'accomplices' and, in many cases, became the pretexts for still more arrests.

Immediate steps were taken to fabricate public support – the indispensable accompaniment to political trials – with the emphasis on Communist Party members. Immediately after Slánský's arrest, before his guilt had been established, before the trial, Gottwald received hundreds of resolutions from Communists, Trade Unionists and even school-children, thanking him for exposing the enemy and demanding the most stringent penalties, including death for the leader of the conspiracy. Of the 2,355 resolutions, letters and telegrams reaching the Party Central Office by 19 December 1951 not one had expressed doubt about Slánský's guilt or about the existence of a plot.

Of the more prominent people arrested on the same day as Slánský we may name Bedřich Geminder, Jarmila Taussigová and Richard Slánský [Rudolf's brother]. In December Eduard Goldstücker was detained, and during the first half of 1952 Margolius, Frejka, Goldmann, Frank, Simone and others. Official or personal contact with Slánský provided grounds for shifting a number of top functionaries in many sectors; one of the casualties was Minister of National Security Kopřiva, who as a 'Slánský man' lost both Gottwald's and Stalin's confidence; at the end of January 1952 he was replaced by Karol Bacílek.

It took a whole year to prepare the trial – planned as the biggest ever political trial in Czechoslovakia and as a full-scale public show.[1] From the outset, when the main job was to conduct long-term interrogations in Ruzyň Prison, the work proceeded according to schedule. The efforts of the Czechoslovak interrogators were matched by those of three Soviet advisers specially sent to 'do' the Slánský trial (Gromov,

---

[1] See a detailed study, 'R. Slánský in Prison' by Dr E. Dvořáková, and an account of 'The Preparation of the Trial of "The Leadership of the Anti-State Conspiratorial Centre led by R. Slánský" ', by V. Brichta.

Morozov and Chernov), and by Beschasnov, chief Soviet adviser to the Czechoslovak Ministry of National Security, with his assistants Yesikov and Galkin. These men personally supervised the investigations, proffered advice and helped to plan the interrogation.

Apart from the false statements extracted from prisoners, Security had a single document in the case – the 'Great Crossing-Sweeper' letter, which had sufficed to get Slánský arrested and into their power. The job now was to obtain the 'evidence', and to this end a 'documentary group' was established to look for the necessary documents in the archives. Most of these were provided by the archives in the Party Central Office, and Antonín Novotný was instrumental in handing them over to Security.

Up to 2 January 1952 Slánský admitted only the political errors he had already mentioned in his self-critical statement to the Central Committee in September 1951. He categorically denied charges of treason, organizing a conspiracy or trying to seize power. As the pressure intensified, however – an agent was planted in his cell in the guise of a fellow prisoner, confrontations were staged, and so on – he realized the hopelessness of his position, and at the end of January he attempted suicide. Breaking-point came with this failure; he began to admit the existence of a 'second centre' and, gradually, he confessed to all that was asked of him. In February Doubek, who was in charge of the interrogation, was invited to Prague Castle to report in person to Gottwald and Zápotocký. Having expressed his satisfaction, Gottwald directed that the investigation should continue according to plan and that nothing should be undertaken without the Soviet advisers.

Thereafter, until August, Slánský was questioned about specific aspects of his alleged criminal activity, with special attention to Trotskyism, Zionism and contacts with Konni Zilliacus. At this stage, too, the 'question-and-answer protocol' was drawn up, this being the first version of the scenario for the trial. Meanwhile the documentary group was collecting extracts from various official sources as 'evidence' against the accused. In addition, 'commissions of experts' began their job of lending credibility to the charge of sabotage. They produced sixty expert assessments and three private reports – all, with rare exceptions, lacking objectivity and a serious approach.

The 'Great Crossing-Sweeper' letter was introduced only at the very end of the interrogation. Having served its purpose as the 'cardinal evidence' for Slánský's arrest, and its utter failure to prove he had contacts abroad being quite clear to both the Czechoslovak interrogators and their Soviet advisers, it appeared during the preliminary investigation and in the court as a document of second-rate importance.

The summer of 1952 saw also the finishing touches to the image of the conspiratorial group about to be put on trial. From various suggestions for a title to describe the group (conspiratorial espionage centre, espionage-conspiracy centre, conspiratorial Zionist espionage centre, to name a few) that of the 'Anti-State Conspiratorial Centre led by R. Slánský' won the day.

There were long discussions about those of the accused who were of Jewish extraction (eleven out of the fourteen selected for the Slánský group). The term 'Jewish nationality', originally proposed by the Soviet advisers [and widely used in the USSR], was superseded by 'Czech nationality, Jewish origin'.

The selection of leaders for the 'Anti-State Conspiratorial Centre' was determined by a number of factors. With no lack of choice among the enormous numbers under arrest, the points taken into account were the kind of statements obtained during interrogation, the likelihood that the person concerned would behave 'well' in court, the impression his testimony would make, and his degree of proximity to Slánský. It was also considered important for the group to include representatives from all the main spheres of public life.

The summer and autumn were spent also in making the final organizational and personnel preparations and in drafting the indictment. On 27 August the Political Secretariat approved Dr Josef Urválek as Chief Prosecutor for the trial, and on 25 October the members of the tribunal (chairman, Dr Jaroslav Novák; members, Dr Karel Trudák and František Stýblo). The prosecutors, judges and defence counsel underwent special briefing before the trial, each being assigned his precise role. They had to promise to adhere faithfully to the documents provided by the interrogators and to follow the scenario of the proceedings.

Meanwhile, on the instructions of the advisers, the accused were memorizing the statements they were to make in court. Although by now they were broken men, to make sure all went well their parts were tape-recorded in advance – a lesson gleaned from the trial of Kostov who, once in court, retracted his previous statements, whereupon he was forbidden to speak and his prepared testimony was read out. Extracts from the recordings were actually played to the Party Presidium! Immediately before the trial, Bacílek held personal talks with the accused (except Slánský), suggesting to them that by keeping to the agreed procedure in court they might earn lighter sentences, appealing to their loyalty to the Party, in whose interest the trial had to take place, and promising that their families would be cared for.

The indictment underwent several changes. The first two versions were drafted on instructions from the Soviet advisers by Doubek and amended according to their wishes by Prchal. When the Political Secretariat discussed the document on 13 November there was no opposition. Some criticism, not directed against the substance of the indictment, was voiced by Čepička and Gottwald; the former considered the indictment weak from the professional point of view, and the evidence for an attempt to assassinate Gottwald seemed to him unconvincing. Gottwald expressed the view that 'activity in the Party ought not to be a matter for prosecution'. Yet both made it quite clear that they agreed with the charges against Slánský, and this was implicit in their other criticisms. Gottwald, for instance, thought it necessary to show Slánský's 'deception, hypocrisy and lying'. Judging from the minutes of the meeting, a sharp attack on Slánský and others was made by Kopecký, who found it necessary to point out that 'Westerners' [people who had been in the West during the war] and Jews were liable to become agents of American imperialism. A pragmatic approach to the affair betrayed fears that the trial might undermine confidence in the Five Year Plan (Zápotocký, Gottwald). A Commission composed of Bacílek, Čepička, Kopecký and Dr Rais was appointed to make the final draft of the indictment, the final editing being done by Gottwald who, in addition to minor amendments, deleted passages accusing Slánský of propagating a Czechoslovak road to socialism.

The Political Secretariat approved a list of defence counsel, added two military judges (General Štella and František Doušek) to the Bench and appointed other commissions to supervise the trial. Members of the Political Commission for directing proceedings were Bacílek as Chairman, Široký, Čepička, Kopecký, Novotný and Rais. The Press Commission, chaired by Kopecký (later Köhler), included Prchal, Klos, Koucký, Vorel and Doubek. Novotný was given the job of working with the Central Party Office to ensure reliable attendance in the public gallery; Bacílek, Kopecký, Rais and Novotný were instructed to arrange direct transmission of the proceedings for members of the Political Secretariat. The Political Commission's work included drawing up a timetable; it required that the proceedings be shortened, thereby reducing the number of witnesses called.

A decision about the sentences was also taken about this time, though there is no record of where and when. However, the customary procedure was followed – a decision was made and handed down by the Minister of Justice to the prosecutors and the Court. That this decision was taken by the political leadership is indicated in a statement made by Čepička in 1963: 'Discussion of the verdicts was conducted in an atmosphere of great responsibility on the part of all, not excluding Gottwald, and I think it did not last long.'

On 20 November 1952 the trial began – staged according to a scenario and timetable prepared in advance. Only once did the Prosecutor leave out a question and the accused, having memorized his sequence of questions and answers, reply to the question he should have been asked, instead of the one actually put to him.

Before the proceedings ended, instructions had already been given for handling any appeals that might be lodged. They were to be heard on 4 December and were to confirm the verdicts. A remarkable feature, apart from the decision that the appeals should be heard in one day, was that the Political

Secretariat decided upon so important a matter without meeting to discuss it; the members merely telephoned their agreement with the arrangements proposed.

The trial was given full radio and press publicity. From the moment it started, the Party and other organizations were mobilized for action. Thousands of resolutions poured in to the Central Committee, the President and the State Court. Thousands of death sentences were passed in factories, offices and other places of work before the Court had even delivered its verdict. And yet there were individuals who had doubts and warned against giving way to irrational moods and passions. Clearly, the long indictment and the clockwork precision of the proceedings had caused some misgivings.

The verdicts, delivered on 27 November 1952, found the accused guilty of multiple charges of high treason, espionage, sabotage and military treason: Slánský, Geminder, Frejka, Frank, Clementis, Reicin, Šváb, Margolius, Fischl, Šling and Simone were sentenced to death, London, Löbl and Hajdů to life imprisonment. No appeals were lodged and the pleas for clemency were rejected. On 3 December 1952 eleven of the fourteen accused went to the scaffold.

With the exception of Slánský, all the victims wrote farewell letters on the eve of their execution. These letters constitute a testimony which is, perhaps, best characterized by Frejka's words in his letter to Gottwald: 'In the last hour of his life, a man does not lie. I beg you, therefore, to believe what I am writing to you. In any case, these lines will reach you after I am no more, so why should I write anything but the truth?' He wrote that he had spoken of himself as an 'agent' only in order to fulfil his obligation to the working people and to the Communist Party – as he had been urged to do by his interrogators. Šváb wrote that he had made his confession because he regarded it 'as his duty and as a political necessity'. Šling wrote: 'I declare truthfully before my death that I have never been a spy.' Simone, who also stressed that a few hours before his death 'even the worst man speaks the truth', said in lines addressed to Gottwald that he had never been 'a traitor or a spy or an agent in the services of a Western or any other intelligence service'.

The farewell letters of the condemned to their families were never delivered, and their letters addressed to Gottwald were handed to him by Bacílek ten days after the executions.

In accordance with a decision of the Political Secretariat taken on 17 February 1953, awards were conferred on a number of the Security men for their services in connection with the trial – fourteen (including Doubek, Košťál, Musil and Moučka) received the Order of the Republic, six received the Order of Labour, forty-seven were decorated For Fortitude, a number were promoted and received financial rewards.

The biggest show trial ever held in Czechoslovakia had ended. But not quite. For on 28 November 1952 Bierut wrote a letter to Gottwald in which he requested permission for 'our Security people to interrogate Slánský and others about their contacts with Gomulka and Field'. (File AN, Box 26, Vol. 4, pp. 78–9.) The request was granted. However, the intention of exploring the Centre's international ramifications was abandoned in the light of world events.

Other trials, known as the 'subsequent' trials, followed the main trial.

In 1953–4, as always, the internal situation in Czechoslovakia was strongly influenced by international factors, particularly political developments in the socialist countries.

Following the worst phase of the Cold War, 1953 inaugurated a new stage marked by the lessening of international tension. The Korean armistice of July 1953 ended the armed conflict between capitalism and socialism which for three years had endangered world peace. In 1954 came the Geneva Agreement on Vietnam.

This did not mean that there were no longer any factors militating against a reduction of international tension. Of importance to Czechoslovakia was the refusal of the imperialist powers to negotiate on the German question, their remilitarization of West Germany and their support for its full membership of Nato. Moreover, by August 1952 the Dulles doctrine of 'liberation' had replaced the unsuccessful tactic of 'containing Communism'.

The political changes in the Soviet Union, however, were the major factor in international relations at this time. Stalin's death in the spring of 1953 ushered in a period marked by efforts to eradicate the 'cult of the personality' and its consequences. Great emphasis was placed on restoring socialist legality. April 1953 saw the rehabilitation of the Moscow doctors, who had been accused of plotting to kill high-ranking Party and State officials. On 6 April 1953 *Pravda* contained an article headed 'Soviet Socialist Legality Is Invulnerable', emphasizing that some members of the Security Police had become isolated from the people and had omitted to serve their interests.

In July a meeting of the Central Committee of the Communist Party of the Soviet Union disclosed the criminal actions of Lavrenti Beria, who was now under arrest. (Beria was executed in December 1953.) The meeting adopted measures to restore socialist legality, to control the work of the Security Police and to democratize Party life. The Central Committee reassessed the Leningrad case and resolved to re-examine the political trials held in 1937, 1938 and other years. These were significant steps taken by the Leninist core of the Central Committee, led by Khrushchev, not merely towards rehabilitating individuals but, primarily, towards restoring the moral and humanistic principles of socialism.

In 1953 there was talk in the German Democratic Republic and in the Hungarian People's Republic about a 'new course' designed to bring rapid improvements in the economic and political life of their countries. Nearly all the People's Democracies were now trying to rid themselves of bureaucracy and apply Leninist principles in the Party and in the development of socialist democracy.

All in all, the policies pursued in the People's Democracies under the heading of a struggle against the personality cult had a number of features in common with the developments in the Soviet Union. They had, of course, their own features emanating from the objective and subjective conditions in the countries concerned. The class struggle assumed various forms, for although, economically and politically, the Five Year Plans had strengthened working-class power in many ways, mistakes made during the early years of socialist reconstruction had weakened it in some of the countries.

Bringing the mistakes of the past to light was, of course, fraught with the danger of a political crisis in all the People's Democracies.

The Central Committee of the Socialist Unity Party in East Germany, assessing the disturbances that took place in Berlin in June 1953, said: 'The enemy has exploited the discontent of sections of our population, caused by our policy over the past year, to engineer provocations.' In Hungary, too, an inadequate analysis of the reasons for mistakes, coupled with lack of unity in the leadership, had produced a complicated situation in the Party.

This explains why the process of regeneration was slower in the political than the economic sphere. In a number of countries (Czechoslovakia, Bulgaria, Romania and to some extent Poland), political trials accompanied by the methods of the personality cult were held as late as 1954. Yet there had already been clear pointers to the illegality of the trials of the early 1950s. On 3 October 1954 the Central Committee of the Hungarian Communist Party concluded that the trials in that country had been mounted 'by means of complicated, unlawful methods of provocation' and that 'the sentences passed on the comrades had been based on false indictments and confessions'. In Czechoslovakia, this news was censored, although it was known that a number of Communists had been arrested and sentenced in connection with the Rajk trial. A little later, another pillar of the indictments in the Slánský and other trials crumbled when the charges of espionage against the Field brothers were withdrawn. In 1954, Ceteka [the Czechoslovak Press Agency] reported that Herman Field had been released and rehabilitated by the Polish Government. In November 1954 Noel Field and his wife were released in Hungary and rehabilitated in full. This signified the collapse of a vital part of the indictment against the 'Centre' and against other Communists (such as Moškovič, Kosta and Kleinová) still held in prison.

A report on the unmasking of Beria was received by the Czechoslovak Party leadership (Zápotocký, Široký, Dolanský,

Bačilek, Čepička, Kopecký, Novotný and Köhler) immediately after a resolution on the subject had been adopted by the Soviet Central Committee. A letter from Khrushchev to Zápotocký, Široký and Novotný dated 19 December 1953 indicates that our leaders received additional information from the Soviet Ambassador, who acquainted them with the charges preferred against Beria. Another detailed report on Beria was given to top Party leaders during talks held in Moscow in April 1954 (according to Zápotocký's notes of the meeting). At the Tenth Congress of the Czechoslovak Party, held in June 1954, Khrushchev, head of the Soviet delegation, supplied the members of the Congress with a detailed report on Party life in the USSR during the Stalin era. Khrushchev also drew attention to the grave violations of socialist legality and the brutal treatment of national groups during World War II.

All this information about the trampling on socialist legality showed that questions of a moral character were involved. This could have influenced the Party's conduct of internal policy. However, the leadership complied only with Khrushchev's explicit request, voiced at the Tenth Congress, to rehabilitate Ludvík Svoboda. The fundamental reason why this was so is that no changes had been made in the political system, distorted as it was by the personality cult, and that the incipient process of political regeneration clashed with political leaders who, through their association with the cult, saw any disclosure of the cult as an attack on their own positions.

The country was now facing serious problems – political, social and economic – and for the first time signs of a crisis in the political system were evident. A drastic currency reform in 1953 lowered the Party's standing with the public. The rapid economic growth during the first Five Year Plan was followed by fluctuations in 1953–4 – a result of the overall concept of the Plan. The growth rate of the national income declined, that of industry dropped substantially, investment declined and a marked imbalance between production and consumption set in.[1]

The situation in the Party leadership was complicated:

[1] More details are given in Information no. 30: V. Škrlant and S. Bálek, 'Contrast between Economic Policy and Actual Economic Growth'.

Gottwald's death was followed by bitter disputes about his successor and about the political course to be followed. These matters were discussed at a conference between the leaderships of the Czechoslovak and Soviet parties held on Novotný's initiative in April 1954. Time, however, was needed before Novotný, who was elected First Secretary of the Party in September 1953, could consolidate his position. Neither in the Party leadership nor in the top echelons of the Security force or the judiciary did changes of personnel lead to changes in the style and methods of work in these offices. Continuity was seen, among other things, in the fact that further trials were submitted to Party Committees for approval. In the functioning of the machinery of coercion, which still remained outside any public control, repression was retained as a valid weapon, and justified as 'class policy'; justice continued to be dispensed behind closed doors. It seems that these facts were partly responsible for the scant attention paid to reports about new features of political life in the Soviet Union, about the state of affairs in the People's Democracies, and about violations of law.

Unfortunately, indications that socialist legality had been violated within Czechoslovakia itself were treated in the same way. There were many such indications – notably letters, complaints and applications sent by condemned men or their relatives to the Party leadership and the Party Control Commission, the President, the Prosecutor-General, the Minister of Justice, individual Party leaders and State officials. During 1953, 102 such communications reached the Central Committee and the President's office, only to be put in the files.

We have selected some of the most important. In 1951 the horrors of the 'Cottage' were revealed. This was a place used by the intelligence sections of the Ministry of National Defence; 'testimonies' extracted there were used to convict many innocent officers. The notorious Mírov camp was abolished at about the same time. Among the most tragic documents, however, are the letters written by the accused in the Slánský trial (3 December 1952), in which many declared that they 'had never been spies or conspirators'.

On 2 December 1952, the day the trial ended, Karel Kreibich, a prominent Party leader, wrote to the Party Secretariat protesting that the indictment against Slánský and the other accused had descended to the worst kind of antisemitism and racialism. This letter, too, was ignored. It found its way into the hands of Bruno Köhler who, on 24 February 1953, two and a half months after it was written, circulated it for the information of members of the Politburo. (A letter from Köhler to Václav Kopecký of 24 December 1952 reads: 'I am sending you for your information a copy of a communication from Comrade Kreibich about the question of Jews in the trial of Slánský and Co.' – ACC CPC, File 100/45.) In another letter, dated 12 November 1955, Kreibich again pointed out that the persecution of people of 'Jewish origin' was continuing in the Party; he condemned the attitude of suspicion and discrimination towards anyone who had been in Britain during the war or who had fought in Spain. Although both letters contained serious allegations against the Party leadership, Kreibich received no reply.

The illegal methods of investigation used at Ruzyň were the subject of a communication from the former Regional Secretary, Stavinoha, to the President. On 4 January 1954 Zápotocký sent this letter to all members of the Political Secretariat, with a covering note in which he cast doubts on Stavinoha's character and his assertions. About the same time Jarmila Taussigová complained to the President – in vain. A second letter was equally unsuccessful. Zápotocký forwarded both complaints to members of the Political Secretariat, with an accompanying note saying he rejected them.

Throughout 1954 the number of complaints about violations of the law and requests for a retrial grew. Among them were letters from Gustav Husák in March 1954, to the Party Presidium and the Prosecutor-General, describing the force used during interrogation and asserting his own innocence. Husák pleaded to be heard by a Party Commission or the Prosecutor.

On 22 October 1954 Josef Smrkovský addressed a letter to Zápotocký and a complaint to Rudolf Barák, Minister of the Interior.

In a letter dated 24 December 1954, addressed to President Zápotocký, Pavel Kavan wrote:

In the testimony which I had to memorize, I stated that . . . I had mediated espionage contacts between Konni Zilliacus, agent of the British Intelligence Service, and Rudolf Slánský, head of . . . the Centre. The whole of this testimony is a lie. It was invented by the investigators at Ruzyň. (ACC CPC, Commission I, Section 1117.)

In September 1954 and on 9 January 1955, Marie Švermová wrote letters to President Zápotocký. In her second letter, she wrote:

I am turning to you once more because, in September 1954, I sent you a detailed account of my case and expressed doubts about the correctness of the methods of interrogation employed by the secret police. I pointed out that my case was not an isolated one. . . . When such methods are used any Party worker can be branded arbitrarily as an enemy and an anti-State criminal. In a letter dated 22 September 1954, I acquainted Minister of the Interior Barák with the grounds for my justified fears. . . . I can declare with absolute certainty that I have never committed any crime against the Party or the State. (ACC CPC, Commission I, Section 1117.)

In December 1953, after his conditional release, Leopold Hofman had an audience with Novotný in the course of which he informed the Party leader about the illegal methods used during interrogation. Dr Outrata made a similar declaration to President Zápotocký when he was brought before him after his arrest in March 1954. (Later, however, the 'Outrata Memorandum' on the trials, dated 9 August 1955, was to be of still greater importance.)

Even this brief summary of just a few of the facts revealed in 1953–4 shows that both the Party leadership and the competent Party and State authorities were in possession of information that should undoubtedly have urged them to discover the truth. The victims, however, received no reply to their complaints. On the contrary, the machinery of repression continued to operate and led to further illegal verdicts and other measures against unjustly accused Communists and members of their families. No Party office, that is neither the Political Secretariat nor the Central Committee, was (except in two cases) informed of these complaints and requests.

In April 1953 the Political Secretariat decided that the families of the 'criminals' condemned in the Slánský and other trials should be moved out of Prague; they were to be settled in two or three districts (for instance the Jeseníky mountains and Krnov) under the constant surveillence of the Ministry of National Security. (ACC CPC, Commission II, Section 36, Report on the Inquiry into Individual Cases of Section 1 of 5 May 1953.)

This entirely illegal measure was suggested by Köhler, Bacílek and Šalga, and approved with the addendum: 'The local police and appointed Party officials shall submit monthly reports on the conduct, work and life of the persons concerned, and Party membership of the members of families of traitors, conspirators and criminals shall be terminated.' (ACC CPC, 02/5, meeting of the Political Secretariat on 7 April 1953.)

On 5 May 1953 the Ministry of National Security (Bacílek) submitted a report to the Political Secretariat on the numbers under arrest, the progress of investigations in the main cases, and the division of these cases into groups.

The first of seven rigged trials to follow that of Slánský's 'Anti-State Conspiratorial Centre' was held on 25–6 May 1953. On 21 April the Political Secretariat had discussed the draft indictment in the case of a group of employees at the Ministry of Foreign Affairs, and on 19 May it examined and approved a report drawn up by the Ministry of National Security concerning the conduct of the trial and the pre-determined verdicts. (ACC CPC, 02/5, meeting of the Political Secretariat, Sections 152 and 156.) In this trial, Professor Eduard Goldstücker was sentenced to life imprisonment and the other accused to long terms in jail, forfeiture of property and loss of civic rights.

Although vital questions of internal policy were under discussion there was no mention of the political trials. The Secretariat, however, was constantly occupied with them.

On 23 September 1953 it received a report about an inquiry into the 'anti-State activity of Jičínský, Outrata, Bárta, Fabinger and others'. (ACC CPC, 03/5, Section 176.)

On 9 October 1953 the Israeli socialist Mordechai Oren, charged with involvement in Slánský's 'Centre', was given a sentence of fifteen years in a secret, illegal trial.

On 19 November 1953 the Political Secretariat discussed the

indictment in the case of 'the anti-State group in Security' (Závodský, Černý, Valeš, Milén, Smolka, Pokorný, Pich-Tůma). On 9 December it discussed preparations for a secret trial of Závodský and his 'accomplices' and approved the sentences recommended. The same meeting discussed the proposed indictment in the case of Dr Haškovec, and a report about preparations to bring a group of Slovak Communists – O. Valášek and others – to trial.

Just before Christmas 1953 the Political Secretariat had another trial on its agenda. On 21 December it approved the indictment and the pre-arranged sentences in the case of the 'Trotskyist Grand Council', involving Václav Vlk, Oldřich Černý, L. Pluhař, Pavel Hrubý, Bohumír Holátko, František Novák and František Roušar. (ACC CPC, 02/5, Section 190.)

The trial took place on 23–5 February 1954, and the seven unjustly accused Communists were sentenced to a total of 103 years' imprisonment, forfeiture of property and loss of civic rights totalling 70 years. A report on this trial was approved by the Secretariat on 22 March.

On 21 December 1953 the trial of Colonel Závodský, of the Ministry of the Interior, and members of Security opened before the Military Senate of the Supreme Court. On 23 December Závodský was illegally sentenced to death in conformity with the verdict agreed beforehand by the Secretariat; four other Communists were given long terms of imprisonment. Závodský's plea for mercy was rejected. On 25 January 1954 the Secretariat was informed of the course and results of these proceedings. Závodský waited under sentence of death until the middle of March. Repeated pleas for clemency for her innocent husband submitted by Mrs Závodská in the first months of 1954 make heartrending reading. They remained unanswered. In a letter of 12 April to President Zápotocký, for instance, she described how she was living in a state of uncertainty about the response to her applications; by then, in point of fact, her husband was no longer alive.

On 30 December 1953 Josef Pavel was committed for trial. Although he had denied all the charges and resisted every pressure to make him 'confess' he, too, was illegally sentenced to twenty-five years in jail.

In the six trials of ten Security officials held between September 1953 and January 1954, one death sentence was passed, nine sentences totalling 149 years' imprisonment, and eight sentences of forfeiture of property, while in two cases the penalty included loss of civic rights for life, and in seven loss of civic rights for a total of 60 years.

The first six months of 1954 saw numerous trials. On 5 January the Political Secretariat discussed charges against Generals Vladimír Drnec, Šimon Drgač and others, and also against D. Benau. On 8 January it gave its approval to the draft indictment of a group of officers (Bedřich Kopold, Otto Hromádko and others), and on 22 February to the charges against Slovak Communists V. Jančík and Koloman Moškovič. (ACC CPC, 02/5, Sections 191 and 196.) In the six trials involving generals and other Army officers which took place in 1954, the sentences passed on eight innocent men totalled 128 years' imprisonment, forfeiture of property in all cases and loss of civic rights for a total of 72 years.

The first big trial in 1954 was that of Marie Švermová and other Party officials. On 30 July 1953, after the Slánský trials, Švermová, who had been kept in custody despite insufficient evidence, was subjected to further interrogation; a report by Lieutenant-Colonel Moučka, in charge of the investigations, claimed that she had admitted her guilt. (In a letter to the Minister of the Interior of 10 December 1953 Moučka wrote: 'On your instructions I am sending the summary of evidence on Marie Švermová of 30 July. Švermová admits to subversive activity, to disrupting the Party, together with Slánský, and to placing hostile persons in high offices.' (ACC CPC, Commission I, Section 287.) On 18 January 1954 the Political Secretariat discussed the draft indictment in the case of Švermová and others, which had been drawn up by the Ministry of the Interior and submitted by Barák. The draft was approved with only a few amendments, the most important of which resulted in the indictment's pinpointing the main offence – participation in a conspiracy. (ACC CPC, 02/5, Section 193, meeting of the Political Secretariat on 18 January 1954.)

At a secret trial held before the Supreme Court on 26–8

January, Švermová was sentenced to life imprisonment and the other accused (Jarmila Taussigová, Mikuláš Landa, Hanuš Lomský, Vítězslav Fuchs, Ervín Polák and Bedřich Hájek) to a total of 113 years. The Court decreed forfeiture of property in every case; one of the accused was deprived of civic rights for life, the others for a total of 60 years. The Prosecutor, Dr Švach, even recommended the death sentence for Švermová.

A report on the proceedings, again submitted by Barák, was discussed by the Political Secretariat on 1 February 1954. It includes this passage:

> Švermová admitted the substance of the charges set down in the summary of evidence. Throughout the interrogation she denied hostile intentions. . . . She was fully implicated by Lomský and Landa. . . . Landa claimed to be completely innocent. He had signed the summary of evidence, he said, solely because he had been in custody for three years. Taussigová, who denied having committed any criminal offence, claimed credit for having helped to unmask Šling and Slánský. There were no disturbances during the proceedings. (ACC CPC, 02/5, Section 196.)

The account contained numerous inaccuracies of which Barák, who had submitted it to the Political Secretariat, was well aware. From the statements made later by three witnesses (Široký, Švach and an employee of the Ministry of Justice, Lenert), we learn that it was found necessary during the proceedings to convene a meeting of the Ministries concerned, at which objections were raised to weaknesses in the case and the opinion was expressed that the trial should be adjourned. (These objections were made by Dr Urválek; Prosecutor Dr Švach opposed them.) After Dr Urválek's report that Švermová had not admitted any guilt in court and that her testimony was no more than a self-critical statement, Barák closed the meeting; according to witnesses, he declared that the Political Secretariat was aware of this and that a decision must be made in accordance with the resolution – that is, to condemn Švermová. (ACC CPC, Commission I, Sections 305, 306 and 307.) The trial of Švermová and others was a classic example of legal proceedings being instituted when the 'misconduct' referred solely to work within the Party.

A most disturbing influence in public life and the administration of the country came with the charges of 'Slovak bourgeois nationalism' which led to the trial in 1954 of Gustav Husák and other Slovak Communists.

The case against these men was prepared by the Ministry of National Security on 23 April 1953. The unsubstantiated charges of penal offences, which included a number of unfounded political accusations, were discussed by the Presidium of the Central Committee on 6 May and by the Political Secretariat on 12 May. Following a proposal to redraft the document, a Commission consisting of Bacílek, Rais, Benada and Gažík was appointed; its composition received the approval of the Presidium on 12 May. That the Party leaders were kept informed of the preparations for the trial is confirmed by a letter of 10 September sent by Bacílek to Novotný, stating that the indictment would have to wait, since Husák was protesting his innocence. This suggests that Bacílek interpreted the redrafting of the indictment as a task 'assigned by the Political Secretariat'. In writing the indictment, the Commission drew on statements made by a number of top Party officials, on instructions issued by the Political Secretariat and the Presidium, and, in particular, on written statements by Široký, dated 6 June, and Bacílek, dated October 1953.

The final draft of the indictment was submitted by Barák to the Political Secretariat; having duly discussed and approved the document on 8 March 1954, the Secretariat instructed Barák and the Prosecutor-General, Václav Aleš, to submit their recommendations concerning the sentences. (ACC CPC, Commission I, Section 201.) On 31 March the Political Secretariat again discussed the staging of the trial and the proposed sentences: Husák, imprisonment for life; Okáli, up to twenty-five years; Horváth, up to twenty-three years; Holdoš, up to twenty years; Novomeský, up to sixteen years. (ACC CPC, Commission I, Section 205.) The final resolution adopted by this meeting recommended that the third paragraph of Novomeský's indictment be reconsidered and that he should receive the mildest sentence. The meeting also approved the suggestion that Novomeský should be released after serving five years (including time spent in custody).

A Political Commission was set up to direct the trial, headed by Pavol David, a member of the Presidium; the other members were Klokoč, Michalička, Melichar, Moučka and Gešo.

Among the indications that the initiative came primarily from political quarters is a letter written by investigator Bohumil Doubek on 29 July 1953, in which he admits that despite all their efforts the Security Service had failed to obtain any fresh evidence; he therefore requested that Minister Bacílek himself, or the political committees, supply the evidence they had promised.

The trial of the 'Slovak bourgeois nationalists' by the Supreme Court was held in Bratislava from 21 to 24 April 1954. The proceedings were conducted as pre-arranged by the Security Service, the Political Secretariat and the Central Committee. Husák was sentenced to life imprisonment, Novomeský to ten years, Okáli to eighteen, Holdoš to thirteen and Horváth to twenty-two. These five innocent men forfeited their property and their civic rights for a total of fifty years.

A report on the trial proceedings was discussed by the Political Secretariat at a meeting held on 16 August, and was approved, despite the fact that the members knew (as did Strechaj, Bacílek and David of the Slovak Presidium) how Husák had refuted the trumped-up charges both during the interrogation and in court.

In June 1954 two further political trials were held – one of economists (Goldmann, Kollár, Jičínský, Bárta, Rudinger and Lewinter), to whose case Smrkovský's was added, and the other of Dr Outrata.

Preparations for the economists' trial were discussed by the Political Secretariat on 10 May. The draft indictment submitted by Barák was not approved; he and Aleš were instructed to go over it, inserting the points made by the Secretariat. What these points were has not been ascertained, since no minutes of the meeting exist. Only the names of those who took part in the discussion are known: Barák, Novotný, Dolanský, Zápotocký, Kopecký and Široký. (ACC CPC, 02/5, Section 212.) The amended indictment was approved by the Politburo on 21 June. (ACC CPC, 02/2.)

The main trial of the economists was held on 7 August; all

the accused received long terms of imprisonment. On 23 August, when the Politburo discussed a report on the proceedings in this case, the Ministry of Justice and the Prosecutor-General were severely criticized for having neglected to submit to the Party organization recommendations concerning the sentences; the resolution passed by the meeting explicitly demanded a statement on this matter. The Politburo further reminded Škoda and Aleš that they were 'obliged, in accordance with a previous resolution of the Political Secretariat, to submit to the Secretariat, in important cases, the views of the Prosecutor-General on recommended sentences before legal proceedings are inaugurated'. (CC archives, 02/5, Section 15.)

This trial was followed by that of Dr Outrata who was originally to have been tried with the economists. For reasons of health his case had to be deferred, and he was tried separately on 5 November.

The eleven innocent members of the economists' group were sentenced to a total of 204 years' imprisonment and in ten cases to forfeiture of property.

These trials condemning economists for alleged sabotage of socialist reconstruction had grave consequences. They pronounced the verdict on a possible alternative development of the Czechoslovak economy; they signalized the virtual exclusion of economic experts of the 'managerial' type, they undermined technical and economic initiative among managers, discouraged enterprise and efforts to achieve economic prosperity; people were now screened for leading posts according to political criteria and many managed to hold down their jobs only thanks to the [inefficient] type of management that had been introduced.

After the main trial and its offshoots came trials of individual Party officials who had not been included in any of the larger groups, and the trial of the 'illegal leadership' of the Social Democrats (Vladimír Götner and others).

Most of the Communists spent months, and many of them years, in prison before being committed for trial. During this period of waiting in hermetic isolation each behaved differently, just as each had behaved differently while at liberty. Some managed to be heroes even in prison. A number of Spanish

Civil War veterans (Josef Pavel, for example), and also Taussigová, Švermová, Husák and Smrkovský, never relinquished the fight for their honour, even under the worst conditions. Broken by physical and mental suffering, morally at a low ebb, they, too, came to the end of their tether and, in those moments, signed 'confessions'. A few days were enough for them to retract. After eight months, Smrkovský repudiated all his previous confessions. Taussigová and Švermová freely admitted their mistakes but refused to confess to premeditated hostile activity. They rejected the argument that the Party needed their confessions. Husák emphatically denied all the charges preferred against him. In their isolation some of the accused (Taussigová, Smrkovský, Husák and others) came to the conclusion that a 'Yagoda affair'[1] was disrupting the Party. These people could not be brought to trial in the 'main period' because there was no guarantee that they would not 'spoil' the carefully staged performance. And when at last they appeared in the dock they defended themselves resolutely – especially Husák.

For a time most of the Communists on trial held out in this way, some perhaps for only a few days (Simone, Frejka), others for weeks or even months. But to fight in isolation against this fearful machine was beyond human endurance. Breaking-point came and they gave up. Some were induced to surrender by the conviction that they were serving the Party (Frank, Frejka, Clementis and to some extent Reicin – perhaps they hoped that the Party would bear this in mind when deciding on their sentences). Many, unable to endure the physical and mental punishment, resigned themselves to their fate and began to confess to whatever was required, however untrue. Their attitude was expressed by Frejka in a letter to Gottwald before his execution:

When after four days I saw that you, Mr President, regarded me as a saboteur and traitor and that this was the view of the Security personnel who, while my case was being investigated, represented the working people in my eyes, I decided that my ideas about

[1] *Genrikh Yagoda, Soviet People's Commissar of the Interior (1934–6) destroyed oppositional groups; he was relieved of his post in 1937 and shot in Moscow on 15 March 1938.*

myself and about what I had wanted to do must have been subjectively wrong. From that day, believe me, Mr President, I – who have been active in the working-class movement for thirty years – looked at myself honestly and mercilessly from the objective standpoint of the Czechoslovak working people and forced myself to see all my activity through the eyes of the investigators; and accordingly I testified against myself as severely as possible the whole time.

From the moment of breakdown many of the accused in the main trial began to write their own indictments. Some, it seems, really believed in Stalin's aphorism, 'when timber is felled, chips begin to fly', and now saw themselves as chips which through some error (and they tried to discover who had actually been responsible for this 'accident') had been cast onto the fire together with real spies and traitors; Frank, Šváb and Frejka were among those who appeared to hold this view.

Some of the victims knew just where they stood. Aware of the methods used by the Security Service, they 'confessed' without delay. They included former members of the Security Service and of military counter-intelligence, and also men whose knowledge of affairs had enabled them to grasp the real nature of similar trials in the USSR and the People's Democracies.

Many of the accused in the main trial, to judge from their farewell letters, believed that they would escape the death sentence, that their lives would be spared. They were obviously strengthened in this belief by their interrogators, and not only by them. Official visits by the Minister of National Security, Bacílek, to many of the prisoners during the investigations, and to most just before trial, led them to believe that their guilt would be judged by their behaviour in court.

From the moment of breakdown some of the prisoners, in addition to testifying willingly against themselves, enlarged the circle of possible offenders. Others, admitting only their own mistakes, fabricated non-existent names or gave the names of those who had been arrested before them. Some tried by obvious falsehoods and absurdities to attract the attention of their one-time friends who were still in influential positions.

Then there were those who, to save their own skins and under the fearful pressure of the prison conditions, submitted completely and collaborated with the Security Service, by acting as stool pigeons in the cells of their former comrades.

In sum, the overwhelming majority believed that by their attitude in prison, whatever it was, they were serving the Party and acting as Communists.

THE MECHANISM FOR ENGINEERING THE TRIALS

The political system was incapable of preventing any external or internal impulses from being absorbed into the machinery that churned out the trials. These impulses included repercussions of the Cold War and the fact that from the moment trials began in the other People's Democracies – starting with the Rajk trial – the conviction grew among leaders in the socialist countries that the centre of a vast international conspiracy was located in Czechoslovakia. In fact suggestions were even made for coordinating the Security forces of the socialist countries under the guidance of the Soviet Security Police. In this connection one should also note the criticisms voiced against Czechoslovakia at a Comecon meeting in October and December 1950, at a meeting on military matters in January 1951, and by Stalin in mid 1951 (in talks with Čepička), as well as Gottwald's resolute declaration that Czechoslovakia would never be a second Yugoslavia. The internal impulses consisted in particular of sectarian trends in policy and manifestations of the abuse of power.

Apart from its failure to prevent the trials, the political system provided the basis from which the mechanism for their engineering was evolved.

This mechanism was developed from within the system, remained a part of it and occupied a special position. It was regarded as the most politically conscious part of the system, and the system in turn influenced its operation. While the numbers involved in the mechanism were not great, its power in the State was immense. It possessed the ability to create the conditions needed for its own long-term existence. Another feature was a relative stability of personnel over nearly ten years, which constituted one of the main reasons for the slow and inadequate rehabilitation. The structure and methods of work made it impossible to uncover the truth either during the trials or after. An instrument of power had come into being, accountable to no one, beyond all control and outside the law; it had placed itself above society and usurped a power to which it had no right. Its very existence was unconstitutional.

There were three main links in this mechanism for the engineering of political trials; political institutions, the Security Service and the judiciary. All three cooperated within a hierarchy of power and authority.

The political section of the mechanism consisted primarily of a small group, who made the immediate decisions about the trials: Gottwald, Zápotocký, at times Široký and Kopřiva (the Minister of National Security), and from 1952 Bacílek, later Barák the Minister of the Interior, and several members of the Political Secretariat, Čepička, Dolanský, Kopecký and Novotný, who in 1954 joined the Politburo. Gottwald played a leading part: the decisions to arrest leading officials usually came from him, he was informed about the results of investigations, and he intervened in the preparation of the big trials.

By statements, resolutions and speeches the political leadership channelled the necessary guidelines to the Security Service and the judiciary and provided the ideological justification for their decisions. These bodies saw their duty to the Party in fulfilling the resolutions and being guided by the views of the top committees and leaders; bound by Party discipline, many were convinced that they were serving the Party even if their actions contradicted its programme. In this respect Šváb's words are revealing: '. . . I decided that what we, the Party leadership, were doing was right; even if it broke the law a thousand times, and even if it was of a criminal nature.'

The political mechanism included the various commissions that participated in various ways in the trials. They were the Commission for the Field–Pavlík case, the Commission for the Šling–Švermová case, the Security Commission and the Party Control Commission. Although the Security Commission and the Party Control Commission were not concerned solely with the political trials, much of their work did have a direct bearing on it. For example, a number of Control Commission documents became the subject of Security investigations and were used as evidence. The Security Commission approved the preparation of the trials (in 1949 and 1950) and the severity of the sentences. Among the political bodies involved in the trials were two departments of the Party Central Committee – one for records and the other for personnel. Both maintained contact with Security and supplied it with personnel reports and individual dossiers. Especially close contacts with the Security Service were maintained by employees of the Records Department, some of whom were recruited to work for the force, although they remained on the Central Committee's payroll.

The special function of the political institutions in this mechanism was that of proclaiming, in general terms, the ideological aims for the other components; at the same time they asserted their dominant status in relation to these components. The relationship, however, was not one-sided; the other components did not play the role of mere passive instruments. They in their turn – especially the Security Service – did more than merely carry out orders; they acted on their own initiative, they supplied the false information on which the political institutions based their decisions, and they also used such information for their own purposes. In this relationship the element of control was completely lost.

The position of the Security Service in relation to the other components was vital. After the war the Party leadership had tried to bring Security under its influence; a number of Party officials were transferred to this sector and, as tensions grew, the Party increasingly used sections of Security to achieve its aims in the fight against its political opponents. In this way a special bond was formed between the Party and Security, whereby Party officials cooperated with Security departments and the Party leadership either exerted direct control or at least intervened in the work.

After February 1948 a change took place in the status and internal organization of the Security Service. New and unaccustomed tasks came to the fore – the staging of political trials. While only part of the Security apparatus was engaged in this work, nevertheless it influenced the work of other sections too. The Service had no previous experience of staging big political trials and this was an undertaking that called for entirely new methods. Political trials are based not on evidence but on directives issued by the leadership; Security, in such cases, is instructed to 'unmask the political designs' of alleged enemies, to deduce these designs from their speeches and articles, and to form a reassessment of their political and other activity; from all this they have to fabricate an alleged threat to the political system. Security was not equipped for this work; the preparation of a political trial presupposed a new type of official – a man politically 'aware' and capable of blind obedience to orders. Consequently, the department most concerned with preparing the trials had to be restaffed.

These personnel changes, inaugurated at the end of 1948, were pushed ahead with renewed vigour when the Ministry of National Security was established. The very act of creating this Ministry was politically mistaken and signified gross interference in the political system. Its staffing, too, was an act of political irresponsibility; the officials placed in charge lacked the abilities required for such important posts.

The main criteria in selecting the many new recruits to the State Security department were 'political awareness and loyalty', with the result that the sections called upon to handle the trials were staffed with unqualified people, some drawn from the People's Militia, others from the Party apparatus and so on. Apart from lack of expertise, they had little experience of life, since most of them were young – ranging in age from twenty to thirty. Being raw and inexperienced, such men were susceptible to 'persuasion', uncritical extremism and, understandably, to ambition and inflated ideas about their status. The responsibility for these men, most of whom believed they were engaged in a 'holy mission', is borne by those who in this way built up the most sensitive sector of State power.

The consequences were grave, affecting both the victims and the fabricators of the trials. One example is that as late as 1963 many employees of the Security Service were wholly unaware that they had violated the law, and pleaded this ignorance in justification, claiming that they had simply carried out the Party's instructions. Many were ignorant of other things as well as of law; they had no idea how to conduct interrogations, how to write out summaries of evidence – in short, the elementary functions of a Security officer. Nor as a rule did their level of political knowledge answer to requirements. They fabricated fantastic charges, juggled with espionage links, invented all kinds of political deviations, mistakes and intentions – all signs of their political immaturity. They compensated for lack of skills by physical and mental torture and by appealing to the Communist consciences of their victims; they competed for the distinction of holding the longest interrogation session. Not all prisoners, however, were subjected to these methods; in some cases a special relationship developed between interrogator and interrogated, with prisoners writing their own depositions and imparting to them a 'political level'.

Pressures on the Security Service were exerted from without by the top leadership, the Party Control Commission, the Soviet Security officers and many others. These pressures resulted in Security undergoing a number of changes; tensions, a feeling of insecurity and suspicion prevailed.

Between 1948 and 1952 the senior staff was changed several times. In 1948 Plaček left and was later arrested; the following year the same fate befell the State Security chief, Jindřich Veselý; in 1950 the Police Force came under a new Minister, Ladislav Kopřiva, while responsibility for State Security was placed in the hands of Šváb and Závodský. Then early in 1951 the entire Security command was arrested; Hora, an official of the Party Control Commission, took over State Security, and Bína, also from the Control Commission, became Deputy Minister. By the end of the year both these men had left their posts, soon followed by Kopřiva, whereupon Prchal became head of State Security, Bacílek was appointed Minister, and later Prchal was named as his Deputy.

These changes were the outcome of the political battle for command of Security, which up to 1951 was viewed with distrust by some Control Commission members and by the Soviet advisers. Each change signified a decline in the political and expert qualifications of the departmental heads of Security, causing deep rifts in the Service.

The appointment of a new chief was always accompanied by an influx of new staff and suspicion towards the existing personnel. With the departure of Plaček, the shadow of distrust fell upon his colleagues. The arrest of the top men in 1951 saw the return of Janoušek and Dr Mudra, the arrival of Klícha, Samec and Keppert, and the consolidation of the position of Smola, Arazin, Holvek (that is, of the Náchod group); on the other hand, those who came with Šváb – Doubek and others – were treated with suspicion. So fierce was the conflict that the Minister himself, Kopřiva, had to speak out in defence of Doubek. Thus various factions took shape within the Service; for example the Jihlava faction (those who had come from Jihlava) and a group round Doubek which was associated with the Party apparatus. The most closely knit faction, it is clear, was that known as the Hradec group, an offshoot of the Náchod Commission which had investigated agents of the Nazi secret police and had then been taken over by the Security Service. It consisted of Dr Smola, Arazin, Holvek, Roček, Dr Mudra and others and maintained contacts with the Party Control Commission and with the Soviet Security Service. Charges against Slánský came mainly from the prisoners interrogated by this group. Another faction, headed by Hošek and including Keppert and Nekvasil, also maintained, through Keppert, contacts with the Soviet Security Service. The speciality of this faction was the indictment of those Security officers who had fought with the International Brigade in Spain.

The characteristic features of the two last-named factions were pathological suspicion and distrust. The Hradec men mistrusted Kopřiva and accused him of collaborating with foreign agents. A bitter struggle was waged among the factions, and the Minister had to intervene. Much remained unexplained – the death of Holvek, for example.

The Czechoslovak Security Service was greatly influenced by Soviet Security. We are not concerned here with the role of the Soviet advisers, which will be described later in this Report.

One last point about the external influences on the Security Service. Our examination is confined to the situation at the centre of State Security. We do not know in any detail about the state of affairs at lower levels, nor do we know anything about those groups that stood apart from the legal sectors and were concerned with Intelligence (for example before Keppert joined State Security). The Prague Party organization and the Prague section of Security played a special role, being in a position to observe much of what was taking place at the centre – a point noted by Novotný at a Presidium meeting on 1 January 1963.

The status accorded the Soviet advisers and the relationship between the Chief Adviser and the Minister made for complications in Security. The advisers enjoyed great prestige; their advice and instructions had the weight of orders and most members of the Service obeyed these orders, convinced of their correctness and usefulness. Many regarded it as natural, even essential, to inform both the Soviet adviser and their own chief, or they informed the adviser first; while some, having confidence only in the advisers, informed them alone. The Minister also accepted the advisers' recommendations as correct and ordered them to be followed. He informed and consulted Gottwald about many matters concerning the trials, usually in the presence of the Chief Adviser. However, the latter often called on Gottwald alone without being accompanied by the Minister. Thus Gottwald was informed earlier by the Soviet side (for example about the case of the 'Great Crossing-Sweeper') than by his Minister.

The role of the Security Service in the mechanism that manufactured the trials affected not only its own internal life but also its relationship with the other cogs in the machine. Its relationship with the political leadership was a complex one; it cannot be described simply as that of subordinate to superior. Security carried out the leadership's decisions – not just general guidelines for combating enemies of the Party, but also specific instructions. On the other hand, Security supplied the documents on which the political leadership based their decisions, and they often relied solely on such information. The Political Secretariat discussed the instructions issued by the Minister concerning the manner of submitting reports on members of the Government, the Central Committee and other officials, and it approved the extent of postal censorship; the political leadership decided which alleged enemies were to be moved from their homes – 'Operation B' – and gave its approval to the arrest of political suspects. Gottwald even took part in the interrogations by answering questions addressed to him by the investigators. The leadership, in its turn, took many decisions regarding personnel only in agreement with Security or with the proviso that that agreement be obtained, and it delegated the screening of some high-ranking officials to Security officers; Security recruited collaborators from the ranks of the Party with the approval of Party officials at various levels; the Personnel Department at the Party Central Office was entrusted by Security with 'special tasks' and so on. Some Central Committee departments – Personnel, Records and the Control Commission – cooperated closely with Security during the mounting of a trial by handing over archives and setting the political tone.

The Security Service's role in mounting a trial was of paramount importance. From the key moment when anyone fell into their hands – when he crossed the border between political accusation and actual arrest – they exercised unlimited power over him, deciding the fate of the prisoner in custody, in the dock, and while serving his sentence.[1] Humiliation and insults, one worse than another, were heaped upon the victims; the brutality reached horrifying proportions, and led to many tragic situations.

This cooperation between the political leadership and the Security Service was seen as a normal consequence of the Party's position of power. Undoubtedly other factors also played a part, for example friendships between political officials and Security officers and, in some cases, fear of the secret police.

The third link in the mechanism was the judiciary. A vital factor in staging the trials was the relationship between power and the law, between the Party and the State. Only the State is entitled to issue general binding rules in legal form, and only the State has the legal right to enforce these rules; this funda-

---

[1] *This was possible because, until 1968, the whole system of prisons and forced labour camps in Czechoslovakia came under the jurisdiction of the Ministry of the Interior and not of the Ministry of Justice, as is normal in advanced countries.*

mental principle was grossly violated. It is clear that the more power is exercised independently of law, the farther the system advances along the road to isolation of the legal order and, ultimately, to disregard for its own laws. After 1948, legal forms were regarded as a formality, important more for appearances than for the actual regulation of social relations. (Kopřiva said in 1963: 'Yes, the arrests contravened the law, but no notice was taken of this at the time. It was only in later years that measures were taken to ensure respect for the law.')

This being the attitude to the law, even laws that had been enacted as instruments in the fight against class enemies were disregarded. And so the way was opened to complete arbitrariness, for the 'rights of the criminal are but another expression for the rights of the innocent'. The trials were more than a violation of the law, they inaugurated a state of misrule throughout our society; they signified a state of complete legal uncertainty even for those on the topmost rung of the power ladder. A strong tendency set in to restrict the State in its inner sovereignty. Its two functions, law-making and law enforcement, were now usurped by the Party leadership, not only by placing Communists in Government posts but also by seeing that only Communists in the top Party posts determined the exercise of State power.

The share of the judiciary in the trials was likewise limited to a small group of officials in the Prosecutor's Office, the courts and the Ministry of Justice, involving especially the Ministers (Čepička, Rais and Škoda) and some Deputy Ministers. The main feature of closed-door procedure was evident in all the trials, large and small; verdicts, that is, were decided not by the courts but by extraneous political bodies such as the Security Commission of the Central Committee, the Security 'fives', the Political Secretariat and 'Commission K'. The judiciary acted as the executor of these orders and decisions, providing them with a semblance of legality. This process, which directly contravened the Constitution, was seen as implementing the Party's leading role.

The introduction of the administration of justice behind closed doors was accompanied by a number of changes in the legal code and the structure of the judiciary. The main role was now accorded to the prosecutor, with the judge merely carrying out his recommendations. Younger men were appointed to the judiciary. Often lacking the necessary qualifications, they were assigned the important posts of prosecutors and judges. This led to a decline in respect for justice and in professional integrity.

Justice behind closed doors signified the complete abolition of the independence of the judges, who were now dependent on the decisions reached by the political authorities. Whether the individual judge was active or passive in the execution of orders, or whether the orders did or did not correspond with his own views, was immaterial. By his conduct he denied the fundamental principle of legal process – the search for objective truth – and delegated his duties and rights to other noncompetent bodies. These actions resulted in a complete degradation of the law.

In the major political trials, the suppression of judicial independence consisted not only in the sentences being decided by bodies outside the court, but also in the fact that the legal proceedings were in the hands of Security and not of the judges and the prosecutor. Judicial officers also deferred to Security and consciously violated the established legal procedure. Legal proceedings were converted into a monstrous farce staged by the secret police. Every detail was stage-managed. The questions asked by the judges and prosecutor had been written down for them, the answers had been memorized by the men in the dock. Witnesses also took the stand with memorized testimonies. Everything followed a scenario rehearsed beforehand, either in part or in full. The task of the defence counsel was to say little and support the indictment. From the moment of arrest to the pronouncement of the verdict, the law was repeatedly violated, and always to the disadvantage of the accused – while the lawyers kept silent. Throughout the performance the judiciary played a sorry role; such conduct served only to degrade the authority of the law.

The prime function of the judiciary in staging the trials was to put the finishing touches to the work of the politicians and Security, to give it some sort of justification, in short to legalize it. Another of its tasks was to publicize the proceedings, thereby fulfilling another political purpose, that of influencing public opinion.

The crowning achievement of the entire mechanism was the organized mass acquiescence in the trials and their verdicts. Numerous resolutions and expressions of gratitude were addressed to the judges in connection with the trials of Milada Horáková and the three Catholic bishops. The peak was reached around the trial of the Centre. Resolutions were passed at public and Party meetings, many of them voicing fierce demands for sentences of death. The political leadership succeeded in generating a mass psychosis designed to confirm the correctness of legal and political decisions.

THE SOCIAL CONSEQUENCES OF THE TRIALS

The trials affected the entire community, impinging on all spheres of life. They were instrumental in shaping society and its outlook; they left a deep imprint on the future.

Among the most monstrous distortions of socialism, they were a manifestation of inhumanity that shook socialism to its foundations both in Czechoslovakia and abroad. The effects were felt in all areas: economic, political and cultural, in the minds of the people, in relations between citizens and in the country's international standing.

The trials were designed to overcome the tension which had arisen as a result of the failure to fulfil the unreal economic targets; they were to prove that the sorry state of the economy was due to the activity of class enemies and their sabotage of efforts to speed up the reconstruction of the Czechoslovak economy and make it independent of the capitalist world. The trumped-up charges and extorted confessions of economic sabotage were so extensive that they raised doubts as to the soundness of the first Five Year Plan. The politicians (especially Zápotocký) feared that the revelations of 'espionage' might shake confidence in the Party's economic policy as such.

The indictments in the case of the 'Centre' and the economists, and the hearings in court, abounded in imaginary crimes and criminal designs by enemies attempting to retard the development of heavy industry. The trials, therefore, helped to support the 'iron and steel' concept of the Czechoslovak economy, their purpose in this respect being to provide evidence that the programme was sound, although in fact its scope exceeded the possibilities of the Czechoslovak economy.

The trials encouraged a subjective approach in economic management. The charges of sabotage that had been fabricated by Security (whose knowledge of economics was negligible), confirmed by the expert assessors and included in the indictments, were then accepted as genuine and as pointing the way to eliminate the shortcomings in the economy. In 1952 the Government was still instructing the competent Ministers and central offices to submit their proposals for overcoming the economic consequences of the Centre's activities. Many Ministries, not lacking imagination in uncovering the results of 'enemy activity', elaborated on the findings of the court, and tried to project into the economic plans for the years ahead schemes for eliminating the results of sabotage.

The prevailing view that the hand of the enemy lay behind every percentage of unfulfilled plan and every economic difficulty yielded two results. The circle of suspects expanded and with it the number of potential victims for future trials, and at the same time the real causes of the shortcomings and economic difficulties remained hidden. The habit of blaming the enemy for everything became so widespread that in 1954 leading officials had to protest against this exaggerated self-deception which was supposed to be the universal panacea for economic ailments, but which, far from curing the illness, in fact made it worse. This self-deception afflicted both the Party activists and economists, as well as a large part of the population; it aroused false hopes that the difficulties would be overcome and, possessed of great vitality, it faded slowly. Nevertheless, the contradiction between unjustified hopes and reality existed; it was not always tackled by an acknowledgement of the facts but often by an appeal for the unmasking of yet more enemies.

The trials helped to consolidate the centralized system of management. People employed in the economic sector were more than ever afraid to make independent decisions, in case they might be prosecuted. The authority of the central offices grew rapidly and the implementation of a central bureaucratic model of management gained support. During the period of the trials the majority of leading economists and those who had conceived the economic policy were removed from office. Many became victims of the trials, others were dismissed for alleged collaboration with the former. These personnel changes took place at the lower levels of the economic sector too. The posts were filled by men with less experience and inferior training, which affected the general level of management.

The impact of the trials was particularly strong in the political arena. They not only provided the most striking illustration of the distortion of the political system but promoted further distortions in their turn. There was a causal relationship between the political system and the trials, and the trials in turn reacted on the system. They bolstered the personality cult of which they were a product. They reinforced the jurisdiction and authority of the select group of leading Party and State officials; they created an atmosphere of terror in which the individual citizen's healthy political activities atrophied and the social function of repression was enhanced; the role of Security and its power grew commensurately. The trials served, in a way, as an apparent confirmation of Security's integrity and as evidence that it was working on the right lines. The conviction grew that enemies in increasing numbers were bent on destroying socialism in Czechoslovakia. A feature of the political system and the status of Security in that system was that Security's ability to stage political trials gave it a basis, continually being renewed, for its privileged position in society, thereby helping to maintain the political system.

The trials degraded politics in the public mind and bred mistrust of political affairs. They were placed in the forefront of political activity and they dominated the political thinking of a large part of the population. This trend, which the Party leadership had initiated and encouraged, ran counter to all principles of humanism, to the genuine interests of socialism and to the Communist Party programme. Such a state of affairs contributed to the atmosphere of fear, made it easier to stigmatize individuals and groups, and encouraged a chronic passivity among the public, a flight from and fear of politics.

The mechanism of manufacturing trials was the ultimate expression of the manipulation of society by the top political group. The manipulation was total: Security officers manipulated the prisoners and also the judiciary and the political officials, the political leadership and Security manipulated each other, the political leadership manipulated the judiciary and the prisoners, while all three – political leadership, Security and judiciary – manipulated the population. They expended a lot of effort, they used all the media at their disposal – the press, books, meetings, conferences, the radio and their own authority – to convince the public of the justness of the trials, to brainwash the population, and to win active public support for their deeds; they invited people to denounce and 'unmask the enemy'. So powerful and so concentrated was this pressure, so pervasive the atmosphere of 'spy mania', that the bulk of the population believed every word they were told. As a result, falsehood replaced truth in their thinking. This conflict contained the germ of a profound social crisis which could not but come to a head the moment the lies were exposed.

The Communist Party especially was hard hit by the trials. Not only did they remove or physically destroy a part of its top leadership, while officials of a new type – executors of orders – took their place; they also paralysed the Party's internal life and created an atmosphere in which it was impossible to apply democratic principles. The system of uncontrollable personal power was reinforced. Where the trials were concerned, the only democratic right left to Party members was to endorse the decisions in the making of which they had no part, and there was no dearth of voices calling for death sentences. Thus for several years the Party lived in the shadow of the political trials, its activities pervaded by the atmosphere of fear – fear on the one hand of ar amified, hostile and treacherous force believed to exist inside the Party and the State, and on the other hand of denunciation as an enemy. The fears haunting the lower echelons of the Party may have been less serious, but the prevailing conditions inside the Party can only be described as abnormal.

The trials influenced, and in some measure determined, the

relationship between the Party and society. On the one hand, they were a product of the bureaucratic, centralistic assertion of the Party's dominant position of power; on the other hand, they reinforced and ostensibly justified these methods. Operating in this way, the Party took over important functions from the State and the public organizations, thereby preventing them from playing their public role or realizing their place and functions in the management of society. The trials were removed from the jurisdiction of the constitutional representative bodies of the State – Government and Parliament – and were directed by the Party leadership, virtually by a small group at the top. This practice inevitably led to the illegal procedures that took on such a fearful aspect in the trials.

The vast scale on which the law was violated engendered feelings of legal insecurity among a large section of the population. The citizen no longer had a guarantee of legal protection; the Constitution had lost its prestige. Violation of the law by State and Party authorities set in motion the vast chain reaction that made possible, and culminated in, the illegal trials, and these in turn maintained and extended this state of affairs. The individual citizen could no longer defend his rights, even over what seemed minor breaches of the law; later, he found he had been deprived of his rights in trials where his life was at stake. The lawlessness was indiscriminate: ordinary citizens holding no official position and men prominent in public life were equally vulnerable. It can be said that the monster trials had their origins in the first occasion that the law was violated in a 'minor case'.

In the cultural sphere, too, the consequences of the trials were many and various. For the most part they were felt indirectly, in the atmosphere and the relationships created by the trials, and in the political attitudes and thinking of the time. To evaluate the state of society as reflected in the arts is, of course, a job for the critics and historians. With their sensitivity to injustice, many artists and writers found the social climate especially hard to bear. Some individuals, and groups, were banned from working, others – the politically committed, men such as Konstantin Biebl, Jiří Frejka and Saša Machov – were driven by the pressures of the day to resignation or suicide. All were haunted by fear, anxiety and the conflict between their conscience and the social reality. Clearly it was an atmosphere not conducive to creative work – a denial of artistic freedom. The frequent political interference and the regiment-ation of the arts, their subordination to the momentary political interests of the leading group, the silencing of many of the foremost writers and artists, all this was a heavy blow to Czechoslovak culture. Many officials in the world of culture assisted in ostracizing prominent men of art and culture and in labelling them as enemies of socialism. Some also shared in creating the oppressive atmosphere and in organizing public approval of the trials. By thinking and acting in this way these men, too, were in fact among the victims of the trials.

The trials played their part in moulding the social attitudes of the Czechs and Slovaks. They presented a simplistic view of the advance towards socialism as being accompanied by a fight against class enemies, traitors and spies; at the same time they affected the image of socialism itself. This confrontation between socialism as the majority of the population had originally seen it and the reality of the mid-1950s constituted a further source of social crisis.

The legal nihilism that had been growing for some time reached its culmination in the trials; it reflected the degree of illegality reached and the decline in the authority of the law. This obliterating of legal consciousness applied not only to the public generally, but especially to the executors of power, while the situation among officers of the judiciary was worst of all.

The trials upset personal relationships, directly and through the atmosphere they helped to create. Officials who had known each other intimately for years no longer trusted one another, friend suspected friend, Communists regarded only certain groups of the population as reliable. Non-Communists, and some Communists as well, became politically suspect. The occasions for coming under the shadow of suspicion and dis-trust were many, and, as suspicions grew stronger, people with-drew into isolation, and friendships cooled. What people did, what they said, the views they expressed and the people they associated with all acquired a new complexion. Many actions and opinions which had hitherto been regarded as perfectly normal and common now gave rise to doubts: they were regarded as potential seeds of treason, enmity and espionage. Every arrest, every faint shadow of suspicion, provided impulses for further denunciations and fresh suspicions to be communicated to the Party and Security. The overwhelming majority of those who acted as informers regarded this role as their civic and Party duty.

The atmosphere of suspicion poisoned the relations between people, between State bodies, between Party and public organizations; it even disturbed the relations between the nations and the nationalities within the country. It affected attitudes towards non-Communists, certain religious groups, farmers, intellectuals and the working class. In human relationships distrust instead of trust was encouraged and indeed practised; this gave rise to tensions in society, stunted its growth, created conditions for a non-stop sequence of political trials and prevented the bulk of the population from making a useful contribution to socialism.

In contributing to a loss of values in society the trials diminished in particular the value of human life, and also such values as honour, responsibility, especially political responsibility, comradeship, friendship, justice and truth – those fundamental principles of Marxist policy. In other words, values which were part of the heritage of Marxism and should have demonstrated the merits of socialism were trampled underfoot. Herein lay one of the most potent sources of the social crisis, which also precipitated a crisis of confidence in which the victims were, at first, certain Party leaders, later all of them (with the exception of Gottwald), and indeed the entire regime.

The trials left a trail of victims – not only those unjustly sentenced or otherwise penalized but also their friends and relations who became subject to persecution. Here, too, was a further source of social crisis and discontent.

Czech and Slovak society was scarred by the trials; many of their consequences were absorbed into its life. If progress was to be made once more, all this had to be put right. The condition was the elimination of the conditions that had nurtured the trials, the righting of wrongs and the restoration to their rightful place in society of those unjustly sentenced or otherwise persecuted.

The Czechoslovak trials were received unfavourably abroad. Progressive public opinion throughout the world, until then sympathetically inclined towards Czechoslovakia, was roused to protest. This deepened Czechoslovakia's isolation, particularly in the spheres of culture and science, and restricted contacts with many leading and progressive scientists and scholars.

TWO

REASSESSMENT AND REHABILITATION

REASSESSMENT UP TO THE TWENTIETH CONGRESS OF THE SOVIET COMMUNIST PARTY

THE inconsistent and incomplete reassessment of the political trials of the 1950s, which has dragged on for the past fifteen years, has made it necessary for this third Commission to consider the history of rehabilitation. For a number of reasons beyond our control it has not yet been possible to clarify all the external and internal factors influencing the course of rehabilitation. A proper analysis will require further historical research. Nevertheless, the work done so far, which has been concentrated on assembling the essential facts, does in our opinion give a clear answer to the key question with regard to rehabilitation: when and to what extent did the Party leadership have at its disposal sufficient facts to begin to right the wrongs caused by the trials?

We have shown that in 1953 and 1954 the Party leadership had enough information from domestic and foreign sources to make it clear that something was seriously wrong. The volume of material continued to grow during the following years; by 1957, for example, the Central Committee, the President's Office and the Prosecutor-General had received a total of 288 complaints which were recorded carefully and filed.

The work of the Commission of Inquiry appointed by the Politburo in January 1955 reflected the attitude adopted by the Party leadership to establishing the truth about the trials. On 10 January Novotný submitted to a meeting of the Politburo his proposals for the composition of the Commission and outlined its task as 'a review of some post-1948 court cases with reference to the sentences'. The meeting fixed the composition of the Commission, made some organizational arrangements and drew up a rough working plan.

The members of what is known as Commission 'A' were:

Barák, chairman, Innemann, secretary, Košťál (Ministry of the Interior), Litera (Ministry of Justice) and Švach (Prosecutor-General's Office).

At the time of his appointment Barák was Minister of the Interior and also a member of the Politburo. His conscience was not burdened with participation in the illegal practices and distortion from the period of the trial of Slánský's 'Anti-State Conspiratorial Centre'; he did, however, share responsibility for the subsequent trials of 1953 and 1954.

The second member was the Deputy Minister of the Interior, Karel Košťál, who had taken an active part in investigating the 'Centre'. He had to be withdrawn from the Commission on 15 August, when it became known that he himself had used illegal methods in getting prisoners to confess to acts they had not committed.

The two other members were the Deputy Prosecutor-General, Dr Švach, and the former Deputy Minister of Justice Dr Litera, both very much 'in the picture' concerning the trial procedure. Švach, for example, had acted as counsel for the prosecution in the trial of Marie Švermová and other Party members. Litera, with the Prosecutor-General, Aleš, had on 9 December 1953 submitted to the Party Secretariat proposals for the secret trial of Závodský and other officials of the Ministry of Security.

Innemann, a pre-war member of the Party, was at the time head of the department at the Party Central Office concerned with government and administration. Marie Kunštátová, a member of the staff at the Central Office, was appointed rapporteur to the Commission.

For the first six weeks the Commission met in the building of the Ministry of the Interior. When the members of the Commission discovered that they were under observation and that their telephones were being tapped, they moved to the Central Committee building.

The Commission did not itself conduct the investigation; it appointed four working groups, each of which included one official from the Central Committee Secretariat, one prosecutor and one official of the Ministry of the Interior. All the members drawn from the Ministries of the Interior and Justice had worked as investigators and prosecutors until the mid-1950s. Those chosen from the Central Office staff were from the lower echelons and were ill-equipped for this job. The working groups submitted reports on their inquiries and made recommendations. Most cases were decided by the Commission, the more important were referred to the Politburo. These decisions, which were ruled by 'political expediency', were final; there was no appeal. That is to say that from the outset the Commission perpetuated the policy of working behind closed doors. The very decision to set up the Barák Commission was yet another violation of socialist justice. This is proved by the resolutions, (a) that only the Politburo should give orders for an inquiry and (b) that inquiries were to be conducted solely by the Commission. There was no legal basis for the existence of this Commission, or for the final decisions on guilt and criminal responsibility being pronounced by the Politburo and the Commission. The powers of the Party Commission were in theory restricted to considering political responsibility and its consequences. But, as we know, in practice the procedure was quite different. The courts were merely the final link in the chain; at closed sessions, without the presence of the public or even of the accused, they obediently pronounced the new verdicts that had been determined˙beforehand and elsewhere.

The Commission was not concerned with rehabilitation, or with endeavouring, objectively and truthfully, to probe the violations of the law and their causes; its chief consideration was to salve the conscience of the Politburo by putting a political full stop to the matter. Consequently the work of the first Barák Commission was confined to political trials other than that of the Anti-State Conspiratorial Centre. The view of the Party leadership was that there should be no tampering with the trial.

The idea behind the appointment of the Commission can be gleaned from a written proposal referred to the Politburo by the Ministry of the Interior. It said:

The Ministry of the Interior hereby submits a proposal for reviewing the sentences passed in certain court cases. This reassessment is not intended as grounds for a sudden wave of releases from prison, but as a gradual re-examination of individual cases, particularly the earlier ones, so that possibly unjust verdicts may be set aside. The Ministry is of the opinion that the present situation and the consolidation of State power, together with an all-round improvement in the quality of its work, allow such a reassessment. (ACC CPC, Commission II, Section 91.)

Even during the Commission's first sessions there was an obvious anxiety to conceal the nature of its work. From the outset the ruling was that documents and other materials were to be acquired in such a way that the purpose for which they were intended should not be revealed to the public. Thus the findings, indeed the existence, of the Barák Commission were long kept hidden from the Party membership and even the Central Committee. Consequently the opportunity to exert any control over the Commission's activities was slight; it became a mere instrument of the Politburo, or rather of certain well-informed members of the latter, in whose subjective views and aims it acquiesced. This explains why the Commission could not deal satisfactorily with the task entrusted to it and why in fact it failed to rehabilitate the people unjustly condemned.

The first case, to which the Politburo gave top priority for investigation by the Commission, was the Švermová trial, as well as cases connected with Noel Field, who had been rehabilitated in Hungary.

The manner, and the findings, of the inquiry into the Švermová trial and that of the regional Party secretaries revealed clearly the leadership's plans with regard to the Commission and its work.

It thus seems necessary to describe in some detail the way in which this trial was handled by the Commission, and to point out the relationship that existed between some members of the Commission and Švermová. Barák, who referred the draft indictment to the Secretariat on 18 January 1954, knew how the trial had been conducted and had attended the interministerial consultation at which objections had been raised about the absence of evidence pointing to any criminal offences on Švermová's part. Košťál, as Doubek's closest collaborator, and also Švach (who had represented the prosecution at the Švermová trial) were well informed about the investigations of her case both before and after the Slánský trial.

Understandably, these circumstances played their part in the inquiry. Existing documents prove that Košťál, Švach and Barák wanted to 'settle' the matter as quietly as possible.

Without analysing the case or thoroughly appraising the facts, Košťál prepared and Innemann submitted to the Commission a recommendation which was accepted: to reduce Švermová's sentence to eight years by way of pardon, to release her conditionally on the occasion of the tenth anniversary of the liberation of Czechoslovakia, and to provide her with a job in an area far from Prague (the Jeseníky mountains were suggested).

The argument used in support of this recommendation is worth noting:

The Communist Party is now sufficiently strong and our Republic is sufficiently consolidated for us to afford a certain degree of leniency. (ACC CPC, Commission II, Section 329.)

The recommendation, however, had been put together in such haste that Barák, although he had approved it, suggested, at the next meeting of the Commission, on 9 February 1955, that Innemann, Košťál and Švach should study the material on Švermová once more and propose two alternative solutions: (a) a reassessment of the verdict or (b) a pardon.

The suggestions were worked out but the Commission adhered to its original proposal of a pardon, as being the most suitable way to dispose of the case. At a meeting held on 23 February it based its attitude on the following arguments:

Neither the Ministry of the Interior nor the Prosecutor-General have at their disposal, nor do they know of, any grounds for a retrial. (ACC CPC, Commission II, Section 329.)

The real reason was disclosed further on in the document:

A Presidential pardon requires no legal proceedings; a recommendation by the Ministry of Justice is sufficient. The Commission recommends the second alternative. . . . This is the simpler way;

the first alternative might be difficult to present to the public. (ACC CPC, Commission I, Section 296.)

The Politburo, however, adopted a different standpoint: the political cases should be resolved by the lodging of a complaint concerning violation of the law and by the holding of a new trial, and only in exceptional cases by a pardon. This was the view taken when another solution of the Švermová trial was discussed on 21 March. At this meeting the Commission's recommendation was amended on the lines that the case was to be handled by means of a complaint of violation of the law. The sentences to be imposed were also decided.

The Politburo's resolution reads:

Comrade Urválek is instructed (1) to submit to the Supreme Court a complaint of violation of the law in the case of Švermová and Co. from the point of view of incorrect assessment of sentence, *bearing in mind as a main guideline that the valid verdict on Slánský and his accomplices is to remain untouched*; and (2) to ensure that the Presidium of the Supreme Court handles the complaint and amends the verdicts. The sentences in the individual cases should be imposed as follows. . . . (ACC CPC, File 02/2, Section 49.)

The inquiry into this first case demonstrated that the Party leadership was continuing its system of policy-making and the conduct of judicial affairs behind closed doors. Guilt or innocence, as well as new sentences, were again decided beforehand by a political body. Švermová and the others were not present at their retrial; they had no opportunity to hear the new indictment or to defend themselves. They were informed that the original verdict had been set aside and a new one pronounced, without being given any reason for the new sentences.

When the Politburo discussed this case, the principle was reiterated:

The trial and valid verdict in the case of Slánský and Co. are not to be touched. (ACC CPC, 02/2, Section 49.)

The method chosen for dealing with the Švermová trial became the 'model' for reinvestigating further cases.

This was so, for instance, in the case of Gejza Pavlík, Charlotte

Pavlíková and Dora Kleinová. The conclusion of the report on Pavlík reads:

After reinvestigation, the working group has reached the conclusion that there is no proof that Pavlík engaged in espionage, or conspired with Field for this purpose. Even if the information that Pavlík disclosed to Field is not mentioned explicitly in the files, we believe that some points could be taken to be State secrets. We recommend, therefore, that through a complaint of violation of the law, the original verdict against Pavlík should be set aside and that Pavlík should be sentenced to seven years for betraying a State secret to an unauthorized person.

As an alternative, the complaint of violation of the law should be restricted to the length of the sentence, Pavlík's sentence should be reduced to ten years and after serving seven years he should be granted a conditional release. (ACC CPC, Commission II, Section 338, ninth session of the Barák Commission.)

Similar alternatives were worked out for Charlotte Pavlíková and Dora Kleinová.

Another case reviewed was that of the Slovak trade unionist Benau. The working group established that Benau had been sentenced to four years on the basis of a confession extorted from him by physical and psychological violence. Yet the final recommendation was in the form of two alternatives.

The Barák Commission, then, guided by the current needs and views of the Party leadership, chose one of the alternatives and amended the material to justify this choice. In Benau's case, the Commission compelled the working group to rewrite its recommendation to bring it into line with the view that the verdict against Benau should not be set aside.

A similar procedure was adopted in the investigation of the guilt of Dr Haškovec, Gottwald's personal physician, who had been sentenced to six years' imprisonment. After studying the documents and interviewing Dr Haškovec, the working committee came to the conclusion that a complaint of violation of the law should be lodged, because the trial had obviously been rigged. The Commission, however, took a different view, recommending that the material should be worked over and a proposal put to the Politburo to confirm the original verdict and deal with the case by means of an amnesty.

Here, too, stress was laid on the importance of 'not tampering' with the Slánský trial. In the document which it prepared for the Politburo the Commission stated:

The Commission regards this as the most suitable method of solving the case, for the granting of an individual pardon or a review of the verdict could provide our enemies with the means for sowing seeds of doubt concerning the Anti-State Conspiratorial Centre. (ACC CPC, Commission II, Section 337.)

The element of political expediency in the Commission's approach is demonstrated in cases where, even after innocence had been established beyond all doubt, the Commission suggested either an endorsement of the verdict or a reduction of the sentence. We summarize the facts from the trials which the Commission reviewed in the first half of 1955.

In the trial of Pavlík and others, the Commission proposed reducing the sentences on Pavlík and Feigl, and endorsing the original verdicts in the cases of Kosta, Nový and Kleinová.

In the cases of Jančík and Kaboš, the Commission proposed to the Politburo that the original verdicts be sustained, claiming that they corresponded to the offences. (ACC CPC, Commission II, Section 337.) Although investigation of the Moškovič trial also showed the charges to have been unjustified, the Commission decided to recommend a new sentence of four years' imprisonment. (ACC CPC, Commission II, Section 341, twelfth session, 4 May 1955.)

Another major case handled by the Commission at this time was the trial of Husák and other members of the group of 'bourgeois nationalists'. The review of this 'case' did not take the Commission long; it was completed in May. After a preliminary examination of the documents, the working group found that

Husák, as a subversive bourgeois nationalist, was rightly condemned but, if his case is to be reviewed objectively, certain deficiencies in the investigations and the trial cannot be overlooked.

Husák had not actually signed a single summary of evidence; the Court had denied the accused the right to defence counsel, it had not heard any of the thirty witnesses whom Husák had wished to call in his defence at the main hearing, and, despite the accused's opposition, it had allowed the Prosecutor's application to read out incriminating testimonies from the Security investigations, by which the Court had violated article 157 of the penal code. Although the working group suggested that some important witnesses named by Husák should be summoned, the Barák Commission questioned only Púll. It then reported:

Since Púll failed to confirm Husák's defence, further witnesses were not summoned, since, unquestionably, they would merely have attested to the subversive activity of Husák and Co. (File 02/2, Vol. 45, Section 61.)

Individuals from the group accused of bourgeois nationalism were also questioned. After this examination, the Commission drew the conclusion that

each of the findings of the Supreme Court was properly substantiated by the evidence of witnesses or by the documents submitted to the Court and, last but not least, by the full confessions of Novomeský, Okáli, Horváth and Holdoš, which in large measure served to convict Husák.

On 25 May the Barák Commission recommended to the Politburo that the verdict of the Supreme Court should stand. The report concludes that the Court

correctly defined the subversive activity of the group of bourgeois nationalists primarily as high treason; for the intrigues of Husák and the others with the reactionary group of the Democratic Party round Lettrich and Ursíny could have had no other aim than to destroy the Republic, an aim necessarily connected with over-throwing the regime of people's democracy and the social order . . . (ACC CPC, 02/2, Section 61.)

On 7 June, the Politburo approved this recommendation. (Ibid.)

The Commission also reviewed the verdict passed on Josef Smrkovský. The examination in this case was typical of the Commission's work during this phase. All the features described above appear again; at the same time it formed a kind of bridge between this phase and the next.

The preliminary proposal to amend the verdict in Smrkovský's case, put to the Commission on 20 April, suggested lodging a complaint for violation of the law regarding the verdict and for a new sentence of four years' imprisonment after a retrial. However, the Commission rejected this proposal and resolved to refer the whole 'case' to the Politburo, but only after a thorough check on Smrkovský's activities during the Nazi occupation and an inquiry into his complaint about methods used in the investigation of his case. (ACC CPC, Commission II, Section 339, tenth session, 20 April 1955.)

After months of diligent investigation, during which the working group studied the material available, interviewing many witnesses, including Smrkovský himself, it decided that the preliminary proposal should be changed. The group established that Smrkovský had been arrested on the basis of unsubstantiated evidence, that during the subsequent investigation he had been beaten to induce him to sign a false confession, and that his whole trial had been rigged. Thus, on the subject of Smrkovský's alleged cooperation with the Gestapo the report says: 'No concrete facts were ascertained which would have justified even the suspicion that Smrkovský had collaborated with the Gestapo.' (ACC CPC, Commission II, Section 343, fifteenth session, 1 June 1955.) This analysis led the working group to propose that Smrkovský should be acquitted on all counts, released and legally rehabilitated.

On 1 June the Barák Commission discussed this new proposal. In Barák's absence, Košťál was the only member to oppose it. He declared that the whole case had been re-examined only with a view to establishing Josef Smrkovský's innocence. At a session on 8 June, Košťál announced that he would submit his own opinion in writing.

The discussions on the Smrkovský case dragged on, with the issue of his guilt or innocence being discussed many times – on 8 and 22 June, and 17, 24 and 25 August. From the above dates we can see that the Commission closed the case after an interval of nearly two months in its work during which new conditions were created by Doubek's arrest. Not until 18 August did it discuss for the second time the working group's proposal that Smrkovský should be acquitted. Yet even with Košťál no longer a member (he had been recalled by the Politburo on 15 August), the Commission came to no final conclusion. It merely resolved that

the final version of the proposal shall be approved after consultation with Comrade Kopřiva (to clarify the circumstances of Smrkovský's arrest) and after ascertaining to what extent Smrkovský's work as Director of State Farms was an indictable offence. (ACC CPC, Commission II, Section 346.)

The final version of the proposal submitted to the Politburo was drafted on 24 and 25 August and contained two prongs: first, that the original verdict should be set aside and Smrkovský sentenced anew to two or three years, and, second, that the Central Committee's decision to deprive Smrkovský of all offices entrusted to him by the Party should be confirmed. (ACC CPC, Commission II, Section 347.)

We do not know exactly what considerations influenced the Commission's ultimate decision. According to the minutes, the Politburo approved this proposal, without any discussion, on 29 September. However, in speaking about these proceedings at a meeting of the Central Committee on 29 May 1968, Novotný said that he and Barák had proposed the rehabilitation of some comrades (including Smrkovský).

When it came before the Politburo we lost. It was argued – and agreed – that, if the existing sentences on Smrkovský, Švermová and Pavlík were quashed, the Supreme Court should be instructed to find other charges to cover the time these comrades had spent in jail. Unfortunately, we were the only two who opposed this.

The working groups ascertained that the law had been grossly violated and illegal methods had been used by Security, as in the cases of Dr Haškovec, Pavlík and others. Josef Smrkovský had also protested strongly against the brutality and the illegal methods used by the Security officers. Although, on the basis of this complaint, the Commission discussed as early as April 1955 the possibility of inquiring into the methods of investigation, no steps were taken for some time. No change took place until the middle of June. By this time the Commission had received fresh information about violations of socialist justice and about trumped-up charges during the trials – notably complaints by Artur London and Vavro Hajdů, two Communists who had been sentenced to life imprisonment in the Slánský trial. London's letter was dated 22 February 1955, and had already been handed to the First Secretary of the Central Committee, Novotný, by Jan Svoboda, in mid-March. It began:

I request most urgently a review of my personal case. . . . I was forced by brutal and underhand methods to sign a false confession of anti-State activity. Trumped-up charges were made against me with the help of false, enforced testimonies and tendentiously worded statements by witnesses . . . falsified summaries of evidence and deliberate distortion of facts and documents. After several months of inhuman physical and moral pressure, I was forced to confess to these fabricated charges. After this 'confession' had been extorted, I was threatened with death and the destruction of my family . . . if I altered my testimony. (ACC CPC, Commission I, Section 395.)

London described his case anew in a conversation with Innemann on 5 July and in a statement sent to Innemann on the following day. (Ibid.)

A letter of 4 May addressed to Široký by Hajdů reached Novotný at the beginning of June. Hajdů wrote: 'After some hesitation, I have resolved to write the whole truth about my case even at the risk that this letter will not reach you directly.' (ACC CPC, Commission I, Section 411.)

Towards the end of June, events gathered momentum. On 22 June the Commission decided that action should be taken against those responsible for the shortcomings in handling Smrkovský's case. (ACC CPC, Commission II, Section 344.) Shortly after this the arrest of Bohumil Doubek was recommended. Košťál quite openly protested against this in a written statement. On 11 July, however, the Politburo approved Doubek's arrest. The reasons were stated as follows:

The inquiries of the Central Committee's Commission have shown that illegal methods of investigation were used in Ruzyň Prison, which constituted a gross violation of socialist justice. The full responsibility for this is borne by Bohumil Doubek who, as Commander of the Investigation Department at Ruzyň from 1950 to 1953, directed the investigations. Ascertained facts give grounds for the suspicion that he deliberately diverted the investigations onto a false trail.

The illegal methods of investigation, the atmosphere of fear, and mutual distrust among the investigators at Ruzyň were described in great detail, and the report concludes by acknowledging that 'as a result of this conduct many innocent persons were condemned'.

The next day, Doubek was arrested. His case was investigated by Švach. Permission to interrogate him was given only by Barák, Švach and Litera. The Deputy Minister of the Interior, Kotál, arranged secret custody and a special guard for Doubek in the Pankrác Prison.

The consequences that would follow from Doubek's arrest were not at first foreseen. It was assumed that his testimony would reveal and confirm the use of incorrect methods during investigation by certain Security officers. But the outcome was far more serious.

After his arrest Doubek was interrogated nearly every day. From 10 to 17 August he wrote a comprehensive testimony. He testified to the use of illegal methods not only by individuals but by State Security as a whole. Even more serious, however, was his more or less accurate account of events from the search for a Czechoslovak Rajk, via the investigation of Šling, to Slánský's arrest, investigation and conviction, an account which showed that the trials had been one big frame-up. 'Whatever Slánský's degree of guilt, the fact is that his role in the conspiracy was prearranged and the investigation of his case followed a predetermined line.' (ACC CPC, Commission II, Section 56.)

Up to this point the guiding line of 'not tampering with the Slánský trial' had been strictly followed in all cases that came up for review (in other words, the indictment and conviction of Slánský and others were to be regarded as correct). Doubek's lengthy testimony was a grave blow to this policy, for he had completely uncovered the mechanism by which Slánský's 'Anti-State Conspiratorial Centre' had been 'created'.

One might have expected that Doubek's detailed testimony

would have caused a full analysis to be made of how these monstrous frame-ups and distortions of justice came about. The Party leadership, however, made no attempt to do this, and indeed had no intention of doing so.

On the contrary, it gave a new twist to Doubek's testimony about the search for enemies inside the Party, about a fabricated conspiracy and extorted confessions. A new, false theory was born, according to which Slánský was actually the cause of the malpractices, mistakes and distortions. Slánský, it appeared, was not the Czechoslovak Rajk, but the Czechoslovak Beria, and it was Slánský himself who had set into motion the mills of illegality which ultimately 'ground' him. This conclusion was not reached immediately after Doubek's arrest but some time afterwards.

On 21 September the Barák Commission discussed the preliminary report on the Doubek investigation and resolved (a) to arrest Doubek's collaborator, Kohoutek, and (b) to rewrite the report and state more precisely the evidence for penal offences committed by Doubek (and possibly by other persons), and how and by whom the evidence had been obtained. (ACC CPC, Commission II, Section 349.)

The report was rewritten in line with these proposals, but on 26 October the Commission decided that 'a special report on Doubek *will not* be submitted to the Politburo'. (ACC CPC, Commission II, Section 351.) Three weeks later, however, the Commission decided to draft an indictment against Doubek and Kohoutek and to produce a report on the participation of Košťál and Moučka. On 23 and 30 November the Commission discussed the outlines of the indictment and recommended that 'after including the proposed amendments in the indictments, it be referred to the Politburo for approval'. (ACC CPC, Commission II, Section 355.)

The outline of the indictment against Doubek had two main features. In the first place, Doubek was charged as an individual. The entire case for the prosecution rested on the endeavour to lay the blame on him and a few other individual members of the Security Service. There was no reference to his having been part of a whole system that not only made his conduct possible but determined it.

In the second place, all questions concerning the Slánský trial were avoided, although Doubek had clearly testified that the trial was a frame-up and had shown up the methods used in the interrogation of Slánský and the other accused. Around this time, Doubek began to testify again about members of 'the Centre' and 'the Centre itself'. (ACC CPC, Commission II, Section 44.)

In other respects the Barák Commission made no change at this stage in its style of work. The working groups continued to rewrite reports on several cases to comply with the prevalent ideological attitudes and political ideas.

This was the case, for example, in the review of the sentences passed on members of the 'Trotskyist Grand Council'. Each report by the Commission was more strongly worded than the last. The first finding expressed the view that 'the Grand Council was not a Trotskyist or an anti-State illegal organization' and proposed reducing the sentences of all the accused and setting aside the indictment against Holátko and Roušar. (ACC CPC, Commission II, Section 349.) The Commission's final report to the Politburo, however, conveyed a diametrically opposite view. It attested to the Trotskyist character of the 'Grand Council' and proposed that the original verdict should stand. (ACC CPC, Commission II, Section 353.)

On 21 November the Politburo discussed the 'Grand Council' case. Its resolution, moved by Novotný, recorded that the report did not adequately describe the political nature of the 'Grand Council' and said little about its hostile, anti-State and anti-Party activities. The report also mentioned, as active participants in meetings of the 'Grand Council', Dvořák and Kálal, who had not been sentenced, and proposed that Party proceedings should be taken against them and that the 'inquiries should decide whether or not to *recommend their arrest*'. In its resolution the Politburo agreed that they should be subjected to Party disciplinary proceedings for participating in the 'Grand Council'. (File 02/2, Vol. 72, Section 88.)

A similar procedure was adopted in the review of Závodský's case. Here, too, the proposals became progressively more stringent. At its meeting of 2 November the Commission considered a document which read:

The conclusion can be drawn that the investigation of Závodský's case was conducted in an improper manner, that his confession was obtained by illegal methods, that in the investigation some facts were distorted, and that his guilt was therefore not proven. As the sentence has been carried out, no purpose would be served by lodging a complaint of violation of the law. (ACC CPC, Commission II, Section 352.)

Although this conclusion is questionable, the document stated that Závodský was innocent. But the Commission's final document, of 7 December, expressed an entirely different opinion:

It cannot be proved that Závodský consciously supported Šváb in his hostile activity, but from the evidence at its disposal the Commission regards it as proven that Závodský as a deputy and later head of the Security Service introduced and used illegal methods and that he bears full responsibility for these. We therefore recommend that the verdict on Závodský should stand. (ACC CPC, Commission II, Section 356.)

In some cases, however, the facts established about false charges were so incontrovertible that the Commission could not ignore them. The Commission therefore recommended that Josef Pavel, Eduard Goldstücker, Pavel Kavan and Karel Dufek should be acquitted on all counts and fully rehabilitated. This was accepted by the Politburo (ACC CPC, File 02/2, Sections 78 and 88.)

At the end of 1955 the Commission drew up an interim report on its work. It completed the indictment in the case of Doubek and Kohoutek with a recommendation that it should be considered by the Politburo. But by the end of the year this document had not even been put on the Politburo's agenda. When in April 1956 it finally came up for discussion the situation had changed and the decision was made not to submit an indictment until further notice. (ACC CPC, Commission II, Section 97.)

At the end of 1955 the Commission began also to examine the first cases from the Slánský trial – those of Artur London and Evžen Löbl. All this indicates that towards the end of that year important behind-the-scenes discussions were taking place on matters which were to influence procedure in further investigations.

The Party leadership had originally expected to present a report on some case reviews to the Central Committee plenum early in 1956, although the inquiry *had not been completed*. Preparations for the plenary session involved working out not only detailed results of the individual cases under review but also a considered attitude to these trials and to the responsibility for them. Now that the resolve 'not to tamper with the Slánský trial' had been broken, such an attitude was all the more necessary.

Consequently, the preparations for the Central Committee meeting saw the emergence and elaboration of the theory about Slánský's responsibility for all the breaches of the law. As far as it is possible to ascertain from the documents, the first reference to Slánský's responsibility for the trial appeared in the survey made by the Barák Commission at the end of November 1955. According to this survey, the facts discovered by the Commission had given rise to the suspicion that someone had been interested in drawing a red herring across the track of the investigations and that this suspicion was borne out by Doubek's testimony. This 'someone', in the authors' view, was Slánský. It was Slánský who had distorted the Central Committee's correct line about intensified class struggle and the consequent need to unmask the enemies inside the Party. It was Slánský who had fathered the attacks on Party cadres. (ACC CPC, Commission II, Section 396.)

This line was developed further in subsequent preparatory reports. An analogy was drawn between Slánský and Beria, according to which Slánský, like Beria, had attempted to usurp 'the leadership of the Party and the State'; Slánský, in fact, had been not the Czechoslovak Rajk, but the Czechoslovak Beria.

According to this line of argument it was Slánský who, acting out his role by introducing Beria-like methods into the Party, placing his own men in key positions and trampling on the Party's basic principles, had finally been unmasked as an agent of imperialism, whose ultimate aim was the restoration of capitalism in Czechoslovakia.

It remained only to explain away the fact that Slánský, as the chief malefactor, had been arrested and sentenced, and that all the political trials (those relating to the 'Centre' and their successors) had taken place after his arrest. So the idea of two phases emerged: one *up to* Slánský's arrest, and one *after* it. It was claimed that in prison Slánský had continued to act as an *agent provocateur* when he put the investigators onto a false trail, as a result of which a number of innocent people had, allegedly, suffered. The fact that all these trials had been staged after Slánský's arrest was accounted for very simply: the fundamental error in the second phase was that Security had continued to work on the lines set by Slánský and to use the illegal methods he had introduced. All these standpoints were summarized thus:

The present examination of the material has confirmed that Slánský and his accomplices were arrested, tried and sentenced according to their deserts as enemies of the Party, the people and the Republic. This fact is not altered by the new approach to the Yugoslav question and to the Field case. (ACC CPC, Commission II, Section 402, draft of a speech made by Novotný at a Central Committee meeting.)

It is hardly necessary to add that this concept conflicted with the established facts. For instance, Doubek had again testified at length about the methods used in interrogating the members of 'the 'Anti-State Conspiratorial Centre'. Kopřiva had repeated at interviews that the smallest group in the Party leadership, the 'fives', decided about the arrests without evidence, simply on the basis of political distrust, suspicion and unverified denunciations.

The Party leadership had neither the will nor the courage to expose the real events of the 1950s. On the contrary, it sought to gloss over the causes of these events on the dubious pretext of preventing any weakening of the Party's authority and of socialism. The harm caused by this attitude became apparent later.

It was in this light that the trials were explained in the draft of an address to be given at a special session of the Central Committee plenum. The Politburo discussed this draft on

28 December. With a note to the effect that this in no way detracted from Slánský's guilt, the draft was accepted, and a decision taken to consult with the Central Committee of the Soviet Communist Party on certain aspects of the Slánský trial. The Politburo also decided not to discuss this matter at an extraordinary plenary session, as had been originally planned, but to combine it with discussions on other matters. (ACC CPC, File 02/2, Section 94.)

In pursuance of this resolution, the draft was sent to Moscow with a request for a consultation. In the meantime, the Politburo decided on 16 January 1956 to convene a meeting of the Central Committee. The third item on the agenda was to be the Politburo report on the review of some of the trials. On 27 January a reply was received from the Soviet Communist Party:

We have studied the draft for an address on the question of re-examining the matter of the Slánský group, to be delivered at a plenary session of the Central Committee of the Czechoslovak Communist Party. In our opinion, to air this problem at a plenum would serve no useful purpose at the present time. We consider it advisable to discuss the matter with you when your delegation comes here for the Twentieth Congress of the Communist Party of the Soviet Union or at any other time that is convenient for you. (ACC CPC, from Novotný's file.)

The draft of Novotný's speech for the plenum was thus submitted but not discussed at the Politburo meeting of 21 January. It was withdrawn from the agenda, as, on advice from Moscow, was the third item on the agenda of the Central Committee's plenary meeting. So, while the Politburo did not discuss this latest sham explanation of the trials, it nevertheless regarded it as the only plausible one and used it as a basis for reviewing further cases. This was illustrated in the review of the first of the 'Centre' cases: those of London, Löbl and Hajdů. Another piece of hair-splitting was used in the London case. Although it was admitted that the charges against him had been trumped up and that London had been forced to sign a false confession, it was stressed that this in no way absolved the other members of the 'Anti-State Conspiratorial

Centre', particularly Slánský, Geminder and Clementis. (ACC CPC, Commission II, Section 358.) No account was taken of Löbl's new comprehensive testimony of October 1955, where he analysed his conviction and denied any kind of guilt. The Commission discussed this case within a fortnight and submitted a report to the Politburo with a recommendation to let the original verdict stand. The Politburo, equally in a hurry to settle the cases of both London and Löbl, approved the recommendation on 2 and 16 January.

Hajdů's case came up for review before the Twentieth Congress of the Soviet Communist Party but was settled after it. By that time a new situation had arisen as a result of revelations and criticisms of the Stalin personality cult made at the Congress.

END OF THE FIRST REASSESSMENT

The Twentieth Congress of the Soviet Communist Party gave an impetus to further acts of rehabilitation. In the first place, the information about the violations of justice and about the Stalin personality cult, which until then had been known only to the top Party leadership, was within a short time after the Congress made known to the majority of Communists; this made it necessary to pay more attention to public opinion when reviewing the political trials. Khrushchev's secret report made clear the wholesale nature of the persecution and the violation of socialist justice, as well as the responsibility of the political leadership headed by Stalin. This led to the logical conclusion that responsibility could not be laid at the door of a handful of men in Security. Khrushchev urged that serious attention be given to the personality cult. Discussions were supposed to remain a Party affair. This inevitably gave rise to contradictions, because the consequences of the cult had affected the whole of society and the wrongs could not be righted by Communists alone but only through the widest participation of the public, whose response would depend in large measure on the degree to which it was kept informed.

The Twentieth Congress led to a change of outlook on numerous aspects of domestic and international affairs. Many actions and attitudes that had hitherto been equated with vacillation, treason or hostility – contacts with Yugoslavia or with Social Democrats, political, scientific and cultural contacts with the capitalist countries, respect for national features, the upholding of national interests in Czechoslovak–Soviet relations and so on – were now seen in a new light. The evaluation of Zionism remained untouched by the general spirit of the Twentieth Congress, evidently because the attitude of the Arab and socialist countries towards Israel remained unchanged, and because antisemitism had not been eradicated. Speaking at a lunch on 1 May 1956, Khrushchev complained that in Poland the Jews accounted for 3 per cent of the population but occupied 70 per cent of the places in the Party and State apparatus.[1] (File 02/2, Vol. 101, Section 118, Point 15.) This circumstance and the intolerance expressed at the Congress over some ideological questions had a negative effect on the reassessment of the trials. For instance, the non-existent law asserting that growth of capital goods must be given priority was defended by labelling all differing views as anti-Leninist, opportunist and extremely harmful. This attitude hindered the rehabilitation of many Czechoslovak economists. Since, as we know, the Twentieth Congress did not go into the origin of the 'personality cult', the main concern was to overcome the extremes of the old political system while preserving the system itself.

The same approach was adopted in Czechoslovakia. Yet without substantial changes in the political system of socialism it was impossible to rehabilitate the innocent and to establish permanent and effective guarantees against attempts to return to the old policy. The same men as before, still holding the reins of power and evading effective democratic control, were

[1] *At the beginning of the 1950s, it was not only in Czechoslovakia that Soviet activists provoked a wave of antisemitism which the Soviet occupiers have tried to resuscitate since August 1968. Antisemitic measures in Poland also have their roots in the antisemitism of the Soviet leaders. This was expressed in monstrous terms at the Cierna nad Tisou discussions between the Soviet leadership and Czechoslovak representatives, and later in Moscow during that fateful week in August 1968.*

naturally incapable of making a radical break with the old policy and of striving sincerely and unreservedly to right the wrongs that had been done.

From the spring of 1954 at latest certain members of the Politburo had known in some detail about the errors in Stalin's policy; but up to March 1956 they had not even partially informed the Central Committee, to let it draw its own political conclusions. We cannot believe that this silence was the desire of the Soviet representatives, for in 1955 open criticism had been levelled at Stalin not only at Central Committee meetings but also at assemblies of Party officials. The procedure of the Czechoslovak Politburo after the Twentieth Congress was based on consultations held in Moscow on 27 February 1956; while adhering to the decisions of this meeting, the Party leadership was satisfied with no more than a formal application of the conclusions of the Twentieth Congress to Czechoslovak conditions. Although, for a time, the Central Committee plenum played a greater part and its members were able to exert a bigger influence on Party policy, the Politburo soon regained its monopoly of power, and within this system more and more power came to be wielded by Novotný in person. This situation was reached by a number of stages.

In the first place, for the sake of maintaining the old political set-up, non-members of the Party were deprived of any say in policy-making or in controlling the conduct of affairs. This came about when, after the Twentieth Congress, the discussions on political issues were kept within the Party and all suggestions for reforming the system through informal public control over the Government were denounced as attempts to restore bourgeois democracy.

The next step was to exclude the rank and file of the Party from any share in making and controlling Party policy. While in April 1956 there had been discussions at all levels, this was an exception without parallel in the 1950s. For a time the rank and file had been able to express its views about the Party line and about any member of the Politburo. But the discussion was brought to a premature conclusion under the pretext that it constituted a threat to the Party and to socialism. The principle was proclaimed that members of the Central

Committee and the regional committees were not accountable to the membership but only to the body to which they belonged; demands for fuller information were therefore refused. (Köhler at the Ostrava Regional Committee on 28 April.)

In the next stage the Politburo again completely dominated the Central Committee plenum and manipulated it to suit its own requirements. In March and April some members of the Central Committee tried to enforce control of the Politburo by the Central Committee plenum and suggested changing the composition of the Politburo to include not only the highest State and Party officials but people from the regions and from industry. These suggestions were rejected out of hand. No new members were appointed to the Politburo even after Čepička's dismissal and the death of Zápotocký; it became a tightly closed group. It disregarded the Central Committee's fundamental rights. The Central Committee alone had the right to approve proposals for new Ministers; yet in April 1956, for example, Novotný allowed the nomination of a new Minister of National Defence to be endorsed solely by members of the Politburo. Only two months later, when members of the Central Committee began to discuss this decision, was a vote taken on the appointment of the new Minister. The renewal of the Politburo's position of power, and the reduction, once again, of the other Party institutions and organizations into the role of mere levers to be used by the Politburo, enabled this body to call a complete halt to the process of political revival, including rehabilitation. Only minor reforms in the management of the economy were permitted. This renewal of the monopoly power of the Politburo was accompanied by a new increase in the authority of the Party Central Office. Novotný submitted a proposal along these lines to the Politburo on 9 July.

Despite its weaknesses, the Twentieth Congress of the Soviet Party had undoubtedly offered an opportunity for an entirely new approach to the reassessment of the trials. Yet neither the Politburo nor the Barák Commission responded to this opportunity. True, in the spring of 1956, with the rank and file voicing its criticism of the distortion of socialism, and with large-scale personnel, organizational and other changes in prospect, some of the innocent were actually rehabilitated with considerable speed. Even in these circumstances, however, the review of trials inflicted renewed injustices. And, as soon as the muzzling of political expression in the Party and among the general public had reached the stage when really the only freedom was to agree with the Party's policy, then rehabilitation ceased.

After the Twentieth Congress Novotný made two important speeches, in which he defined the principles underlying the approach to the trials. These were speeches made at a meeting of the political staff of the Central Committee Secretariat and at a plenary session of the Central Committee in March. On each occasion he repeated the central theme of the report on the review of political trials discussed by the Politburo on 28 December 1955.

In a speech delivered on 29 March Novotný, as an attempted explanation of why there had been violations of justice in Czechoslovakia, repeated the assertion that it was Slánský in the first place who had introduced in Czechoslovakia methods similar to those employed by Beria in the Soviet Union. He also announced that following reviews of their trials London, Goldstücker, Kavan, Dufek and Pavel had been released once their innocence had been established, and that in a number of cases disproportionately heavy sentences had been reduced. He pointed particularly to the case of Marie Švermová. Švermová, he claimed, had been guilty of supporting Šling's hostile personnel policy by concealing her knowledge of his designs and by hiding secret documents for him. Novotný therefore regarded the revised sentence of ten years passed on Švermová as proportionate. He announced, too, that Josef Smrkovský's sentence had been reduced to three years; he was, it seemed, guilty of negligence which had enabled class enemies to damage the State Farms in his charge. In his enumeration of the incorrect policies at the time of the trials Novotný included the attitude to the Spanish War veterans, antisemitism and the fabricated charges against Yugoslavia. He stated that the sentences of a whole group of convicted persons had been confirmed but did not specify the number involved.

The new interpretation of the guilt of Slánský, Švermová, Smrkovský and others was thus disseminated throughout the

Party. Novotný's speech set the tone by blaming violations of the law on the activities of Security officers, especially Slánský, and drawing a veil over the real responsibility of the top Party leadership. The speech gave the impression that wrongs were being righted and that it was now just a matter of proceeding with the review of the trials on the same lines. This helped to perpetuate the method of assessing cases behind closed doors.

After the Twentieth Congress of the Soviet Communist Party, Commission 'A', set up in January 1955, continued its work on the trials, and a new Commission 'C' was appointed, also under Barák's leadership. The latter Commission derived from a motion submitted by Novotný to the Politburo on 5 May. The meeting resolved:

1. That a Commission of the Central Committee be set up to review the Slánský trial, the members being: Barák (chairman), Hruška, Innemann, Bakula and Mlejnek; and that the Commission be instructed to begin work immediately in order to complete the review and submit a report to the Politburo by 20 May 1956.

2. That certain members of the Political Secretariat should 'express an opinion on that period and on the circumstances surrounding the investigation of Slánský'.

Notes on the discussion show that Novotný suggested that Zápotocký, Čepička and Široký should express their opinions. (File 02/2, Vol. 92, Section 110, Point 31.) None of these men nor any others who had been members of the Politburo at the time of the trials availed themselves of this opportunity.

It appears that the obvious impossibility of justifying the charges preferred at this, the major trial, ruled out, after the Soviet Twentieth Congress, any attempt to defend the overall correctness of the verdicts unless a reassessment 'confirmed' them in some way. That is why Novotný declared in one breath, at the conclusion of the Central Committee on 20 April, that the Politburo had appointed a new Commission to review the Slánský trial and that 'we have no doubt about Slánský's guilt'. (ACC CPC, File 01, Section 50, p. 112, minutes of CC meetings, 19 and 20 April 1956.) The review of the Slánský trial was obviously one aspect of the change of needs resulting from a change of policy. Many things which for reasons of policy had been necessary in 1952 – for example, the charges against Yugoslavia and against Konni Zilliacus – had become obstacles by 1956.

In the report by Commission 'C' discussed by the Politburo on 6 June, Barák explained the necessity for a review of the Slánský trial:

Facts have come to light proving that Slánský implemented a number of illegal measures and that innocent persons were arrested on his initiative. This was also the reason why it was necessary to inquire into the whole Slánský affair. . . . The indictment against Slánský and his accomplices, the whole trial, its course and justification cannot remain in their original form. It would be historically incorrect. . . . The whole trial was considerably exaggerated and complicated by political problems arising from the international situation at that time and in particular our conflict with Yugoslavia. (File 02/2, Vol. 105, Section 122, Point 2.)

Two-member groups were appointed to draft reports on individuals sentenced in the Slánský trial. One of the two was always a member of the political Commission headed by Barák. They were kept busy by their various duties, with the result that some of them were unable to devote sufficient time to studying the documents. Barák was in a better position, since he could rely on his staff at the Ministry of the Interior, whose assistance he used to confirm the original verdicts. Hruška substituted his own recollections for a proper study of the documents; in some cases his recollections were used as evidence against the accused, in place of these missing documents. Of the five men picked to work with the Barák Commission, one was from the Central Committee apparatus, the others from the investigatory sections of the Ministry of the Interior and the Military Prosecutor's Office. The main burden of drafting the reports fell on these men. Where they failed to comply with the demands made by the members of the main Commission and tried to adhere to the verified facts, the final drafts of the reports were drawn up by the Commission itself.

In considering the reports from its working groups on individual cases Commission 'C' invariably decided to underline the gravity of the original charges. Not a single resolution adopted by the Commission recommended deleting unsubstantiated charges, and the documents prove that Barák and Hruška were particularly zealous in piling on the accusations.

At the Commission's sixth meeting held on 25 April, a resolution was passed in connection with Slánský: 'The whole affair must be viewed as a matter of penal offences committed by individuals. No such thing as a Centre ever existed.' (Commission II, Section 377.) On 6 June the Politburo discussed the preliminary report of the Commission and recommended the inclusion of an extract from it in Novotný's speech to the coming Party Conference. This report reiterated that there had been no conspiracy and no Centre, but that Slánský and his accomplices bore some measure of guilt, and that none of them could be fully rehabilitated. The point was merely to make a just assessment of their sentences. 'It is already clear that we shall not carry out any rehabilitation in the case of Slánský and others.' (Ibid.) This categorical statement was made after two months' work, when the review was still in its initial stage, and was repeated in substance in Novotný's address to the Party Conference in June. Again, as in 1951, Slánský and the other Communists were publicly judged in advance, and, just as at that time State Security had confirmed the correctness of the statements made by the top Party functionaries, so now the Barák Commission fabricated revised versions of their guilt.

We will cite a few cases to illustrate the Commission's procedure.

In the case of Josef Frank, the view that he had not deserved the death sentence was expressed by Mlejnek at a meeting on 25 April. Yet at its next session, on 14 May, when considering a draft report on Frank, the Commission referred the document back with the comment that 'the report must be precisely formulated, particularly so that his genuine guilt and its evaluation should stand out'. (Ibid.) On 21 May the Commission again rejected the draft and insisted on a re-examination of matters that might help to retain some charges against Frank. On 6 March 1957 the report was returned for the third time, because its findings – that the death sentence passed on Frank had been illegal and that as a Party official he should have been charged only with political responsibility – were evidently unacceptable to the Commission. The resolution adopted at this session criticized the report for its non-legal approach and demanded that articles of the law be quoted (Commission II, Section 379, twentieth session) – i.e. that political responsibility be converted into criminal responsibility. On 29 May 1957 the Commission finally approved the report on Frank in these words:

The report will emphasize his responsibility for the sector entrusted to him and will stress that, although he must have known a number of things about Slánský's activity, he failed to inform the competent comrades. (Ibid., twenty-second session.)

This was the version accepted by the Politburo on 23 September. While the death sentence was regarded as unjustified, Frank was still held responsible for sabotage in the economic sector, for economic damage which had been 'caused by the activity of hostile Zionist functionaries' and for mistakes in personnel policy. (Commission II, Section 383.)

On 9 April 1957 the Commission discussed Geminder's case for the fourth time. The draft report from the working group contained the following findings:

Not a single point in the indictment against Geminder has been satisfactorily proved; some of the charges – for example, espionage contacts with Zilliacus, forming a Trotskyist group in the Ministry of Foreign Affairs, a number of cases concerning personnel at the Ministry – were unequivocally refuted. [He had made mistakes, but] there is no proof that he acted with intention or that he was a deliberate enemy.

In this instance also the Commission referred the report back for amendment and adopted the following resolution:

Contacts with Zilliacus, Zionists and Trotskyists (dating from pre-war days) need to be elucidated. According to Hruška, Geminder maintained contacts with Neurath, that is to say also with Zinoviev, as early as 1925–8. . . . Slánský was aware of his shortcomings, and because of this Geminder became his willing tool. (Commission II, Section 379, twenty-first session.)

Finally, on 23 August, the report on Geminder was accepted. It claimed that the lapse of time had made it impossible to examine the question of motivation, but that it was clear that Geminder had made many mistakes. He had created an atmosphere of fear at Party Central Office; he had blindly obeyed Slánský's instructions; he had enabled members of the Jewish bourgeoisie to emigrate to Israel, and so on. The report claimed that he had been partly to blame for his own sentence and that he had been responsible for convicting others, having willingly testified at interrogations. (Ibid., twenty-third session.)

On 23 September the Politburo accepted the Commission's recommendations on Geminder. His correspondence with Zilliacus was also defined as a penal offence, because, it was alleged, he had in the process betrayed State secrets. Nevertheless, the report approved by the Politburo said that this could not be proved as the letters were sealed.

The case of Reicin was first discussed by the Commission at its eleventh session on 28 May 1956. Information was provided on a report made by military assessors. All the monstrous fabrications about sabotage and military espionage remained in the document before the Commission, but Reicin's guilt on these counts was viewed less strictly and part of the blame was transferred to the former Minister of National Defence, General Ludvík Svoboda, and his deputies. According to item (b),

the main offenders in sabotaging the Czechoslovak Army were General Svoboda, then Minister of National Defence, General Boček (Chief of Staff), Generals Drgač, Procházka, Vicherek and Paleček and other officers from different commands. There is no justification for the charge of sabotage against Reicin because he had no influence on that sector of the Czechoslovak Army.

In another passage, the report reads:

The charge of espionage must be seen in the light of a finding by a Ministry of National Defence Commission which clearly states that it was carried out with the knowledge of, or on direct instructions from, the former Minister of National Defence, General Svoboda, the Chief of Staff General Boček, and General Drgač.

In its resolution on the proposals for action on the Reicin case the Commission recommended adding to the draft Reicin's responsibility for the Fifth Department, and clarifying his relations with Píka, the case of the Štěchovice archives[1] and contacts with the Gestapo. A report on the statement by the military assessors will be included in a special report on Reicin. (Commission I, Section 378, eleventh session.)

The sole comment needed here is that Hruška, a member of the Barák Commission, had been one of the military assessors in 1952.

This report on Reicin was approved by the Commission on 30 August 1957, and by the Politburo on 23 September. A new statement by military assessors made in 1957 at the request of Commission 'A', however, refuted all the charges in the 1952 report, except for an accusation concerning shortcomings in personnel. In allowing the sentence on Reicin to stand it was therefore argued that he had probably betrayed secrets to the Gestapo; this 'cannot be proved beyond doubt, but there are grounds for serious suspicion'. He was made responsible for the looting of the Štěchovice archives by the Americans, for using illegal methods in military intelligence and for errors in Party work in the Army. It was also alleged that he had concealed the existence of documents, which he had received in 1939, relating to Šling's espionage contacts. The report admitted that these documents had not been located but that Hruška had vouched for their content. On these grounds the Politburo decided to let the sentence stand. (Commission II, Section 383.)

The review of Frejka's case proceeded comparatively smoothly. The Commission discussed the first version of the report on 22 November 1956 and resolved that 'the review should be based mainly on the assessors' reports, which concern all the other economists as well'. (Commission II, Section 378, eighteenth session.) These instructions were observed. The economic assessors refused to amend their 1952 report, and new reports made in 1956 were therefore rejected. The Commission accepted the recommendation on Frejka on 23 August 1957. While acquitting him of high treason and espionage the report claimed that he had caused damage tantamount to sabotage.

---

[1] *Nazi archives containing lists of Czechoslovak collaborators. After the war they were removed by the Americans; some were later returned.*

The Politburo endorsed this recommendation on 23 September and decided not to change the verdict.

The findings of the review of Šváb's case came before the Commission on 30 August. The report found that Šváb had not been guilty of high treason but had been responsible for 'hostile and damaging methods', which could be defined as sabotage, and consequently that there was no reason to amend the verdict. Barák spoke very critically:

The weakness of this report lies in the fact that the greater part of it – over twenty pages – is devoted to explaining that high treason was not proven. It would have been more fitting to dwell on the positive proofs of Šváb's sabotage in Security so that the conclusion would have been a logical culmination of the report.

A resolution was adopted on the lines proposed by Barák:

The material must be redrafted and shortened, especially the passages where the original indictment is not confirmed, and the part dealing with hostile methods in Security and the Party apparatus should be expanded, because the original investigation was not pursued in this direction. (Commission II, Section 379, twenty-fourth session.)

The report was amended by the mechanical deletion of the sentences which stated that the charges against Šváb had not been confirmed.

The first draft report on Šling was submitted on 21 May 1956. His espionage contact with Voska in 1939 was taken as proven. The report claimed that Šling had left England as an agent of the bourgeoisie acting on direct instructions from Dr Beneš. It stated, however, that no proof had been found of his espionage through the Trust Fund[1] or that he had continued espionage after 1945. Charges that he had introduced anti-Party methods in Brno and had supported former capitalists were sustained. The Commission rejected the draft and suggested that

the report should be rewritten and espionage contacts with Voska should be re-examined. The Trust Fund is put in an incorrect light. It must be stated that it was Šling who began to accuse a number of people. (Commission II, Section 377, ninth session.)

[1] *A fund to aid Czechoslovak refugees in Britain during the war.*

The new version, discussed on 4 June 1956, asserted that there were grounds for suspecting that Šling, in addition to his subversive activity, had conducted espionage, but this could not be proved. Apart from the famous letter of 17 April 1939, Šling's cooperation with Voska had not been confirmed. This fact increased the doubts about Šling's espionage during World War II. The report also said that no evidence had been found for the claim that Šling had cooperated with Slánský on a platform inimical to the Party or the State. The report was rejected by the Commission, and Hruška was instructed to rewrite it himself, particularly the references to espionage contacts with Voska and through the Trust Fund. (Commission II, Section 378, thirteenth session.) The final version, accepted by the Politburo on 23 September, stated that, 'although there are now no direct proofs, it can be assumed that Šling continued working for the British Intelligence Service in Czechoslovakia after 1945'. The charges against Šling of anti-Party activity in Brno and finding jobs for capitalist sympathizers remained. The original verdict was unchanged.

The report on Slánský was discussed at the last session of the Commission, on 5 September 1957, as a result of a decision, made on 22 November 1956, that the Slánský case could not be closed without establishing the guilt of those accused with him. The report made a critical analysis of the methods used in the investigation, which had not aimed at ascertaining the objective truth. It granted the probability that Slánský had aspired to the highest post in the land – that of President of the Republic. The draft report stated:

Slánský was found guilty by the State court of the crimes of high treason, espionage, sabotage and military treason. The inquiry has found no evidence that any of these crimes was committed – including the principal charge in the indictment, treasonable conspiracy in the Anti-State Conspiratorial Centre. On the other hand, it has been ascertained that Slánský caused grave damage to the Party and that he must be held responsible for personnel policy and for the activities of Šváb and Frejka.

The assertions about damage caused by Slánský were made in general terms. The most serious charge was 'that he caused harmful methods to penetrate into Party work'.

The Commission expressed strong dissatisfaction with this report and resolved

that the report be redrafted in line with comments made during the session. . . . The verdict should be dealt with briefly, the points that have been confirmed should be enlarged upon, including his responsibility in performing his office as Secretary-General of the Party and, in particular, the new findings concerning his criminal offences. The purely legal approach of the report deserves criticism. The Commission finds that if this approach is adopted various charges have to be dropped, and that the aim should therefore be to supply a résumé of the section on Slánský's personality contained in Part II of the Commission's report. Comrades Barák and Innemann will prepare a résumé for the next session of the Commission. The verdict is to stand. (Commission, Vol. 14, Section 380.)

The amended report, accepted by the Politburo on 23 September, found Slánský guilty of

(a) finding positions for elements alien to the Party;

(b) responsibility for the treason committed by some persons appointed by the Cadre Commission of the Ministry of Foreign Affairs;

(c) political responsibility for shortcomings in arrangements for Jewish emigration;

(d) (probably, although espionage contacts with Zilliacus were not proven) disclosing confidential information;

(e) responsibility, with Švermová, for Šling's subversive activities;

(f) violating socialist legality, for which he had not been sentenced;

(g) responsibility, with Reicin, for shortcomings in purging the High Command of the Army;

(h) responsibility for harmful methods in Party work.

In short, the new construction put on Slánský's case by the reassessment presented the former Secretary-General once more as the source of all the evil in past Party activity and the absolute personification of wickedness.

Although, from the outset, the Commission had maintained that it was concerned solely with the crimes of individuals and that no Centre had existed, the report on the trial accepted by the Politburo on 23 September accused the men convicted in the Slánský trial of placing each other in top positions, and of supporting each other while also serving Slánský's aims. Slánský had inaugurated and directed the security 'fives', and had interfered in Army affairs through Reicin, in the economic sphere through Frejka, in international affairs through Geminder. (Commission II, Section 383.) Thus, even after the 'Centre' idea had been abandoned, the group tried with Slánský was viewed as an anti-Party, factional and criminal group. (Commission II, Vol. 14, Section 380.)

Thus Commission 'C' fulfilled its intention of not carrying out any rehabilitation. All the death sentences, with the exception of Frank's, were confirmed as warranted. But no steps were taken to rehabilitate even Frank in the eyes of the law and the Party.

In the procedure adopted by Commission 'A' and other institutions concerned with the later assessments of trials one can discern the influence of the political changes occurring in the country. While the influence of the Twentieth Congress was not reflected in the methods of the Barák Commissions, the political developments at the Congress had brought to the fore the question of responsibility for the unlawful and despotic methods; and – a new feature – the question was frequently and sharply posed at the lower levels in the Party. The Commission, however, continued to evade the issue of the responsibility of the top Party and State leadership. This was the approach, for instance, in the case of Doubek and Kohoutek. Officials of the Prosecutor's office stated in a draft report issued in March 1956:

We should point out that, as instructed by the Deputy Prosecutor-General, Dr Švach, our investigations in the cases concerned have not gone beyond the criminal activity of Doubek and Kohoutek; criminal offences by other persons could not, therefore, be fully demonstrated by the investigations conducted so far. (Commission II, Vol. 13, Section 363.)

Under the influence of mounting criticism from below, the Politburo decided, on considering the Barák Commission's report, to call to account Major Zdražil and General Kokeš of the military judiciary. On 26 March Košťál, Prchal and Moučka were dismissed. Barák and Novotný were to find them suitable positions, to make further inquiries into the conduct of employees of the Ministry of the Interior and then to submit a report to the Politburo. (Commission II, Vol. 7, Section 126.) However, no such report ever appeared and, except in the case of Doubek and Kohoutek, no criminal proceedings were instituted.

The final report on the Doubek-Kohoutek investigation was referred to the Politburo on 23 April. After that date, at least, no member of the Politburo could plead ignorance of how the Slánský trial was fabricated or of the unlawful methods used against the accused in the subsequent trials also. Every subsequent decision by the Politburo concerning the trials must be judged from the viewpoint that its members knew the truth about the conduct of these trials in Czechoslovakia. But even in the case of Doubek and Kohoutek the Politburo decided 'not to submit an indictment until further notice'. (File 02/2, Vol. 95, Section 114, Point 2.) Contrary to the law, their detention was extended without their cases being brought to court. The motives for this could only have been political – probably fear of holding a trial of this nature in the spring of 1956. In February 1957 a dispute arose in the Commission about further procedure. The following are extracts from the minutes:

Comrade Barák claimed that custody was illegal and that no court could sentence Doubek and Kohoutek. Comrades Švach, Litera and Innemann insisted, on the contrary, that the Court would probably impose the heaviest possible sentence because its duty would be clear. . . . [Barák reiterated:] To bring Doubek and Kohoutek to trial would be tantamount to clearing Slánský, Taussigová and Šváb. The two investigators were simply obeying orders; consequently no court can sentence them. . . . The beginning of the unlawful methods, for which Doubek and Kohoutek are accused, dates from that time [1949]. The responsibility rests with Slánský, Šváb, Taussigová, Závodský, Kopřiva, Köhler, Gottwald and others of the Party apparatus, who intervened in the investigations. (Commission II, Vol. 13, Section 373.)

This dispute obviously reflects the conflicting interests of Security and the Party apparatus. Barák was evidently concerned that neither the Security officers nor Köhler and other leading Party representatives should be held responsible. The conflict ended in a compromise.

On 9 April 1957 the Politburo consented to Doubek and Kohoutek being committed for trial. The report before this meeting named sixty-four Security officers, of whom it had been proved or might be assumed that they had used unlawful methods of investigation. The Politburo, however, regarded it as adequate punishment to dismiss them from office or to take disciplinary measures. On Barák's insistence, however, these two points were deleted from the resolution. (File 02/2, Vol. 135, Section 176, Point 16.) At this session, Barák was delegated to inquire into the awards conferred for services rendered during the trials. (At Novotný's request, this was not included in the minutes – ibid.) Prchal, Košťál and other Security officers were allowed to retain their medals; this was intended as an expression of their partial rehabilitation. (Commission II, Vol. 37, Section 558.)

On 11 June 1957 the Politburo considered a report on the trial of Doubek and Kohoutek; it noted information given by the Prosecutor-General, Jan Bartuška, that they would come under the amnesty and that Doubek would have served half his sentence by 12 July 1958, and Kohoutek by 26 January 1958. (File 02/2, Vol. 142, Section 185, Point 29.) A few months after their trial the two men were released.

All the officers of State Security imprisoned in the early 1950s, with the exception of Josef Pavel, were held responsible for violations of socialist legality. The report submitted to the Politburo by the Barák Commission on 11 September 1956 stated that 'the original investigation of criminal offences committed by these persons did not consider responsibility for inadmissible methods in security work'. (File 02/2, Vol. 115, Section 138, Point 5.) It has been proved that some of those convicted were, in fact, guilty of using such methods. Now, however, it was politically expedient to call them to account so that it could, if necessary, be argued that those responsible for the unlawful methods had been punished; at the same time it could be shown that they had not served prison sentences without justification. But they were treated leniently. Party membership was restored – a quite exceptional step – to Smoček, who was fully rehabilitated, and to Pokorný (even though he had received a new sentence of six months). In the case of Plaček, held responsible for issuing the order to murder P. Konečný, the verdict was confirmed, but a resolution was passed that the Secretariat should, at a convenient moment, instruct the Prosecutor-General to grant him a conditional release. (File 02/2, Vol. 115, Section 138.)

Plaček was released on 16 April 1957. This was used as an argument for applying the same tactics in the case of Pich-Tůma who had committed the murder. A report on Vaš, a former officer of Reicin's Fifth Department of the Army High Command, said that he had given orders for the murder of de Backer during a rigged escape. On the Politburo's recommendation Vaš was acquitted of the original charges and released on 21 September 1956. (File 02/2, Vol. 103, Section 120, Point 14.) On the other hand, the verdict on the former head of the Fifth Department, Mírovský, was confirmed, not because he had broken the law (the report claimed, for instance, that his provocation of Generals Kemr and Kolařík could not be regarded as a criminal offence), but because there were suspicions about his activities during the German occupation. (File 02/2, Vol. 107, Section 125, Point 23.)

In short, the men who had trampled on the law, and killed or removed from their posts numbers of highly qualified people devoted to the Party, were judged very leniently in all cases where the actions could be attributed to over-zealous conduct of the class struggle and extreme political vigilance. Such exaggerated behaviour was usually seen in the Party as adherence to Communist principles. On the other hand, the worst sin for a Party member and the height of 'opportunism' was to 'underestimate the enemy' and display a lack of vigilance. Consequently, the victims of despotism and unlawfulness were always suspect, even after rehabilitation, as can be seen from numerous resolutions passed by the Politburo and from speeches by Novotný.

A renewed campaign for greater political vigilance in the unmasking of enemies within the Party and in society generally, publicly proclaimed after the events in Poznan[1] (editorial in *Rude Pravo* of 2 July 1956), had a most adverse effect on the reviewing of trials. At a meeting of regional secretaries of the Party held on 30 and 31 August 1956, Vasil Bilak attacked the policy of reviewing all the trials, and Pavol Tonhauser criticized the courts for their leniency. This turn in the situation was strongly reflected in the Barák Commission.

Whereas, in the spring of 1956, the cases of some generals had been speedily settled (Klapálek, Svoboda and Hromádko had been legally rehabilitated), decisions concerning the remaining generals hung fire for a further two years. General Novák, whose rehabilitation had not come through, was granted a remittance of the remainder of his sentence by a presidential pardon on 17 September 1956. The Barák Commission stalled in the cases of Generals Drgač, Drnec and Bulander, despite the fact that the military assessors' report of 1952 (Hruška, Kratochvíl and Thoř) had been invalidated by a subsequent report of August 1957. Later, on 15 April 1958, after the Barák Commission had been dissolved, the Politburo criticized the Prosecutor-General's Office (which was subordinated to the decision of the Politburo) for dilatoriness in this matter and decreed that the generals be granted a conditional release. (File 02/2, Section 235, Point 9.) This dilatoriness which the Politburo suddenly noticed in 1958 derived from resolutions of its own making. On 19 November 1956, at the suggestion of Barák and Bartuška, it had discussed a document stating that during the preceding six days forty men sentenced for counter-revolutionary activity had been conditionally released, and concluding:

Undoubtedly this state of affairs is undesirable in the present situation; temporary measures must therefore be taken to ensure that persons serving sentences for counter-revolutionary activity are not granted a conditional release and that in these cases there should be no remission of sentences.

The report by Barák and Bartuška further stated that in future remission of sentence would be granted solely on the decision of the Prosecutor-General:

[1] *A town in Poland where in June 1956 workers revolted against oppressive labour conditions; the uprising was put down by the Army.*

Under the present internal regulations this applies to persons sentenced at trials with organized attendance by the public, in cases where the Supreme Court was the court of first instance, and in all cases where the accused were clergymen.

The same applied to the military section of the Prosecutor's Office in decisions concerning persons sentenced to more than ten years. To ensure that people convicted of counter-revolutionary offences should not, for the present, be released, the Prosecutor-General made the following provision:

The Prosecutor-General reserves the exclusive right to pronounce a decision in all cases of persons sentenced for counter-revolutionary activity.... Internal instructions have been issued by the Prosecutor-General (mainly the Military Prosecutor) that for the time being no recommendations for conditional release or remission of sentence will be approved in cases of persons convicted for the above criminal offences.

The Politburo took note of this decision without discussing it. (File 02/2, Vol. 122, Section 144, Point 13.)

The militant campaign against 'liberalism', which in the ideological and political fields reached its height at the Communist Party conference in 1956, was now increasingly impinging on the reviews of trials. Over-simplification of the class approach caused grave damage throughout the community. While the revelations of despotism made at the Soviet Twentieth Congress no longer allowed the repetition of the trials in their original form and number, the same political aims were pursued in changes of personnel, in the mass screening of senior officials for their class background and political reliability, and in the isolation of those who were a thorn in the flesh of officialdom.

Liberalism in the sphere of the judiciary was criticized by Jiří Hendrych and other members of the Central Committee at a session in June 1957, and by Novotný at a meeting of Party district secretaries on 27 June. Submitting a progress report about the judiciary to the Politburo on 20 June, the Minister of Justice, Škoda, reduced the purport of the Party Conference resolution about reinforcing socialist legality to a matter of fighting liberalism. He described the situation as follows:

Tendencies towards leniency have also been detected in the prosecution of counter-revolutionary offences. This liberalism is particularly dangerous because after the Party conference the courts were flooded with applications for retrials (1,717) and an even larger number (about 14,000) was submitted to other institutions.

Consequently all courts had received two circulars from the Ministry explaining 'the correct class interpretation of the new laws'.

Communists working in Security, the judiciary and the Prosecutors' offices attended joint meetings in all regions to discuss the common fight against liberalism. Contrary to the conference resolution requiring that Security, the Prosecutors' offices and the courts should keep a check on each other, Škoda urged 'the closest cooperation and a merciless approach to enemies of our regime'. Bartuška announced that such mutual control would be correct 'only if all parties see penal policy in the same light'. (File 02/2, Vol. 143, Section 189, Point 7.)

In a report on the Supreme Court, Minister Škoda criticized the judges for their exaggerated mistrust of the findings in both the earlier and the current investigations carried out by Security, and for relying in controversial cases solely on evidence given in court. This, said Škoda, was particularly dangerous where counter-revolutionary criminal offences were concerned. (Ibid.) These reports and speeches by Škoda and Bartuška can only be interpreted as a call to persist in the infamous judicial methods of the early 1950s. Their attitude had the full support of the Politburo.

After the events in Poznan and Hungary, the fusing of Party and Security methods advanced once more. Party conclusions were made on the basis of information provided by Security and Military Intelligence. Party members who had become unpopular with leading officials because of their forthright criticism of faults and errors were shadowed, although there was no evidence that they had infringed the law. All the members of the Politburo were aware of this. On 5 April 1957, apropos a report on the situation among Slovak intellectuals, Karol Bacílek mentioned that information on the 'factional activity' of Pavlík and other writers had been

provided by Security. Pavlík was expelled from the Party
without any justification and several writers were disciplined.
(File 02/2, Vol. 135, Section 176, Point 19).

Security maintained its superior position vis-à-vis the courts
and the Prosecutor's Office, and these institutions were powerless to control the operation of the Security officers. In April
1956 the Central Committee was not properly informed about
the background to the trials; nevertheless, the discussion
touched on the mechanism that had made the trials possible.
The Central Committee established, quite rightly, that one of
the main factors was the unlawful conduct of investigations,
especially the linking of the operational and investigatory
branches of Security. It therefore resolved to 'institute examining
magistrates in order to improve the quality of investigation
and guarantee the reliability of evidence'. (ACC CPC, File 01,
Section 50.) By 18 May the Politburo was already considering
recommendations from the Ministry of Justice and the Prosecutor-General's Office for amending the regulations governing
penal proceedings; the institution of independent examining
magistrates occupied a key place in this proposal. Barák
submitted his own version, representing the standpoint of the
Ministry of the Interior, which acknowledged that examining
magistrates were indispensable, but added the rider that their
jurisdiction in investigating anti-State offences should be kept
to an absolute minimum. This, he claimed, was justified by the
necessity for 'secret detention and secret investigations' in such
cases. This was tantamount to a call for connivance at breaches
of the law. The Politburo made no definite statement on the
matter. The Party conference in June supported 'the appointment of examining magistrates under the jurisdiction of the
Prosecutor's Office'. (ACC CPC, File 02/2, Section 95.)

In October 1956 the Politburo interpreted the conference
resolution in its own way: it instituted, under the jurisdiction
of the Prosecutor, investigators to supervise the investigation
of criminal offences against the State but decided not to
appoint special investigators for other offences. The position
of Security remained unaffected, since the Prosecutor's
investigators did not conduct the investigation of offences
against the State. In short, the Central Committee resolution

of April and the conference resolution of June were not properly implemented. (ACC CPC, File 02/2, Vol. 103, Section 119, Point 5; File 02/2, Vol. 104, Section 121, Point 6; File 02/2, Vol. 121, Section 154, Point 7.)

The Ministry of the Interior, with its blend of Party and Security methods, occupied a special position in the political system. Barák and Novotný were the two men most fully informed about the internal situation. After the dismissal of Čepička, Novotný intervened in Army affairs to a greater degree than previously. He did so through the Party apparatus and through a Military Defence Commission, set up on 2 April 1957, of which he was chairman. He influenced Security mainly through Barák, with whom he worked in close co-operation. Not even in the Politburo did Novotný bother to discuss reports on the conduct of Security work and the build-up of the Security apparatus.

Ruthless action against those who demanded genuine rehabilitation for the innocent grew in direct ratio to the increasing power of Novotný and Barák, the Party apparatus and the Ministry of the Interior (although there were other causes, too). This action was taken with the connivance of the Politburo, the Central Committee and the regional and district Party secretaries, who never raised any objections at national assemblies, although they, too, received appeals for help from people who had been unjustly sentenced.

The Barák Commission was particularly severe in its treatment of 'bourgeois nationalists', 'Trotskyists' and 'economists'. Of these groups only a few individuals were released in 1956–7, most of them through a presidential pardon. With one exception, no prisoner was granted a conditional release after serving half his sentence. In the later 1950s no member of these groups was rehabilitated. They spent the longest terms in prison and the majority of them were only released after serving their sentences or under the amnesty of May 1960.

Of the group of eleven economists sentenced in 1954, Dr Outrata was the first whose case came up for review. In view of his serious heart condition his sentence was interrupted for six months from March 1955. At the end of the six months, the Prosecutor-General, Aleš, although in possession of a doctor's certificate drawing attention to the possibility of [Outrata's] sudden death, submitted the following proposal to the Politburo:

Further interruption of the sentence is not expected to influence the course of the illness. The Prosecutor-General therefore proposes to summon Outrata to serve the rest of his sentence and will not extend the interruption of sentence for health reasons. (File 02/2, Vol. 70, Section 86.)

The Politburo turned down this suggestion: Outrata remained at liberty, though under the constant threat of having to return to prison. On 4 January 1956 the Barák Commission, after considering a report on his trial, endorsed the verdict. The main argument for the claim that Outrata had deliberately damaged the interests of the Republic was his class origin: 'Outrata's whole past . . . is such that it gives no grounds for accepting his defence, which is not substantiated by conclusive evidence.' (Commission II, Vol. 13, Section 360.) Three days later the Politburo decided to let the sentence stand but to remit the remainder via a presidential pardon.

Decisions relating to the other leading economists were taken after the Party Conference, by which time the political atmosphere was growing increasingly unconducive to just settlements. On 11 July the Commission discussed the working group's recommendation in the cases of Goldmann and Jičínský. The group rejected charges that the two had deliberately damaged the national interest, and turned down the assessors' reports used against them at the trial, stating:

On the basis of investigations during which thirty-six witnesses were heard, new reports were received from assessors, documents and dossiers in the case were studied, and all the other defendants were questioned. . . . The Commission finds that there were no grounds for convicting Goldmann and Jičínský for high treason, sabotage and military treason (espionage). As far as damage caused by negligence is concerned, the court should decide the extent of their guilt. (Commission II, Vol. 13, Section 368.)

The Commission decided to consult Dolanský and to discuss the assessors' report with the Commission of Government experts before referring this recommendation to the Politburo.

This gave the original assessors a welcome opportunity to reaffirm their dubious expertise. The amended version of the report on Goldmann and Jičínský states that assessor Púček reiterated his original viewpoint that the economists had deliberately planned a low output of iron ore and so on. Consequently, this second report no longer rejected the verdict on Goldmann and Jičínský out of hand, but recommended that, in view of 'certain errors', there should be a retrial. (Commission II, Vol. 13, Section 372.) The Politburo approved the retrial, but since its resolution of 19 November 1956 was still valid the finding of the Court was not reached until 22 March 1958, when Goldmann's sentence was reduced from twenty to eight years and Jičínský's from twenty-two to six years.

The story was repeated in the cases of Fabinger and Rudinger.

After reviewing the verdicts on Eisler and Kárný, the Barák Commission recommended disciplinary proceedings against the former examining magistrate Engelsman on the grounds that in 1949 he had failed to comply with the orders issued under the closed-door system of judicial procedure. In a report approved by the Politburo on 26 March 1957, we read:

During the original investigation and the conviction of Eisler in 1949 there were serious errors; the examining magistrate of the State Court, Dr Engelsman, weighted the investigation in Eisler's favour. . . . It has been ascertained that Dr Engelsman disagreed with the instructions from the Ministry of Justice to accelerate the investigation and conduct it along the right lines, and that for wholly inexplicable reasons he took the case to Frejka.

The Politburo therefore decided to transfer Engelsman to other work and to initiate Party proceedings against him. (File 02/2, Vol. 134, Section 174, Point 15.) This procedure was a clear defence of the old form of behind-the-scenes justice, perpetuation of which was condoned by the Politburo.

In the case of Bárta reduction of sentence only was approved, while on 11 June the Politburo decided to instigate Party disciplinary proceedings against V. Pavlan 'for encouraging witnesses to testify in defence of Bárta, and to submit a report to the Central Committee Secretariat'. The Commission's report on which this decision was based stated:

Pavlan called all the witnesses whom Mrs Bártová allegedly produced to testify to Bárta's innocence. This shows that Bárta and his family were still intriguing to sway the results of the investigations in his favour. . . . Pavlan's conduct is a serious infringement of Party discipline, and we therefore recommend that Party disciplinary proceedings be taken against him. (File 02/2, Vol. 142, Section 185.)

So, while neither the Commission nor the Politburo had called to account a single witness for perjury in the trials, those who had been ready to speak on behalf of the victims were persecuted and intimidated.

The Barák Commission 'A' completed its work in September 1957, without completing the reviews of a number of verdicts (the generals, economists and others). By then the Prosecutor-General had at his disposal a smoothly operating mechanism capable of keeping matters firmly in hand and of obeying higher political directives unswervingly, regardless of facts, valid laws and principles. When the two Barák Commissions had been wound up and a summary report of their work had been approved, in the course of a brief discussion during which Barák, Bacílek, Široký and Dolanský referred briefly to the findings, Novotný made a closing statement:

Rehabilitation is out; a monster trial was needed with Slánský as the centre piece. Things did not happen by chance. Personal matters played their part. Čepička played an evil and dirty role – only Gottwald could throw light on the affair. . . . What would have happened if Slánský had remained General Secretary – a repetition of Hungary last year. The Central Committee report should confirm guilt . . . collect the documents, keep them safe, so no one can get at them. (File 02/2, Vol. 153, Section 201, Point 9, brief and incomplete minutes of the discussion.)

Once the Politburo had approved the recommendations of the Barák Commission and the results of the review had proved unfavourable for the applicant, he could no longer hope for a just settlement – only, at best, for a conditional release, or in exceptional cases for a presidential remission of sentence or an amnesty.

We have shown that the review in 1955 of the trial of 'bourgeois nationalists' was a farce, staged at the expense of the convicted men. Later, after the Twentieth Congress of the Soviet Communist Party, this trial was described as having been reviewed and found correct; all the doubts expressed by so many Party members as to its legality were brushed aside.

Široký, addressing a Central Committee meeting, said:

In connection with violation of socialist legality, the question is frequently raised in Slovakia whether Husák, Clementis and Novomeský were justly sentenced. It should be emphasized that, as far as the Central Committee is aware, none of these men was sentenced for holding deviant ideological and political views. The Party was, however, fully justified in waging a sharp ideological and political struggle against their bourgeois nationalist outlook. They were tried and sentenced, not for these errors or for an incorrect attitude on any issue, even the most vital, but because their actions constituted a threat to the results of the Slovak National Uprising, to the fruits of victory won by the Slovak people over Hitlerite fascism, a threat to our socialist endeavour.

The resolutions adopted at this meeting were in tune with this speech.

At a meeting of the Slovak Central Committee on 13 July, Bacílek too referred, in a manner typical of the accusations bandied about during the 1950s, to the treachery of Husák and his accomplices, adding as a new argument that 'under the false slogan of extending the jurisdiction of the national committees they actually restricted the rights of the Slovak national bodies'. The guilt of the 'bourgeois nationalists' was reaffirmed again and again at Party meetings, and all the efforts of the convicted men to get their wrongs redressed were fruitless.

On 27 April 1956, for example, Husák again addressed himself to Novotný with a plea for a Party and State inquiry into his case, backing it up with details of the ruthless and illegal treatment he had received. No reply was forthcoming. In May 1957 he addressed to the Prosecutor-General a request for a review, but the letter was held back at Leopoldov Prison[1] on the pretext that it exceeded the four pages that prisoners

[1] *In the large, old prison at Leopoldov in Slovakia, victims of the political trials were detained alongside criminals and Fascists from World War II, without any of the concessions common for political prisoners in civilized countries.*

were allowed to write. In June 1957 he again applied to the Prosecutor-General for a review, adding a request for a court hearing. This time he never even learnt whether the letter had been delivered. (File 02/2, Vol. 241, Section 322.)

Holdoš, in a letter to the Politburo shortly before the Twentieth Congress, complained that physical and psychological violence had been used during his interrogation, and that false evidence had been given by intimidated witnesses. He requested a hearing before a Party committee where he could produce facts to refute the falsehoods contained in the police evidence. On 20 January 1957 Holdoš wrote to Široký and again demanded an opportunity to inform the Central Committee, or a body named by it, about his case, or to obtain by some other means a retrial with a defence counsel, as permitted by law. In 1956 Okáli and Horváth had addressed similar letters to Novotný and the President.

The men accused in this trial also [that of the 'bourgeois nationalists'] retracted their previous testimonies. Novomeský, for example, informed the Party Control Commission that his statements about Clementis contained in the summary of evidence in 1952 were untrue and at variance with his original testimony. He emphatically denied the assertion at the end of the summary that the bourgeois nationalists had sought to restore capitalism and incite Slovak opposition to the Czech nation, and that the group had established contact with Western imperialists. On 19 September 1956 Horváth also retracted his evidence against Clementis.

The very foundations of the indictment and verdict of the Supreme Court against the group of 'bourgeois nationalists' cracked when the main witnesses in this trial, Nový, Löbl and Hložková, retracted their evidence. Yet, even when the reviews of other cases brought to light new facts showing that the charges preferred against the bourgeois nationalists had been fabricated, the Barák Commission never reconsidered their case as a whole.

Of the five men sentenced in April 1954 as bourgeois nationalists, only two had been released by 1960. Novomeský was granted a conditional release in February 1956 after serving half of his sentence.

Holdoš's release followed in April 1957. A few weeks earlier the Politburo had confirmed the original verdict but recommended a presidential pardon. (File 02/3, Vol. 133, Section 173, Point 6.)

In 1956 the case of Marie Švermová came up for re-examination after her daughter, Mrs Kopoldová, had applied for a conditional release. Švermová, reluctant to accept this solution, insisted on complete rehabilitation; this, however, was unacceptable to the Politburo. On 21 September, therefore, the Politburo approved a conditional release suggested by Barák, with the proviso that it should first be announced at a Central Committee meeting. (File 02/2, Vol. 112, Section 133.) Towards the end of this meeting, held on 27 September, Barák explained that Švermová's good conduct had earned her conditional release after serving half her sentence. This was being announced to the Central Committee, he said, in order to avoid any impression that Švermová was being rehabilitated because of wrongful conviction. None of those present expressed the slightest misgivings about this procedure.

Among those who fought hardest for rehabilitation was Smrkovský, whose original sentence had been set aside in 1955, whereupon he was given a new sentence of three years. After his release, Smrkovský was told by Novotný that his rehabilitation would be considered by the Central Committee and that he would be called for a consultation beforehand. When this invitation failed to materialize, Smrkovský, in February 1956, sent to all members of the Politburo a request for his case to be heard by the Central Committee in his presence. In his letter he declared that the decision to impose a new sentence in 1955 had been made by the Party, and was a mere pretext for branding him as an offender and preventing him from resuming his proper place in public and Party life. (File 02/2, Vol. 92, Section 110.)

It was a matter of course that Smrkovský was not invited to attend the meeting of the Central Committee on 29 February 1956. In his address on this occasion Novotný reiterated the newly fabricated charges against Smrkovský on which the verdict of 1955 had been based, thereby giving them wide currency within the Party and outside. Smrkovský quite justifiably decided to put the facts of his case before Party members. On 8 April he drafted a letter intended for circulation inside the Party, but after consultation with the District Secretary he dropped the idea. His letter came before the Politburo on 16 April. After Novotný, Fierlinger and Zápotocký had expressed their views it was decided that 'Smrkovský, despite his anti-Party attitude, will be invited to a Politburo meeting'. (File 02/2, Vol. 94, Section 112, Point 23.) This, unfortunately, was not the first time that the Politburo had described an effort in the cause of truth as anti-Party conduct.

But even this decision, adopted by the Politburo on 16 April, was not implemented. It was not until 20 October that a mere two members of the Politburo – Barák and Novotný – discussed his case with Smrkovský. Barák told him that 'the Court is independent and the Party cannot influence its decisions'. (File 02/2, Vol. 51, Section 197, Point 20.) Naturally, both Barák and Novotný knew perfectly well that without instructions from the Politburo, or at least its consent, the Court could do nothing, and when Smrkovský's application for a retrial, dated 27 October 1956, remained unanswered he realized that he had been deceived. On 21 August 1957, in another letter to the Politburo, he wrote:

It is common knowledge that the Supreme Court and the Prosecutor-General make no decisions without the concurrence of the highest Party authorities. This has been so in my case; who, then, bears the responsibility for the fact that it has not yet been settled? The Politburo and the Party Control Commission!

He demanded that the Politburo instruct the Prosecutor-General to lodge an objection to the verdict of 15 October 1955. (Ibid.) Novotný passed this letter to the Politburo merely for information without any suggestion that action should be taken. So for the time being Smrkovský's fight for rehabilitation remained fruitless.

True, the international situation did, for a time, favour some progress in rehabilitation. The Twentieth Congress of the Soviet Communist Party had called on the other Communist Parties to establish contact and cooperate with Social Democratic parties in the capitalist countries, and this obliged the Politburo to make a public rebuttal of certain charges brought at the trials. For instance, the Israeli Socialist, Mordechai Oren, arrested in 1951 and sentenced to fifteen years' imprisonment, was released on 13 May 1956. But in this instance the indictment was not set aside; after his release, therefore, he demanded a review of his case. In his book, *A Political Prisoner in Prague*, he writes:

Through the Czechoslovak Embassy, I addressed detailed letters to the President of the Czechoslovak Republic, the Minister of Justice, the President of the Supreme Court and the Central Committee of the Czechoslovak Communist Party. After more than two years – in December 1958 – I received a reply from the Prague Supreme Court. . . . This body had the effrontery to claim that my show trial had been perfectly legal and there were no grounds for a review. The Czechoslovak judiciary refused to see justice done and thus clear itself of this stain on its honour.

In June 1956 Novotný, in a speech at the Party Conference, cleared Zilliacus of the charge of espionage. Zilliacus, regarding this as his rehabilitation in Czechoslovakia, expressed the wish to renew social contacts with Czechoslovak representatives. (File 02/2, Vol. 115, Section 138, Point 22.) Zilliacus's rehabilitation helped those who had been sentenced for having had contact with him. With the subsequent deterioration in the international situation after the Anglo-French Suez adventure and the events in Hungary, however, contacts with Zilliacus again acquired their former connotation in reassessments of the trials. In many cases, the giving of information to Zilliacus in the immediate post-war years was described as a betrayal of State secrets.

Wishing to establish contact between the Czechoslovak Communist Party and Social Democrats abroad, the Politburo decided to review all the trials of former Social Democrats held since 1948. (File 02/2, Vol. 92, Section 110, Point 32). However, this decision was not implemented. After talks between Jiří Hájek and Morgan Phillips, Secretary-General of the British Labour Party, who was expected to visit Czechoslovakia in the spring of 1956, the Politburo decided on 9 April to postpone the trial of Bohumil Laušman, due to open the following day –

10 April. This was because, in January, Morgan Phillips had insisted on the release of imprisoned Social Democrats as a condition for holding discussions with Communist Parties. (File 02/2, Vol. 92, Section 111, Point 11.)

Laušman had been in the custody of the Ministry of the Interior since 26 December 1953, and of the State Prosecutor since 2 April 1954. On 15 May 1954 he made a public statement. On 19 December 1955 the Politburo decided on a secret trial. Laušman was accused (a) of organizing an underground movement among right-wing Social Democrats, (b) of espionage and the transmission of slanderous reports, and (c) of leaving the country illegally on 31 December 1949 and continuing his espionage activities against Czechoslovakia in capitalist countries up to 23 December 1953.[1] (File 02/2, Vol. 142, Section 186, Point 15.)

On 28 May 1956 the Politburo decided that Laušman should be released. According to a subsequent report by Barák, this could not be done because Laušman had tried to contact his family in order to agree on messages by which they would know when to apply for his release. On this ludicrous pretext he was detained in custody. (File 02/2, Vol. 142, Section 186, Point 15.) Laušman now found himself in a hopeless position. He had not been released and he had not been sentenced,

[1] *Laušman's son-in-law, Major Nechanský, was arrested in 1948 and executed one year later. Laušman was warned that a warrant was out for his arrest. He tried to escape with his wife and daughter. Only Laušman managed to get away; his wife and daughter were imprisoned. Laušman worked for a time as an economic expert in Yugoslavia, before moving to Salzburg in the hope of helping his family. (His wife had spent six years in a concentration camp during the war.) On 23 December 1953 he was lured by an Austrian citizen to a meeting with two Czechoslovak Security officers, abducted and conveyed over the Austrian border to Prague. In May 1954 he made a public statement declaring that he had returned to Czechoslovakia voluntarily. He did this because the Minister of the Interior, Barák, had promised that in return he and his wife and daughter would be released.*

On 8 May 1963 Laušman was given some cigarettes by one of the prison staff, which – according to his fellow prisoner – were doctored. He also drank a cup of tea brought from the prison sick-bay, had an attack of cramp and lost consciousness. No medical attention was administered all night. At five o'clock next morning the doctor entered the cell and diagnosed death from heart failure. This and other circumstances connected with Laušman's death have never been investigated. His case remains one of the most shocking of all those involved in the political trials, particularly when we remember the tragic fate of his whole family.

although the investigation had been concluded. In August he began a hunger strike in the desperate hope of forcing a decision in his case. On 21 August Barák informed the Politburo:

Laušman has recently been finding his imprisonment hard to endure, probably because of uncertainty about his fate. He has not yet been informed of the decision not to take his case to court. (File 02/2, Vol. 133, Section 134, Point 22.)

At this point the Politburo decided to transfer Laušman from prison to a place where he was under guard but enjoyed greater freedom. Laušman, in fact, became a special prisoner of the Politburo, which kept him is prison without any court proceedings. In making this decision all the Politburo members present at the meeting deliberately broke the law. Political considerations can in no way justify their action, which involved keeping a man in custody indefinitely after completion of the investigation. On 7 September Barák promised Laušman that he would be taken to his country cottage before employment was found for him.

On 18 June 1957, the changed international situation having caused a loss of interest in contact with the Social Democrats, Barák finally produced a new proposal for the Politburo's consideration – that Laušman be committed for trial because, so he said, Security had succeeded in discovering espionage documents concealed in a picture once owned by the prisoner. (File 02/2, Vol. 142, Section 186, Point 15.) This highly dubious suggestion was clearly intended as a pretext for disposing of a case that had become gravely embarrassing.

A report on the Laušman trial, which had been held in Prague on 2 September 1957 and had resulted in a sentence of seventeen years' imprisonment, was given to the Politburo by Bartuška and Škoda on 14 November. According to their statement, the indictment had been approved by the Politburo on 19 December 1955 (yet on 28 May 1956 it had decided to release Laušman!) and again on 18 June 1957. On the second occasion the meeting had not discussed the indictment but had merely accepted Barák's statement offering as the only fresh argument for a trial the business of the picture.

Laušman had made no appeal against the sentence. The Regional Prosecutor, however, had referred the case to the Supreme Court which, on 1 November, had added the penalty of forfeiture of property. (File 02/2, Vol. 159, Section 215, Point 10.)

Determined efforts to secure rehabilitation for Dr Nebesář of the former Social Democratic Party, who had been Chairman of the National Bank after 1945, were made by Fierlinger. Nebesář's innocence was clear. All the 'evidence' of espionage had lost its validity. Yet Barák opposed rehabilitation, justifying his attitude by citing new information acquired by Security from intelligence sources. The other members of the Politburo agreed with Barák. Dr Nebesář, too, applied to the Supreme Court for rehabilitation, but the competent official informed him that, in the event of the Court not setting aside his original verdict but merely reducing his sentence, he would not be eligible under the new sentence for a presidential pardon and would have to serve the remainder of his term. (File 02/2, Vol. 140, Section 183, Point 10.)

Fierlinger's protest was the sole example of a member of the Politburo taking a stand against an unjust review of a court verdict. He did not, however, adopt a similar attitude in other, less obvious, cases.

The 1955-7 period of the reviewing of trials was brought to a close at a Central Committee meeting on 2 October 1957. In a short speech, Barák gave an original account of the genesis of the trials and summarized the findings arrived at in re-examinations of some of the most important cases. The conclusions followed the lines of earlier Politburo resolutions. Attention was focussed on the group around Slánský. The term 'anti-Party and anti-State conspiratorial centre' was replaced by a new formulation: 'Slánský was the instigator, organizer and head of an anti-Party, factional and criminal group which he gathered around himself.' Praising the Party leadership, Barák declared: 'Our Party did not embark on an indiscriminate rehabilitation programme which would have discredited policy.' He demonstrated this by the following figures:

The Commission reviewed 300 cases and recommended retrials in 52 cases. Altogether 6,678 requests for reinvestigation were received.

The Prosecutor's Office submitted 211 cases for review. The various Commissions examined a total of 6,978 cases. Recommendations for retrials were made in 263 cases (i.e. 2·6 per cent).

Only 50 verdicts were considered to have been entirely unjustified and in 213 cases the original sentence was found to have been disproportionately severe. In the rest of the 6,715 cases, i.e. 97·4 per cent, the original charges and the decisions of the courts were justified and correct.

Novotný, too, spoke at the Central Committee meeting; he supported Barák's report as a 'true and factual review of all the individual cases', and declared that it provided an excellent assessment of the situation in the years 1948–52. Novotný also expressed himself emphatically about Zionism and the danger it represented:

One must see the issue of Zionism in this whole group and in the whole grouping of these people. We ought not to forget what kind of people found their way into high Party posts after 1945. . . . Finally we learned that a pact had been made with the State of Israel. . . . It was made by people who, in many cases, had played leading roles in pre-war Zionist organizations and were linked with international capital. (File 01, Vol. 58, Section 58.)

The quite brief discussion at the Central Committee focussed on those who were dissatisfied with the reviews of the trials. Harus, noting that the Party cards of six rehabilitated people had been returned to them, continued:

In such cases where guilt has not been proved but absolute innocence and an unblemished Party record has also not been established, the Party must, independently of the judicial rehabilitation, reserve the right to decide its attitude to members – and members to it – irrespective of the court findings.

Referring to dissatisfaction among the rehabilitated, he said:

Even those whose membership has been restored and who have received considerable sums in compensation fail to recognize this rehabilitation and compensation as meaning they should, after all, self-critically admit their guilt for having come under suspicion of participating in the policy of the Slánský regime, within the Party and outside it.

Developing this theme, Novotný applied the anti-Party label to those who did not agree with the trial verdicts. A number of these people were saying:

We have been legally rehabilitated, so first of all give us back the posts we had before, compensation, full political rehabilitation and I don't know what else.

As for their efforts to defend their interests through the Union of Anti-Fascist Fighters, Novotný said:

A number of these people have actually organized groups with the intention of undermining Party policy and sowing mistrust of the Party leadership and individual functionaries . . . a number of these people and Comrades whose Party cards have been returned, and others grouped round them. They are grouping on an anti-Party platform. . . . They must subordinate their interests to the Party. . . . In 1948 the Party had to be tough, if it really wanted to destroy the old order and enforce the new line. There was no choice, and we must be tough now, too, for if we were to ease up, Comrades, I don't know what the results would be.

The report was discussed at this Central Committee meeting of 2 October at the very end of the agenda, late in the afternoon on the third day. The discussion lasted less than two hours. The role of the Central Committee was lamentable. Not a single member asked for detailed information or expressed doubts. Only Ďuriš objected that not all members of the Political Secretariat had participated in some of the decisions to the same degree; Čepička, he said, could explain a lot. No one protested at the antisemitic tone of Novotný's speech. The Politburo manipulated the meeting as it wished, getting it to rubber-stamp what was needed.

It is also not without interest that this part of the proceedings is not properly covered by the published minutes, which merely state briefly that the Central Committee discussed and approved unanimously the Commission's report, and name those who submitted the report, and who spoke in the discussion.

The Party, as an organization, was informed of the reviews of trials in a similar manner. On 7 October, a week after the Central Committee had met, a national conference of district secretaries was convened. Towards the end of a speech on the Party's tasks, Novotný referred to this matter. He was pleased, he said, to be able to inform the gathering that the Party had not resorted to sweeping rehabilitation 'which would have discredited the Party's policy and the entire system of people's democracy'. He again pointed to the danger of what might have happened had Slánský managed to seize power in the Party and the State: 'We would inevitably have been faced . . . with the prospect of a coup in our country, the prospect of a counter-revolutionary outbreak.' (File 018, Section 115.)

Similar information to that contained in Novotný's speech (sometimes even less specific) was sent to the district committees, while Party branches were told nothing.

The Barák Commission was finally wound up on 22 November 1957 with the adoption by the Politburo of the following resolution:

1. The review of political trials in Commissions should be regarded as complete, and further cases should be referred to State bodies.

2. Commission members should not in future accept complaints but should pass them on to Party and State institutions.

3. Findings concerning personnel and other matters should not be communicated to other institutions, but 'should be submitted to the First Secretary'.

4. Documents should be handed in. The documents in the case of Slánský and others should be deposited in sealed parcels; the right to dispose of them was reserved to the Politburo.

The work of the Barák Commissions, and of the Politburo at the time, can by no means be described as constituting rehabilitation. Of the negligible number rehabilitated by the courts, only a few individuals were granted Party rehabilitation and not one was given a post corresponding to his qualifications, or even at approximately the same level as the one held before his arrest. In reviews of the trials new charges were fabricated against people already unjustly convicted; indeed, new trials were held, and once again the Politburo determined the sentences. Although the Politburo had known since 1955, when Doubek testified, how the 'Centre' trial had been staged, new allegations about the guilt and responsibility of Slánský and others were spread abroad. With a few exceptions, the Politburo succeeded in deceiving the Party anew. The way was blocked to uncovering the true causes of the illegal practice – a step which would inevitably have resulted in substantial changes in the deformed political system. The mechanism that had produced the trials was more or less intact, though now it was supposed to deal with rehabilitation. In these circumstances the results could only be negative. What was more, the existing system could not guarantee the public a sense of legal security or rule out a return to the days of wholesale violations of justice.

REASSESSMENT, 1958-62

The Party leadership assumed that the October 1957 meeting of the Central Committee had rung down the curtain on the political trials, that it would never again have to consider their legal or political aspects. Evidently in order to avoid any revival of interest in the subject, the Commission's report was withheld from the Party rank and file, and the general public was kept even more in the dark. One of the arguments used to justify this omission was that the subject of the trials might have overshadowed an open letter to members on the completion of socialist reconstruction in Czechoslovakia, also approved at the October meeting.

Many Party members, however, realizing how inconsistent and short-sighted this policy was, voiced their criticism. Although the number of critical voices tended to fluctuate, they never disappeared altogether. In the period immediately following the October meeting, in an atmosphere of tense ideological campaigning against revisionism, there were comparatively few critical voices; this was due in part to the fact that few Party officials had even an approximate idea of the facts encountered by the Commission, and they could therefore hardly imagine how profoundly the facts conflicted with the conclusions drawn from the inquiry. Moreover, the Party leadership was obviously impatient of criticism, and the harshest penalties were meted out to members who objected to the way the trials had been reviewed or expressed doubts about the trials themselves. Usually these cases were handled by the Party Control Commission, the Secretariat or even the Politburo.

This fact is indicative of the interest shown by these top Party committees in matters concerning the trials. Even while the Commission was still working, such procedure was quite common. In April 1957, for example, Comrades Kühnl and Kusí, of the School of Economics, were expelled from the Party, mainly because of their attitude to the trials. In October 1957 the Secretariat expelled Mrs Kreibichová, the wife of a founding member of the Party, for much the same reason. A report to the Politburo on Kreibichová stated that she had repeatedly tried to get Rudinger rehabilitated. The report continued:

She maintained the necessity of fighting for a public retrial (of the 'Anti-State Centre'). The whole Party bore responsibility for the executions and the torture of innocent people by Gestapo methods. . . . In her speeches she made a point of referring to Comrades Novotný and Kopecký as antisemites.

On 22 October the Politburo confirmed Kreibichová's expulsion from the Party. (ACC CPC, File 02/2, Section 207.)

Disagreement with the way the Party had applied the conclusions of the Twentieth Congress to Czechoslovak conditions was voiced by some Slovak intellectuals, especially writers: they were dissatisfied with the slow pace of the democratization process and the leadership's attitude to the Slánský trial and that of the 'bourgeois nationalists'. On 22 March the Party Bureau appointed a Commission, composed of Jeleň, Michalička, Šebesta, Lörincz and Šmíd, to investigate anti-Party views. The Commission found that incorrect views were held by some individuals (Pavlík, Špitzer, Kupec and Štítnický) and expressed the conviction that the lack of confidence in the Party fostered by some individuals, like Comrade Pavlík, and the inadequate fight against incorrect views, were preventing the intelligentsia from taking a more active part in building socialism. 'This is also the main obstacle to a consistent implementation of the conclusions drawn by our Party after the

Soviet Twentieth Congress. This is why it is necessary to take action against those who hold these views.' When the Central Committee met in April 1957 'incorrect views' had become 'anti-Party and factional activity'. According to Bacílek, the substance of Pavlík's anti-Party activity was that

he did not agree with the Party decisions concerning the application of the resolutions adopted at the Twentieth Congress of the Soviet Party and as an example he cited the application of these resolutions in Poland. . . . He regarded the Husák trial as illegal and claimed that Husák might have made some political errors, but had not committed crimes. (ACC, CP of Slovakia, File of the CC Plenum.)

Pavlík was expelled from the Party and deprived of his university professorship. He was also barred from publishing his work. Party penalties were imposed on Špitzer (a reprimand and dismissal from his post as editor-in-chief of the Slovak weekly, *Kulturny Život*) and Štítnický (a reprimand).

In the text of an address to be delivered at the Slovak Party Congress, submitted to the Politburo by Novotný on 24 April, Pavlík was already referred to as the Slovak Nagy and a bourgeois nationalist:

You, Pavlík and other individuals, just you prove that the policy of our Party does not spring from the needs of the people! And just tell us what you mean to do, what your aims are. Admit that you wanted to be the Slovak Nagy . . . that you are bourgeois nationalists. (ACC CPC, File 02/3, Section 178.)

At the beginning of 1958 (at a Central Committee meeting on 9 January) Pavlík's activity was redefined as 'revisionism tinged with bourgeois nationalism'. (ACC CP of Slovakia, File of the CC Plenum.)

The attitude to the trials played a similar part in discussions on the 'case' of the Military Political Academy in Prague. On 16 September 1958 a report submitted to the Politburo by a special commission headed by Ladislav Štoll stated that, besides expressing revisionist trends in . discussions after the Twentieth Congress, the Military Academy had '. . . grossly exaggerated the consequences of the personality cult'. The Politburo closed this case by dismissing the head of the Academy and his deputy and transferring eight teachers to other sectors of the Army. (ACC CPC, File 02/2, Section 259.) [1]

On 13 November 1957 President Zápotocký died. Six days later, Antonín Novotný, First Secretary of the Communist Party, was elected President. An amnesty was announced on 1 December in honour of the presidential election. At the time the number of prisoners under investigation was six thousand, and 26,412 were serving sentences. The Politburo discussed the proposed amnesty on 26 November after consulting the Deputy Minister of the Interior (Kotál), and Švach and Samek, deputizing for the Prosecutor-General. A total of 3,102 prisoners, from both categories, were to be released. Some sentences were to be reduced. The amnesty covered mainly ordinary criminals; it applied only to those political prisoners who had less than six months of their sentence to serve. Barák, Bartuška and Škoda were appointed to a Commission to deal with borderline cases. (ACC CPC, File 02/2, Section 215.)

After a discussion on 28 November, the Politburo recommended some extension of the amnesty; ultimately the releases numbered 4,811, even this falling short of the figure for penal offences under the 1955 amnesty, due to the limited range of cases falling within its scope. (Politburo meeting, 28 March, ACC CPC, File 02/2, Section 232.)

Meeting in October 1957 to consider the findings of the reassessments of the main trials, the Central Committee stipulated that socialist legality must be fully restored. This decision also assumed that those who had violated legality in the past would be prosecuted.

On 10 December the Politburo discussed the situation in the Ministry of Justice. The result was a purely formal organizational change and the reduction of the number of deputy ministers from six to four, while the only demotion was that of the former Prosecutor-General and later Deputy Prosecutor-General Aleš, who was transferred to the department for international law. (Aleš was recalled from his post as Deputy Prosecutor-General by the Politburo on 17 December.)

Similar paradoxical measures were carried out in the

---

[1] *After the occupation of Czechoslovakia by Soviet troops, the Military Academy was again sharply criticized; it was dissolved in July 1969.*

Ministry of the Interior. The former head of the investigations department, Lieutenant-Colonel Doubek, had been taken into custody on 12 July 1955; on 17 May 1957 he had been sentenced to nine years' imprisonment (together with Captain Kohoutek). But by 17 December 1957 the Politburo was already reviewing his case. Novotný recommended a pardon, pointing out that 'with regard to these circumstances [family reasons – Commission's note], and to the fact that most of the other employees of Security who used the same methods or bore responsibility for the use of these methods for which Doubek was sentenced have not been prosecuted, I regard it as feasible to reduce Doubek's sentence'. The Politburo resolved 'to instruct the competent prosecutor to recommend conditional release so that Doubek can be free before Christmas'. (ACC CPC, File 02/2, Section 218.)[1]

The handling of this case, especially the attitude of the Politburo, gives the clearest indication of the sense of collective guilt and responsibility for the crimes committed. The consideration shown towards Doubek (who was home for Christmas) was absent from the Politburo's treatment of the trial of Valášek and others. A week before it considered the Doubek case, the Politburo had had before it a report about the review of this trial, showing that a number of the original charges had been distorted and giving new facts which confirmed that some Slovak Security officers had introduced illegal methods of investigation. The report recommended that a complaint of violation of the law should be lodged at the Supreme Court only after the investigation of guilt had been completed. The Politburo returned to the case six months later and resolved to lodge a complaint of violation of the law, but at the same time to let Valášek and the others stand trial anew for these violations. (ACC CPC, File 02/2, Sections 217 and 247.)

Doubek was released after two years in custody and six months in jail. Valášek and his fellow accused were to be put

[1] After his release, Doubek was appointed to a top job in Čedok, the State travel agency, and in this capacity was one of Czechoslovakia's representatives at the Brussels Expo 1958. While Doubek enjoyed his liberty, the majority of his victims still had to serve two or three years in prison.

on trial again after two years in custody and serving five years of their sentence.

Similar treatment was meted out by the Politburo to nearly all the victims of the various political trials and to their families. In June 1957 Marie Švermová twice addressed letters to President Zápotocký requesting remission of the additional penalties, since deprivation of civic rights prevented her from claiming a pension. 'You will appreciate,' she wrote, 'that it is not easy for me to ask for remission of additional penalties, but as there is no hope of my case being settled in the near future I have no alternative.' Not until 27 December did the Politburo consider and accede to this request. Švermová was granted a widow's pension of 450 crowns a month. Three years later, in September 1960, her right to a retirement pension of 1,600 crowns a month was recognized. (ACC CPC, File 02/2, Sections 219 and 357.)

The Politburo approached the matter of a pension for Dr Alexej Čepička, former Minister of National Defence, first Deputy Prime Minister and member of the Politburo (until 20 April 1956), quite differently. Čepička had gradually been deprived of high offices until he eventually retired. On 10 November 1959 the Politburo decided that his state of health warranted a monthly pension of 3,000 crowns for a period of one year. And at the very time of raising Švermová's pension to 1,600 crowns it approved the continued payment of a personal pension of 3,000 crowns a month to Čepička. (ACC CPC, File 02/2, Section 364.)

The double yardstick which the Politburo applied to the victims of the trials and to their architects is evident at almost every turn. Nor did it ever return to a victim's case of its own accord; such matters were included on its agenda only after applications by those persecuted.

The treatment of Mrs Franková, widow of Josef Frank, who had been unjustly condemned and executed, is tragically typical. In January 1958 she begged the Politburo to allow her to return to Prague to live with her daughter. In her letter she pointed out that she had been directed to live in the village of Holčovice near Krnov. She described the conditions under which her daughter's family was living; she had been evicted from her flat and had to move with her husband and child into one room measuring thirteen feet by six. Only after receiving this desperate letter did the Politburo decide, on 11 February, to allow Mrs Franková to move to Prague. Instructions were given to the Mayor of Prague to find a suitable flat where she could live with her daughter's family. The Politburo also directed the Ministry of Social Insurance to pay Frank's son an orphan's pension of 240 crowns a month (the equivalent of the minimum pension for an orphan who had lost both parents). (ACC CPC, File 02/2, Section 226.)

In the spring of 1958 the draft programme of the League of Communists of Yugoslavia was published; in the summer months another wave of anti-revisionism swept Czechoslovakia. The campaign preceding the Czechoslovak Party's Eleventh Congress was coloured by this atmosphere, and the policy of repressive class power was strongly emphasized.

An element in this hard-line approach was the so-called 'class political screening' of 1958. In the early stages it involved only the central State administration and research institutes, where some personnel changes were made. Eight hundred and forty-four people in the Czech lands and 485 people in Slovakia were dismissed from the Administration and the central economic sector for reasons of class and political unreliability; 4,302 were demoted (988 in Slovakia) and 1,089 were pensioned off (146 in Slovakia). Most of those who failed to pass the screening test were not members of the Party. Gradually these strict requirements concerning class origin and political reliability spread to the regional and district authorities. (ACC CPC, File 02/2, Section 241.) Although this campaign was not as sweeping as when the administrative machine was restaffed in the early 1950s, it encouraged the growth of sectarianism in the Party, increased the feeling of insecurity among State employees, and was accompanied by a general heightening of tension.

Altogether, the Politburo, mainly on the initiative of the Minister of the Interior, Barák, was especially concerned at this time with the activity of classes hostile to socialism, and underlined the need for political vigilance. According to a report received by the Politburo on 30 June 1958, 90 per cent of the *kulaks* were convinced that an anti-socialist coup would be effected in Czechoslovakia during that year. The largest quantity of illegally held arms so far was stated to have been discovered in May. (ACC CPC, File 02/2, Section 247.) This atmosphere, together with the political backwash of the drive to end collectivization in the countryside, gradually led to any consideration of matters connected with the trials, even individual cases, complaints and requests, being stopped. If any of these subjects did happen to get onto the Politburo's agenda, they were judged on the whole from the standpoint of the intensified class policy pursued at the time of the Eleventh Congress.

Although the Barák report of 1957 had already substantially demonstrated the illegality of the trials, the top power groups were apprehensive lest rehabilitation should threaten their own positions. The courts, therefore, were instructed to proceed with the retrials of peripheral cases. The accused were to be acquitted of high treason and espionage but sentenced for sabotage or abuse of authority; only in exceptional cases were they to be acquitted entirely. Evidently the results of these retrials were directly influenced by the Commission for individual cases (appointed by the Politburo on 25 November, to prepare for the amnesty), composed of Barák, Bartuška and Škoda, who consulted Novotný on major decisions. Individuals who had been prominent in the 'subsequent' trials were to be given shorter sentences in their retrials, though the sentences were to be long enough at least to cover the time already served. In short, the leadership was not at all concerned with rehabilitation but merely with reviewing certain verdicts, an attitude which in effect inaugurated another wave of illegality.

Some cases were reviewed in 1958. On 22 March the Presidium of the Supreme Court set aside the Court's original verdict of 1954 on Goldmann and eight other economists, and sentenced them to between six and twelve years' imprisonment for sabotage or under the law on the protection of national enterprises. (ACC CPC, File 02/2, Section 454.)

On 7 July the Presidium of the Supreme Court set aside the original verdict of 1954 on Generals Bulander and Drgač and sentenced them for abuse of authority: Bulander to eight years and Drgač to six. Drnec was acquitted. (ACC CPC, File 02/2, Section 454.)

On 2 October the Supreme Court set aside the original verdict pronounced in 1953 on Valášek and nine police officers in Slovakia and imposed new sentences – from six to seventeen years – for sabotage. (ACC CPC, File 02/2, Section 454.)

On 15 July the original verdict on Richard Slánský [Rudolf's brother] was set aside and he was sentenced to seven years for abuse of authority and for military treason. (He was released on 28 August 1958.)

On 14 February the original verdict on Oskar Langer was set aside and he was found guilty of treason and sentenced to twelve years in prison. (He was released under the amnesty of 9 May 1960.)

On 18 March the original verdict on B. Biehal was set aside and his case referred for further consideration. He was acquitted on 29 January 1959.

'Rehabilitation', however, was still usually confined to granting conditional release through a pardon without any review of the trials. A few people were released conditionally in 1959: B. Hájek-Karpeles (on 26 November for a probationary period of ten years), V. Jančík (on 18 March), R. Viktorín (on 12 March for a probationary period of three years), František Kollár (on 14 May for a probationary period of three years), V. Sedmík (12 June) and Horváth (21 December). These steps indicated the Party leadership's intention to complete the whole 'rehabilitation' process gradually and with the least possible fuss.

At the beginning of 1959, the Prosecutor-General notified the Party leadership that Ervín Polák and Mikuláš Landa were due for conditional release, having served half their sentences. The Prosecutor-General was acting in accord with the Politburo resolution of 21 March 1955 to the effect that all those convicted in the Švermová trial should be considered for conditional release after serving half their sentences. On 13 January, however, the Politburo supported the Prosecutor-General's standpoint that the behaviour of the prisoners and their work did not warrant conditional release. (ACC CPC, File 02/3, Section 275.)

The increasing use of repressive methods by the Administration was mirrored in the decisions of the Supreme Court. On 17 March the Politburo considered a report which stated that the Supreme Court was successfully combating liberalism in the judiciary, but criticized it for some shortcomings:

In 1958 the Presidium of the Supreme Court was obliged in eleven cases involving breaches of the law to correct *political* errors by the Appeal Courts of the Supreme Court. Although the President intervened to correct these particular errors, this alone could not lead to an overall and permanent improvement, because the leading officials of the Supreme Court failed to analyse the causes of these errors, or to draw general conclusions from them which could have served as *political* guidance to the Appeal Courts. (ACC CPC, File 02/2, Section 286.)

Urválek, the main prosecutor at the Slánský trial, remained President of the Supreme Court: indeed, he was not relieved of this office until a resolution to that effect was adopted by the Presidium of the Central Committee on 5 March 1963.

On 17 March 1959 the Politburo discussed a reply by Czechoslovak Spanish War veterans to a letter received from British veterans. The Czechoslovak veterans stated that none of them was guilty of espionage; they regarded with the utmost suspicion the explanation that the illegal measures taken against them had been inspired by reactionaries and the 'Anti-State Conspiratorial Centre' (Slánský and Taussigová). This, of course, put the validity of the trials in question. The letter also expressed the view that the Slánský trial should be reviewed. The Politburo refused to approve this letter and decided that a Party institution should send a reply to Britain.

At this time the Politburo was faced with very strong demands for a thorough review of the trials. Foremost among these demands were letters from Smrkovský (communicated to the Politburo on 3 September 1957 and 12 June 1958) and from Husák (discussed on 8 December 1959).

In the letter placed before the meeting of the Politburo on 12 June 1958, with all members present, Smrkovský wrote:

In October 1955 I was released from jail. Since then I have sent numerous letters to the Central Committee, describing the unlawful treatment to which I was subjected. Civil laws, the Party rules and Leninist norms were all violated in my case. . . . Appealing to the Party rules and Leninist norms of Party life, I demand to be summoned before the Eleventh Congress. Let the offences I am supposed to have committed be stated clearly and let me, at last, be given the opportunity to defend myself publicly. (ACC CPC, File 02/2, Section 244.)

Husák wrote the letter to Novotný from Ruzyň Prison on 23 September 1959; the letter, discussed by the Politburo on 8 December, said:

I have never acted with intent to harm the Party or committed criminal offences against the Czechoslovak Republic. I not merely assert this; I can prove it. From my first day in prison, for nine whole years, I offered these proofs in all quarters to which I have been allowed to address myself. I have never found an ear that was willing to listen or the slightest human understanding.

David, Kopecký, Novotný, Široký and Fierlinger took part in the discussion. (ACC CPC, File 02/2, Section 322.) The Politburo finally resolved

to return to the Husák case in connection with the proposal to grant political pardons on the occasion of the fifteenth anniversary of the liberation of Czechoslovakia by the Soviet Army. (ACC CPC, File 02/2, Section 322.)

So gradually the Politburo, too, began to realize that its overall position with regard to the reviewing of trials was now untenable, but it still lacked the courage to take any practical steps. The tendency was to evade the issue of political responsibility for the trials and the illegal sentencing of the accused. Thus advantage was taken of the amnesty of 9 May 1960, which extended, for the first time, to leading Communists still serving their illegal sentences. In any case, this amnesty was the most comprehensive to date. Its scope was determined not only by the anniversary but also by the announcement that socialism had triumphed in Czechoslovakia.

On 1 April 1960 the number of persons serving sentences for 'anti-State' (including political) offences was 8,708. The total of prisoners convicted for criminal offences was 22,214. The amnesty applied to both categories. On 26 April the Politburo discussed and approved a list of names of prominent person-alities of the different political parties, ex-members of previous governments and so on. All who were covered by the amnesty were released, with the exception of a few leaders of the Slovak State, with regard to whom Karol Bacílek raised objections. (ACC CPC, File 02/2, Section 341.)

Of the seventy-two convicted in the main trials, the re-maining eleven Party functionaries were released under the amnesty, but probationary periods of various lengths were imposed (the shortest three years, the longest, Löbl's, ten); in most cases the additional penalties were not remitted.

In time most of the victims were granted conditional release, the original verdicts, including the additional penalties, being sustained. These penalties, particularly loss of civic rights, caused them great hardship, and their frequent applications and complaints to government offices and the courts, mainly concerning pension rights, continually brought rehabilitation into focus. Evidently in an attempt to stop this, the Politburo decided on 7 February 1961 that the remaining additional penalties should be remitted without the main sentences imposed under the original verdicts being set aside. The Party leadership may have assumed that the Central Committee meeting in October 1957 had closed the chapter of the political trials, but this naïve notion was disproved by the Politburo's own actions. It was forced to deal with the problem in one form or another nearly every month.

Party members still raised critical voices at the slow and inadequate rectification of injustices, but pressure mostly took the form of complaints and applications from the trial victims and their families, sent to the Central Committee, the President's Office and the Prosecutor-General. In 1958 these bodies received forty-five appeals, in 1959 thirty-four, in 1960 twenty-four, in 1961 twenty-two and in 1963 thirty.

The Twenty-Second Congress of the Soviet Communist Party in October 1961 made a strong impact. It was in discussing the outcome of this Congress that a considerable number of Czechoslovak Party members turned again to the question of Stalinism and its consequences in Czechoslovakia. The subject of the trials became once more a foremost issue in the Party.

The Politburo discussed them when preparing for the coming meeting of the Central Committee. Speaking about the violations of the law revealed by the Twenty-Second Congress, Hendrych told the Politburo on 14 November:

It is not a matter of a fight against a group [i.e. Molotov and Malenkov – Commission's note], because that has been won; the main thing is that it is of importance to us. . . . I spoke to Comrade Kozlov when the statutes were drawn up. I'd like to tell you one thing that stuck in my mind when I was talking to him, and that was when he said: 'At present we have no worries about the future. We have got Comrade Khrushchev and he won't allow such things to happen. But Comrade Khrushchev is getting on, goodness knows how things will turn out, and so we must ensure a strong collective leadership for the future.' From that I gathered that they, too, are concerned that such things should not be repeated; that it was necessary to tell the Party everything, in order to amass some sort of antibodies against any repetition. (ACC CPC, File 02/2, Section 417.)

It looked, after the Twenty-Second Congress of the Soviet Party, as though the Politburo would be forced to return to the whole problem of the trials and to make up its mind about a thorough reassessment. Yet its members, evidently too well aware of their own responsibility, still lacked the courage to take this step. Their personal ties and dependence on each other led them to the unanimous decision not to bring up the matter and, indeed, to reaffirm that on the whole it had been settled for good. This was the tone of Novotný's speech to the Central Committee meeting on 15 November 1961, where he repeated the 1955 theory about the similarity between Beria and Slánský. Novotný claimed:

Where people who had committed no crimes against the Party or the Republic were persecuted under Slánský or as a result of other illegal acts, we have redressed their wrongs. These people have been fully rehabilitated and compensated, their Party membership has been restored; they enjoy our full confidence and are again working in Party, State or public organizations or in scientific institutes. . . . If there are still any outstanding cases of violation of socialist legality, the Party will judge them fairly. . . . And we reject as completely unjustified the irresponsible demands for the rehabilitation of those who were themselves guilty of gross violations of socialist legality at the height of the Slánský era. . . . Many of them should realize that they were caught between the millstones (which they themselves had helped to set in motion) and that they bear responsibility for violating the standards of Party conduct and the legal code. Therefore, when considering their 'innocence' let them first of all examine their deeds. We see no reason why our Party, which has taken a consistent Leninist path in eradicating the personality cult, should change its attitude in these cases. (ACC CPC, File 01, Section 81, p. 11.)

The discussion following Novotný's address and, as the very next item on the programme (evidently with the intention of diverting attention to economic matters), a speech by Šimůnek, which continued after Hendrych had spoken, concentrated on the economy and on youth questions. No member of the Central Committee made an issue of the trials; only a few of the speakers alluded to them briefly, while basically identifying themselves with Novotný's standpoint.

The Politburo, aware of its grave responsibility for the trials, displayed a lenient attitude to anyone who had operated in the power system of the time. The appointment of the President of the Supreme Court was on the 18 August agenda and again the Politburo agreed on Urválek's candidature:

Comrade Urválek still shows some shortcomings, mainly lack of initiative, promptness and consistency in handling the organizational and personnel problems of the Supreme Court. Although these shortcomings remain in Comrade Urválek's work, the Supreme Court does, on the whole, direct judicial practice correctly from the political and legal points of view. (ACC CPC, File 02/2, Section 414.)

Leniency in this respect was counterbalanced by ruthlessness in answer to criticism of the trials. On 10 October 1961 the Politburo discussed the report of a special commission that had been investigating the case of Lukeš and others. Prominent among the accusations levelled against this group was the issue of the trials, which they regarded as illegal, while they considered the rehabilitation to be slow and inadequate. This was part of a wider criticism of the policy pursued by the Party leadership, a critical attitude which these men had arrived at individually. Most of them were scholars, with considerable political knowledge. To characterize as a 'group' these Communists, who met only occasionally and some of whom hardly knew each other, was a political move and the first sign that another wave of trials might be expected. Indeed, the Politburo actually discussed the possibility of a trial, although in the end the idea was dropped; it was resolved merely to expel seven of the 'group' from the Party and demote them to manual work, while six were reprimanded, three were summoned to interviews and two cases were referred for further investigation. (ACC CPC, File 02/2, Section 412.)

Their attitude to the trials also lay behind a personal quarrel between Barák and Novotný, which by the end of January 1962 had developed into an open clash. We cannot yet give an exhaustive account of the dispute between the two top politicians, but from the material available it would seem that Barák had been getting ready for a showdown with Novotný. He intended, for his own political advancement, to attack Novotný's policies at the forthcoming meeting of the Central Committee in February. Just at that time Novotný had discovered that, when leaving the Ministry of the Interior, Barák had failed to account for a sum of money in foreign currency and that he had taken from the archives documents on the politicial trials, transferring them to his office in the Government building. Novotný, therefore, gave orders for the safe in charge of Barák's secretary, Jenyš, to be searched. Reporting to the Politburo, Novotný said:

The safe contained foreign currency and the files of Moscow meetings, documents relating to the Slánský trial and other papers which only Barák, as a member of the Politburo and Minister of the Interior, could have had in his possession. They were papers that should either have remained at the Ministry of the Interior or been handed over to the Central Committee. (ACC CPC, File 02/2, Section 427.)

From this account, and from the minutes of the Politburo, it is clear that Barák had in his hands a number of documents concerning the part played by top politicians in staging the trials, as well as intelligence reports on the conduct and former attitudes of certain members of the Politburo; in all probability he intended to use them in his criticism of Novotný's regime. (Mention was made at the Politburo meeting of materials concerning Široký.) This was confirmed by Hendrych at a subsequent Politburo meeting on 27 November, when he said: 'Barák kept the documents so that he could produce them whenever it suited him. He counted on becoming head of the State – such were his ambitions.' (ACC CPC, Commission II, Vol. 35, p. 541.) Although it was clear that this dispute was predominantly political, the Politburo resolved on 30 January 1962, in Barák's absence, to hand his case over to the courts and to indict him for embezzlement of State funds and abuse of his official position. On 3 April, when considering the indictment and preparations for the trial, it resolved

to extend the indictment to include the political implications of Barák's actions, those of a political adventurer who deliberately deceived the Party and the Government, slandered comrades and sowed doubt in the public mind towards the Central Committee and the Government, all this to further his own career.

A further part of the resolution, to which the words 'NOT TO BE INCLUDED IN THE MINUTES' are appended in Novotný's handwriting, eloquently confirms the Politburo's awareness of the political nature of the case:

The Politburo is of the opinion that it is not in the interests of Party policy for Barák's case to be presented as a political one, and suggests that the Prosecutor should recommend a sentence of fifteen years' imprisonment for his criminal offences. (ACC CPC, File 02/2, Section 435.)

The arrest and conviction of Rudolf Barák, who had headed the 1955–7 Commission entrusted with reviewing the trials, enabled Novotný and other members of the Politburo to comply with demands by many members of the Czechoslovak Party and with the suggestions emanating from some leading people in the Soviet Party (whose names have not yet been definitely established; perhaps Andropov?) to appoint a new Rehabilitation Commission.

REHABILITATION

On 30 August 1962 Antonín Novotný submitted to the Politburo a recommendation to 're-examine the trials of people who formerly occupied important political office'. (ACC CPC, File 02/2, Vol. 362, Section 454.) He explained the proposal by pointing out that 'some people who were sentenced in political trials held between 1948 and 1954 are still turning to various institutions with the request that their cases should be reinvestigated and they themselves rehabilitated'. (Ibid., Appendix III.)

In a report to the Politburo of 21 November 1962 the Rehabilitation Commission justified the re-examination of the trials by stressing that new facts had come to light which underlined the inconsistent handling of many cases. (Ibid., Commission II, Vol. 23, Section 487.)

Novotný, in his report to the Twelfth Party Congress, was more precise:

After the dismissal of Rudolf Barák, new information came to light and made new inferences possible. Although, as chairman of the 1955-7 Commission for reviewing the political trials and as Minister of the Interior, Barák was aware of ominous indications and facts, he made no systematic investigation and failed to explain to the Politburo and the Central Committee the significant circumstances which threw new light on the assessment of some of the trials and some of the charges. By protecting certain offenders in this way, Barák hoped to strengthen his position at the Ministry of the Interior. He speculated on using this knowledge in the furtherance of his own career. (*Twelfth Congress of the CPC*, Prague, 1962, pp. 64–6.)

The Report of the Commission for Reviewing the Political Trials over the Years 1949–1954, submitted to the Central Committee meeting on 3–4 April 1963, stated:

The passage of time has made this review imperative. More and more facts are encountered testifying to inconsistency in the work of the first Commission, headed by Rudolf Barák, which was charged in 1955-7 with examining the violations of socialist legality in

1949–53 and with submitting the appropriate recommendations for remedying them.

In a speech by Novotný at the April meeting of the Central Committee we find the following line of argument:

The assessment of the personality cult era made by the Central Committee on 15 November 1961, in the light of the more profound approach at the Twenty-Second Congress of the Soviet Communist Party and of our new findings, was essentially correct.

However, to enable us to examine the period of the personality cult in detail and with all its implications in the light of the new facts, we appointed a Commission which was to report to our Twelfth Congress.

What have we discovered recently, Comrades? That this Commission [the Barák Commission], having made a substantially correct political evaluation of the period, failed to draw and submit the right conclusions derived from the facts it had ascertained.

To establish objectively the motives that prompted the setting up of the 'Kolder Commission' is important for appraising the political responsibility of the Party leadership at the time in question for the inconsistent and protracted procedures adopted over the solution of this tragic problem.

Until the summer of 1962 the Party had seen fit to handle the subject of the trials by the method chosen in connection with the fifteenth anniversary of liberation – legally under the amnesty, and on Party lines, by discussing cases with the Control Commission. This method virtually ruled out any consistent rehabilitation; witness Novotný's address at the November 1961 Central Committee meeting:

Naturally the Central Committee continues to maintain absolutely firmly and openly the view that legally and in the Party justice must be done wherever the law has been infringed. And therefore, if there are still any outstanding cases of violation of socialist legality, the Party will judge them fairly. But under no circumstances will we allow anyone to exploit matters already settled for the purpose of demagogic attacks on our Party. And we reject as completely unjustified the irresponsible demands for the rehabilitation of those who were themselves guilty of gross violations of socialist legality at the height of the Slánský era, people who inflicted wrongs and used force, or who initiated the anti-Leninist methods that were once introduced into the Party and Government and were justly punished under the law or the Party rules. Many of them should realize that they were caught between the millstones (which they themselves had helped to set in motion) and that they bear responsibility for violating the standards of Party conduct and the legal code. Therefore, when considering their 'innocence' let them first of all examine their deeds. We see no reason why our Party, which has taken a consistent Leninist path in eradicating the personality cult, should change its attitude in these cases. (Ibid., p. 11.)

Novotný's 'mill' theory forestalled questions concerning the responsibility of those who had held top Party positions at the time of the trials and during the first stage of their review.

This explains why after the Twenty-Second Congress of the Soviet Communist Party, which again dealt with violations of legality, there was no move by the Czechoslovak Party leadership to settle the question of the Czechoslovak trials. We have no evidence that any member of the Politburo, apart from Novotný, called for a re-examination of the political trials. (The members at the time were Bacílek, Barák until 1962, David, Dolanský, Fierlinger, Hendrych, Novotný, Široký, Hlína, Jankovcová, Köhler, Kolder and Strechaj.)

Even if we allow that the decision to recommend a further review of the trials was a response to demands by individuals for re-examination of their cases, to impulses from the Soviet Twenty-Second Congress in October 1961, to the Party discussion that followed, and to the signs that the handling of the cases by the courts and the Prosecutor's office was slow and perfunctory, it does seem, nevertheless, that the main reason for appointing the Commission (unless there was some other reason yet to be discovered) derived from two circumstances: the case of Rudolf Barák, former Minister of the Interior and member of the Politburo, which was in fact mentioned in the resolution recommending a further review, and the preparations for the Twelfth Party Congress.

The Twelfth Congress was convened against a background of growing conflict with the Communist Party of China. This had come sharply into focus at the Twenty-Second Soviet Congress. Indeed, it may be said that the renewed discussion of the tragic results of the personality cult in the USSR and the international Communist movement was largely a response to criticisms levelled by the Chinese Communists at the conclusions of the Twentieth Congress, particularly the attacks on Stalin.

It can be assumed that Novotný had similar reasons for including on the agenda of the Twelfth Congress the consequences of the personality cult in Czechoslovakia.

Novotný proposed (on 4 September 1962) the establishment of a special Central Committee Commission to reinvestigate the trials of 1948–54 and 'to make recommendations to the Central Committee from the standpoint of the law and of the Party'. (ACC CPC, File 02/2, Vol. 362, Section 454.)

(Insofar as the references are from files deposited in the archives of the Central Committee of the Czechoslovak Communist Party, only the files and archives sections are quoted henceforth.)

The members of the Commission were Drahomír Kolder (chairman), Alexander Dubček, Pavel Hron, Jozef Lenárt, Pavol Majling, Miroslav Pastyřík, Václav Prchlík, Lubomír Štrougal, Bohuslav Laštovička, Helena Leflerová and Václav Škoda. (Ibid.) Pastyřík was later dropped and replaced by Miroslav Mamula.

Novotný mentioned a number of trials in his proposal, but the majority were not examined by the Commission. When and where it was decided to omit some of the trials is not clear from the documents at hand.

On 11 September the Politburo approved with minor amendments the terms of reference for the Commission put forward by Kolder. It also endorsed the proposed procedure for inquiries to be conducted by the Prosecutor's Office and the Supreme Court.

Responsibility for groups of trials was divided among the members of the Commission. Kolder, Štrougal and Mamula were responsible for the 'main' trials (during Mamula's illness he was replaced by Procházka); the 'economists' were Majling's responsibility, the 'military' Prchlík's, 'other political parties' Škoda's, and a group added later under the heading 'Ministry of Foreign Affairs personnel' was allotted to Laštovička and Leflerová. The latter, however, was too busy to participate in the work of the Commission. (File 02/2, Vol. 363, Section 455.) Dubček was later added to the group in charge of the 'main' trials, Kunštátová, who had worked with the Barák Commission, was a member of the new Commission and acted as rapporteur. (Ibid.)

The Commission started work on 12 September 1962, and at this first meeting Kolder submitted a working programme which differed – in the grouping of the cases – quite substantially from the arrangement decided on by the Politburo on the previous day.

The inquiry into the Slánský trial was now confined to Slánský, Geminder, Frank, Šváb and Šling. The remaining cases from the main trial were allotted to other groups. (Commission II, Vol. 22, Section 489.) Why and by whom the decision was made to change the membership of the groups is not clear from the documents studied.

There may have been good practical reasons for the change. But it involved a danger that important links in the different cases would be broken, links deriving from the fact that the groups allegedly forming the 'Centre' and its offshoots were artificial constructions. The inquiry could take this turn only because the aim was still to fix political responsibility and guilt, in some cases even to give a clearer definition of criminal responsibility. With this approach the charges of conspiracy could be dropped in almost all cases while letting individual accusations of errors and shortcomings stand. This method of work may have been adopted fortuitously, but its consequences were bound to be serious. There was a danger that the new review of the trials and the new phase of rehabilitation would become merely another exercise in 'redefining' the trials, in making them more objective – and this would happen whatever the intentions of the Commission members.

When the methods of work were discussed, particular importance was attached to the inquiries to be conducted by the Prosecutor-General and the Supreme Court.

The Prosecutor-General and the Supreme Court were to ascertain whether the trials had been conducted correctly from the legal point of view, whether the investigations had been properly carried out; they were to assess the authenticity of the evidence, appraise the verdicts in the light of the evidence thus assessed, and recommend legal and political action.

Their findings were to be weighed by a panel drawn from the Prosecutor-General's Office (Bartuška, Ozimý, Samek, Švach, David and Dlouhý) and members of the Supreme Court Presidium (Urválek, Pastorek, Flajzar and Stýblo). Their recommendations were to be submitted to the Central Committee Commission. Some of the officials of the Prosecutor's Office and the Court (for example, Urválek, Švach, Flajzar and Stýblo) had taken part in the trials of the 1950s. (Ibid.)

The Commission had to work in the knowledge that the Politburo had decided to complete the inquiry by 25 November 1962. That left little time for each case. At the suggestion of Urválek and Bartuška, the reports on the cases of Nový, Goldstücker, Pavlík and others were to be handed to the Commission by 4 October, that is within less than a month. The other cases were to be investigated at weekly intervals.

The Commission worked under Novotný's personal supervision. A Politburo resolution bound Kolder 'to inform Comrade Novotný of the Commission's deliberations and to submit the conclusions regularly to the Politburo'. (Ibid.)

In his statement of September 1968 on the Commission's work, Kolder referred to this resolution:

At first Comrade Novotný was surprised at our findings. He was critical and suspicious, but gradually he changed his attitude. Nevertheless, he maintained very strong reservations about the political activity of Slánský, Švermová, Clementis and the Slovak comrades. Novotný's unrelenting attitude is evident in the relevant passages of the April Central Committee resolution and in his speech at that meeting.[1]

This statement by Kolder was also signed by Majling; Hron added some comments expressing his agreement. The available records do not contradict the statement.

Some embarrassment was caused by the fact that Urválek, who had been Prosecutor in the Slánský trial, was now, as

---

[1] The Central Committee Commission for Completing Party Rehabilitation, Information No. 5, October 1968: Kolder's statement on the Commission's work and Hron's standpoint on its report.

President of the Supreme Court, to play a prominent part in the inquiry.

The Commission decided that Kolder should have a talk with Urválek. The record of the talk, held on 13 September, the day after the Commission's session, reads:

Comrade Kolder informed Comrade Urválek about the Politburo's decision to reassess cases that had been before the courts and also about the tasks assigned to him at the Commission's meeting of 12 September. He informed Comrade Urválek that the Party was fully aware of his previous work as Prosecutor in some of the cases now under review, but that he had the full confidence of the Party.

We expect that Comrade Urválek will do all in his power to assist in the reassessment.

In a further conversation Comrade Urválek explained the judicial proceedings that can be adopted in reassessing penal offences and what is permissible under the criminal code. This information was to be communicated by Bartuška and Urválek at the next session of the Commission. (Commission II, Vol. 22, Section 489.)

Urválek frequently attended the meetings of the Commission. Innemann, whose experience, the Commission decided, could be of great value, was invited to attend regularly and he was made a member of the editorial group. So there were now two members who had served on the Barák Commission; the other was Kunštátová, and both were in the 'editorial group'.

Innemann pointed out that 'a number of cases handled at the beginning of 1955, when Karel Košťál was still a member of the previous Commission, were not properly investigated'. (Ibid.) He referred particularly in this connection to the cases of Švermová, Moškovič, Jančík, Langer, Kaboš, Pavlík and Husák.

The Commission submitted its first report to the Politburo on 27 November 1962. It had considered individual cases; the procedure adopted and the difficulties faced can best be illustrated by reference to the most complex case, that of Slánský. The findings of the legal investigation of the case were summarized in a report by the Prosecutor's Office and the Supreme Court (submitted to the Commission by Bartuška and Urválek) in the words, 'the verdict must be regarded as illegal *in toto*'. (Commission II, Vol. 22, Section 490.)

The report continues:

Although it is impossible in the light of the documents at our disposal to arrive at firm conclusions, there are some serious indications that other offences may have been committed. However, the investigation has not provided sufficient evidence and no final decision about possible criminal responsibility or the offences that may have been committed can be made without further inquiry. Since Rudolf Slánský is dead, no legal proceedings can be taken nor can the circumstances be investigated. There remains the possibility of an inquiry on Party lines, which would make possible a final political decision.

The serious indications are substantially the following:

1. Violation of the law in Military Intelligence;

2. Slánský's part in the Security 'fives' and his responsibility for the work of the Records Department and Party Control for the methods employed by Security including violations of the law;

3. Placing people with bourgeois backgrounds and class enemies in the administration and the economic sector;

4. The suspicion that Slánský, with Geminder, supported Zionist organizations, either actively or by refraining from taking measures against them, although his attention had been drawn to their hostile activities. (Milan Reiman's testimony.)

Similarly, the working group found that 'Slánský would have to be held criminally responsible for violations of the law during his term of office as Secretary-General, particularly in Security and the Army'. (Commission II, Vol. 22, Section 490.)

In short, both reports endorsed the standpoint on the Slánský case adopted at the end of 1955 and after the Twentieth Congress and by the Barák Commission in 1957, a view also endorsed by Novotný at the Central Committee meeting in November 1961.

As far as can be ascertained from the records, some members of the Commission expressed similar views; for example, that 'the testimonies were extorted, but this does not mean that all the charges are invalid'. (Laštovička and Škoda.)

These views were challenged by Prchlík, Kolder, Majling and Štrougal, who asked, for instance: 'Why were others not charged with responsibility?' Majling, however, in common with Laštovička, conceded that Slánský had shown a 'Zionist bourgeois attitude'. Urválek even expressed the view that they 'might still work round to treason'. (Ibid., Section 491.)

In a later statement the Commission expressed the view that Slánský's mistakes should not have been judged outside the Party, but that 'his guilt was such that it justified relieving him of all his public offices and questioning his membership of the Central Committee and the Party'. And it repeated the claim that after the Soviet Twentieth Congress he would 'have been charged with criminal responsibility'. (Ibid.)

The fifth meeting was mainly concerned with documents in the Šling case. The working group stated that, since the review of the Slánský case had eliminated the charge of membership of a subversive movement, they had investigated the following questions:

1. Šling's alleged hostile activities while abroad;
2. His alleged espionage for the Anglo-American intelligence services in 1945;
3. The affair of the 'generals' group in Brno, allegedly formed by Šling;
4. Employing in the Brno region administrators with hostile views.

The group then reported that the charge of espionage was not substantiated, but it found Šling guilty of concealing his contact with Voska, the Patzaks and Bělina: 'Šling's letter to Voska of 17 April 1939,' the report concluded, 'is evidence that he was serving the leadership of the bourgeois resistance and it should be classified as activity inimical to the Party.' (Commission II, Vol. 22, Section 491.)

Furthermore, the group stated that no evidence had been found to support the charge of espionage in 1945-50; it would therefore have to be dropped. The same went for the charge in connection with the 'generals' group'. This opened the way to a solution of the Bulander case.

The working group summed up its uncompromising negative attitude to Šling's political activity in Brno in the words: 'Šling conducted objectively hostile activities in the Brno region. He caused considerable political and economic damage, for which he fully deserved to bear criminal responsibility.' (Ibid.)

Similarly, the report by the Prosecutor-General and Supreme Court stated that 'illegal methods were employed in the investigation', and 'Šling's criminal activity was substantially exaggerated and distorted', but that 'criminal offences, for which the law valid at the time set a maximum penalty of life imprisonment, can be taken as proven'. (Ibid.)

Urválek contributed to the discussion with the statement that 'a retrial can also be held *in camera*' – in effect an invitation to proceed with rehabilitation by the old secretive methods.

The Commission followed a similar procedure in a number of other cases. General and political issues were given increasing prominence. The establishment of responsibility for the trials and assessment of the results of the reviews came to be the main issue, involving the question of full Party rehabilitation for all the victims and confronting Novotný's published statements on trials with the Commission's findings. These matters featured at a meeting of the Politburo on 27 November to consider the Commission's first report. The Commission assumed that members of the Politburo would help to clarify the question of responsibility, since many of them had been in the top Party leadership at the time of the trials. These expectations, however, were not fulfilled.

Indeed, while the matter was still under discussion in the Politburo, the attitude of these leaders proved embarrassing. While as former members of the leadership they admitted responsibility, nearly all of them denied any knowledge of what had actually been taking place. As for the fact that the re-assessment started in 1955 had failed, after seven years, to reach a satisfactory conclusion, they blamed Barák for deliberate obstruction.

Široký, for example, said:

As far as our responsibility is concerned, I should like to say: we belonged to the leadership. It is true that I did not raise objections to any case. I did not criticize violations either of the Party rules or of socialist legality. I did not speak out because I had not the slightest doubt that, if there was evidence that so-and-so was an agent, then there was evidence against all of them.

Fierlinger declared that in his view

Čepička was the villain of the piece.

Dolanský said:

I agree that not only Gottwald but the entire leadership was responsible. But the fact is that we knew nothing about these things. In a Party that was fighting the bourgeoisie, we were accustomed not to ask questions. If someone, even the General Secretary, did something illegal, it was not done to question it. Those were the conspiratorial methods.

Bruno Köhler declared:

In my view the report is on the whole correct. I must say that much of what is contained in it is news to me.

Hendrych was mainly concerned with the question – the most urgent from his point of view – why matters had not been brought to a conclusion after the Twentieth Congress.

I should like to say one thing, Comrades; that much of the blame for not seeing things through to the end rests with Barák. There should have been more about that in the documents. Look here, Comrades, apart from the assessment on matters of principle, only one charge has been withdrawn, that of espionage. We have re-habilitated some people, reduced the sentences of others; instead of ten years we have given them three. Someone had been in for five years; we gave him five so that it worked out exactly right. That's how it was and for that Barák is to blame. So I put the question of his responsibility.

Novotný spoke as follows about the responsibility for the trials and the inconsistent rehabilitation:

Slánský was one of the first to introduce Beria's methods into Security. I repeat: Slánský, Šváb and the whole Security 'five' were the ones who introduced the Beria methods.
     The other thing, and I insist on this, is the mill I mentioned at our November meeting. He called up spirits and then they stifled him. It turned against us. Then it was just a matter of various cliques settling personal accounts. This can best be demonstrated in Security.
     This report poses a question that all of us should answer. Who is guilty? I don't think everyone has replied to that. That, I think, must be said. It's not a matter of characterizing this man or that,

but of answering the question: who is guilty? It's from that we have to draw conclusions.

I don't want to say it was Comrade Bacílek. You were surely the only one who did not know what was happening at the Ministry. Frankly, this must be a relief to you, but terrible things were going on behind your back of which you knew nothing.

Kolder spoke towards the end. His attitude contrasted quite sharply with that of Novotný, especially his assessment of Gottwald's responsibility. Kolder stressed this responsibility much more and excused it less than Novotný had done. On the other hand, he took a more lenient view of Slánský's responsibility. On the whole he agreed about Zápotocký's responsibility, but he judged that of Čepička more severely.

Kolder then addressed himself to the old Party leaders:

Comrades of the old leadership, we have to put the question to you: how is it that a Party of such revolutionary experience and with such standing in the international working-class movement could have countenanced these things?

No reply was forthcoming from the 'old' members of the Politburo.

The immediate steps to be taken in the light of the Commission's findings were clearly indicated by Novotný:

However, I suggest that we don't lop off heads, that we don't return to that. Fix the scales of punishment to fit the people concerned. If we don't cut off the head of the man at the top how, after all, can we behead the others? Somebody gave the orders. It was a system. So we should decide in proportion to guilt.

In the end the Commission lacked the courage or the determination to include in its report the question of the personal responsibility of those who had been members of the Politburo at the time. Consequently, for the time being its work served no useful purpose; indeed it was in a way a cloak for manipulating the Party Congress, since the excuse that 'things' were under investigation prevented any real discussion of the interpretation advanced by Novotný.

Novotný referred briefly to the deformed quality of political life during the period of the personality cult, with specific reference to the trials and the process of reassessment and rehabilitation. His statement was in line with the Politburo resolution of 27 November that 'the Congress report should refer to these matters in accordance with the November meeting of the Central Committee'. But, in view of the findings already known from the Commission's report, what he did was tantamount to misinforming the Congress and suppressing the established facts. As a result the subject received hardly any attention.

The section of the Twelfth Congress report on these questions reads:

In view of the gravity of the matter and with a view to writing *finis* to the personality cult in our country, a Central Committee Commission is studying all the documents of the day. Its findings will be concerned mainly with the conduct of the Party and the top leadership of the Party and Government, and finally it will consider individual cases. The inquiry has already confirmed that on the whole the assessment made at the Central Committee meeting last November was correct. This is further proof that our Party is resolved to deal uncompromisingly with any violation of socialist legality and to eradicate all remnants of the personality cult. (*Twelfth Congress of the CPC*, Prague, 1962, p. 66.)

Hron's comment on the work of the Kolder Commission, expressed in October 1968, shows that the Commission knew much more about the subject of personal responsibility than it disclosed.

In the course of the inquiry there were many personal meetings with Comrade Novotný; for example, a meeting at Lány before the Twelfth Congress, which I attended, recommended that some responsible functionaries of the 1950s – Bacílek, David, Köhler – should not be re-elected to the Central Committee and, more particularly, that they should not be elected to the Presidium or as secretaries. This recommendation was not carried out. (Documents of the Commission for Completing Party Rehabilitation, Information No. 5, Kolder's view of his Commission's work and Hron's attitude to this report, October 1968, p. 14.)

The next phase in the Commission's work dated, not, in effect, from the Congress but from the Politburo meeting in

November 1962. On 19 December Kolder informed the Commission about the discussion of its documents at this meeting; he also submitted a programme for the Commission's further work.

Some weak points in the reports were to be further considered. The aim was clearly to strengthen the arguments supporting Novotný's concept of responsibility for the political trials. Consequently Slánský's role in relation to Security, the Army, the Records Department and the Defence Department was to be re-examined. More substantial evidence was to be provided concerning Čepička's responsibility for judicial proceedings behind closed doors.

The programme was approved and a deadline for the majority of the tasks was fixed for January. The reports on the individual cases and the summary report were to be completed during February.

There are no records of the meetings held between 19 December 1962 and 7 March 1963, and no documents, apart from the register of those present, are in the files. Kunštátová, who did not attend these meetings, later put the following note in the files:

> During my absence minutes of the meetings held on 29 January 12 and 27 February and 7 March were to have been kept by my deputy, Comrade Müller. According to Müller and Kolder, the comrades decided not to keep minutes of these meetings. They said that mainly organizational matters were discussed.
>
> Papers which I received as a member of the Commission were passed on to the comrades for redrafting and some of them were handed to Comrade Novotný for his information.
>
> For these reasons no documents are enclosed.
>
> M. Kunštátová.
>
> (Commission II, Vol. 24, Section 499.)

It is unlikely that 'mainly organizational matters' were on the programme at that late date, because on 13 March the Commission was already discussing the chairman's address and the draft of its report. So the minutes omit the most important period of its work. This deficiency makes it impossible to reconstruct the process which produced the final wording of the documents submitted to the Central Committee meeting in April 1963.

The minutes of the meeting on 13 March at which the draft report was discussed state laconically: '3. The Commission's report. No important comments.' (Ibid., Section 501.) The address was to state more precisely whether leading officials had known that innocent people had been arrested, whether and how these things could have been prevented, and further to demonstrate Baštovanský's responsibilities in the cases of Husák and Clementis. Degrees of responsibility were to be differentiated and Gottwald's basic responsibility was to be stressed. Evidently the draft of the address had a fairly smooth passage. As these documents, apart from the introduction to the final report, were not discussed later by the Commission, it can be assumed that they were approved by this meeting.

The Presidium discussed this report on 26 March and again on 1 April 1963. The discussion on 26 March was divided into two parts. In the first, after an introduction by Kolder, the 'old' members of the Presidium spoke (Bacílek, Hendrych, Fierlinger, Široký, Dolanský, Jankovcová, Novotný). The effect of their contributions is summarized by the remark addressed to them by Hron in the second part of the meeting: 'Comrades, in my opinion, some members of the Presidium have not fulfilled the expectations of the Commission and have not helped to analyse its findings.'

Although the injustice of the verdict on Slánský is implied in the Kolder Commission's report, Novotný claimed that 'those deviations in the Party, his careerism, or that reading of *The Paris Prefect* I told you about and the methods used could really have earned him the rope'. Hendrych, like Novotný when discussing the Barák report in 1957, revived the antisemitic note. 'Really,' he said, 'there was something abnormal about Slánský's personnel policy; when we look at the Central Committee apparatus, particularly its Economic Commission, it's obvious it wasn't normal. They were all Jews. That's how it is.' (Commission II, Vol. 35, Section 542.) No member of the Presidium opposed these views.

While Presidium members knew the basic facts about the trial and the reassessment, the question of responsibility was, in effect, narrowed down to a small group (Gottwald, Zápotocký, Čepička, Barák, Bacílek, Köhler, and, in part, Široký). Kapek, Dubček, Lenárt, and Kolder were not satisfied with this.

The discussion continued on 1 April, when the draft resolution and conclusions were submitted to the Presidium. Along with exchanges on phraseology and factual accuracy, the question again arose of the political responsibility of those in the Party leadership who had been members at the time of the trials and later when they were reviewed. Even if most of them admitted responsibility each construed it in his own way. Novotný, for example, announced towards the end:

> If the Presidium declines responsibility, I shall announce resignation at the next meeting of the Central Committee. Comrades, is this possible? Comrade Bacílek, you were Minister of the Interior. You are silent. That really is the limit. Tell me, how can you act like this? (Commission II, Vol. 35, Section 543.)

In this atmosphere and under mounting pressure a resolution was finally adopted on Bacílek, Köhler and Gustav Bareš. At the close, Dolanský asked to be relieved of his office. Some members of the Presidium, Fierlinger for example, regarded this as a 'provocation' and 'demonstration'. The resolution then carried in this atmosphere was submitted to the Central Committee on 3 and 4 April. These decisions about the 'living' remained more or less on the lines proposed by Novotný.

The Central Committee meeting opened with a speech by Hendrych on agricultural production in the regions and districts. Only towards the end of the first day did Novotný present 'a report on the violation of Party principles and socialist legality during the personality cult'. In the evening copies of the Commission's report were handed to the members. They were not allowed to take it out of the building and were required to return it immediately after reading it.

On the second day the chairman, Hendrych, announced that there would be a 'discussion on Comrade Novotný's address and on agriculture'. (File 01, Section 89, minutes of CC meeting, 3 and 4 April 1963.) Kolder spoke first, as chairman of the Commission. Then there were various contributions on the trials and on agriculture. Later, with a series of speeches by long-standing members of the leadership (Široký, Dolanský, Köhler and Fierlinger) a new note was introduced, although the discussion was still interlarded with other contributions. The discussion was wound up by Novotný who, after the resolution had been passed, proposed changes of personnel. It can be said that the whole course of the meeting was dominated by Novotný. It was chaired by Hendrych. Dubček, Hron, Lenárt, Emil Chlebec, Jankovcová, Vratislav Krutina and Škoda were denied the opportunity to speak; they presented their contributions in writing.

The main measures agreed in the resolution were:

1. To confirm the expulsions from the Central Committee and the Party of Slánsky, Šling, Reicin and Taussigová.

2. To confirm the expulsion from the Central Committee and dismissal from their posts of Švermová, Smrkovský, Lomský, Nový, Moškovič, Novomeský, Husák, Fuchs, Dubová and Clementis. To deprive Geminder [retrospectively] of his post.

3. To restore Party membership to Frank, Švermová, Smrkovský, Geminder, Lomský, Polák, Fuchs, Frejka, Löbl, Margolius, Husák, Novomeský, Nový, Dubová, Simone, Moškovič and Clementis.

4. To expel from the Party Kopřiva and Čepička. (Ibid.)

The meeting further resolved to recall Bacílek from his post as First Secretary of the Slovak Communist Party and as a member of the Presidium of the Central Committee of the Czechoslovak Communist Party. He was allowed to retain his offices as a member of the Presidium of the Central Committee of the Slovak Party, as a Deputy to the National Assembly and to the Slovak National Council. Köhler was recalled from his post of Secretary of the Central Committee and member of the Secretariat but allowed to remain a Deputy to the National Assembly. Bareš was to receive a Party reprimand.

The resolution also included the following:

On the basis of facts ascertained during the review of the political trials held between 1949 and 1954, the Central Committee resolved:

1. To approve the report of the Central Committee Commission empowered to review the trials of 1949-54 and its conclusions.

2. That in the light of the inquiry the following measures have to be taken:

(a) To tighten up systematic control by the Central Committee of the Ministries of the Interior and National Defence, the courts and the Prosecutor's Office: to establish the principle that the Minister of the Interior and the Minister of National Defence shall not be members of the Politburo.

(b) To instruct the Party Control Commission to settle the outstanding cases of Party membership in the light of the findings of the Commission empowered to review the trials and to report to the Central Committee.

(c) To instruct the Supreme Court and the Prosecutor-General to complete the judicial consideration of the remaining cases in accordance with the Commission's findings and to draw conclusions for the theory and practice of law in the courts and Prosecutor's Office.

(d) To instruct the Minister of the Interior systematically to implement in his area of jurisdiction the conclusions already drawn on the instructions of the Central Committee regarding the work of Security.

(e) To instruct the Minister of Justice to take the necessary steps to assist the families of those unjustly charged.

The Kolder Commission merits praise for its work. It helped very considerably to elucidate questions concerning the political trials, particularly individual cases. In a number of cases it led to complete legal and Party rehabilitation. It smashed the fabricated network of charges of hostile activity; it attempted to pose the question of responsibility and to suggest action in this respect. For the first time some serious steps were taken regarding the responsibility of Security and the judiciary. Thanks to this Commission the Party learnt the first authentic facts about the trials.

Although the Commission did much useful work it displayed a certain inconsistency. There may have been various reasons for this, but everything points to the fact that on the fundamentals it accepted Novotný's views.

The inconsistency of the Commission can be seen in:

1. Its choice of collaborators, for example Urválek, who had been directly engaged in the political trials, and Innemann and Kunštátová, all previously members of the Barák Commission.

2. Its handling of the Party rehabilitation of Slánský and

others; allowing Party penalties (expulsion from the Central Committee) to stand in a number of cases; maintaining the charge of bourgeois nationalism.

3. Its failure, knowing that the trials of Party functionaries had been illegal, to inform the Central Committee that the other political trials had been staged in a similar way.

4. Its one-sided and incomplete conclusions about political responsibility, which it restricted to a small group of officials, most of whom had already been in conflict with members of the Politburo and had been expelled from the Party.

5. Its ignoring of Novotný's responsibility as a member of the Political Secretariat and of the Political Commission for the 'Centre' trial and his responsibility as First Secretary of the Central Committee for the 'subsequent' trials.

We should mention in this connection that, when informing the Central Committee in May 1963 about the results of Party rehabilitation, Hendrych replied to questions and critical voices about Novotný's role by saying:

It was, in fact, because of his correct attitude to the harmful methods which Slánský and others introduced into Party work that Comrade Novotný was brought onto the Central Committee. That is the truth, and if we cast our minds back to Novotný's critical speeches we see that they were perfectly sound and there is no need to retract anything from them today.

What is more, I should like to add that after Comrade Novotný joined the Central Committee a halt was called to the common practice of submitting Party documents to Security, handing over members of the Central Committee to Security for investigation, and so on. (ACC CPC, File of the CC meeting.)

The Kolder Commission had collected sufficient evidence to disprove this information, which in fact can be qualified as deliberate misinformation.

The Commission frequently and unsuccessfully requested those leading functionaries who had held high office at the time of the trials to submit written reports and to assist the Commission. Discussions of the Commission's report in the Presidium in March and April 1963 were also fruitless. This was one of the reasons why, despite the Commission's valuable work, its inquiry into the trials, the responsibility for them and the process of rehabilitation remained a compromise.

As a result, the Party failed to come to terms with the tragic heritage of the political trials. The inquiry failed to signalize any fundamental change either in Party policy or in the composition of its top leadership. In this respect, the entire leadership elected at the Twelfth Party Congress and the Commission of Inquiry bears a share of the political responsibility. The degree of responsibility varies for different individuals, but it is undeniable.

The Kolder Commission did succeed in advancing matters, but it remained in effect merely one stage in the endeavour to make a clean break with the legacy of the trials and the period of violations of the law.

On 4 May 1963 the Secretariat approved the text of a communiqué on the Central Committee meeting and a press statement on personnel changes. The communiqué (no more than three typewritten pages) on the main conclusions of the Central Committee meeting stated:

It was appreciated that the Party had justly assessed the guilt or innocence of the functionaries dismissed at that time and that it had strictly differentiated between their cases. The whole truth has been revealed and the Party has gained new vigour in its struggle for socialism and communism. (ACC CPC, Commission II, Section 556.)

Then, on 7 May, the Presidium approved the final recommendations of the Commission of Inquiry. It instructed the Prosecutor-General and the Supreme Court to settle all matters concerning the imprisonment of wives and relatives of those rehabilitated; the Party Control Commission and Department I were directed to renew the Party membership and settle the personal affairs of these people. The Departments of Defence and Security, Department IX and the Party Control Commission were instructed to begin Party investigations of all employees of the Ministries of Security and Justice who had used illegal methods and violated the law.

Between April 1963 and the end of 1967, a total of 387 members were reinstated in the Party. A further forty victims of the trials had their membership restored at a meeting of the Central Committee on 3 and 4 April 1963. All those who were reinstated in the Party received financial compensation, and suitable accommodation was provided for them.

Between May and December 1964 Party penalties were imposed on forty-seven Communists employed by Security: four were expelled from the Party, sixteen received a reprimand with warning, ten a reprimand, sixteen were criticized at Party meetings, one application for renewed membership was refused.

On 1 August the Presidium approved a report on the responsibility of the judges, prosecutors and defence counsel who had taken part in the trials. Švach, Hloušek and Flajzar were dismissed and demoted to lower-paid jobs in the judiciary; another ten employees of the judiciary were downgraded and four lawyers were dismissed. (ACC CPC, 02/1, Section 32.)

The responsibility of the Communists among the legal assessors was judged at a meeting of the Secretariat on 20 December. It was decided that six should receive a reprimand, three a rebuke and the other eight should be criticized at Party meetings. The resolution was implemented.

By 16 July 1968 fifty-eight employees of the Ministry of the Interior had been dismissed and two demoted. The decorations conferred for services in the trials were confiscated in sixty-six cases: three Orders of the Republic, fifteen Orders of Labour and forty-eight awards 'For Fortitude'.

As in 1956, so now in 1963 attention centred on the position of Security in the penal system. In December the Politburo discussed a number of legal amendments to the penal and detention systems. The foremost legal experts were asked their opinion of these measures, and they unanimously recommended the appointments of examining magistrates who should be independent of Security and the Prosecutor's Office. However, their suggestions were not accepted, and the Politburo approved only changes of an organizational nature. Investigators attached to the Prosecutors' Offices were to be responsible for a limited range of general indictable offences, but even then they were not to handle cases that had already been clarified by the police. No changes were made in the investigation of anti-State offences; they remained in the hands of State Security. (ACC CPC, File 02/1, Vol. 46, Section 50.) Despite the clearly stated resolutions of the Central Committee and the Party Conference of 1956, the essential part of the mechanism of the political trials dating from the 1950s remained intact – that of investigation, a stage at which evidence should be collected with maximum objectivity as a basis for court decisions. This mechanism can again quite easily produce political trials built on violations of the law, because no institutional safeguards have been set up.

The Kolder Commission was followed shortly afterwards by the 'Barnabite Commission' appointed to 'express an impartial political and ideological opinion on the justification for the criticism of bourgeois nationalism voiced at the Ninth Congress of the Slovak Party and after it'. This Commission was established by decision of the Presidium on 22 June 1963, its members being Jozef Lenárt (chairman), Vasil Bilak, Rudolf Cvik, Matej Lúčan, Jozef Való, Viliam Šalgovič, Bohuslav Graca, Petr Colotka, Josef Macek, Ivan Skála, Jaroslav Kladiva, J. Šimek and Miroslav Klír. When on 17 September Lenárt became Prime Minister, Koucký took over the chairmanship of the Commission, to which Sabolčik and Laštovička were coopted.

Why yet another Commission of Inquiry? In the first place, because the Slovak Communists, who had been only partially rehabilitated by the April Central Committee meeting, were demanding genuine rehabilitation and, in the second place, because the matter had really become a national issue in Slovakia. Criticism of inconsistency in tackling the problem was voiced not only at Party meetings but also in the press; the Slovak Communists regarded it as part of the rehabilitation of the Slovak nation and the Slovak Party. Even the dismissal of Karol Bacílek and the election of Alexander Dubček as First Secretary of the Slovak Party failed to halt this movement. Although Novotný and other members of the Presidium tried to prevent the complete rehabilitation of the Slovak Communists convicted of bourgeois nationalism, they were gradually compelled by the pressure of public opinion in Slovakia and the hard facts amassed by the 'Barnabite Commission'[1] to change their standpoint. Speaking in Košice on 12 June 1963, Novotný was still able to launch a strong attack on Husák, Novomeský and others.

In the eyes of the Party, they remained guilty of violating the principle of Party unity. . . . My view is that the criticism of nationalism in Slovakia, expressed at the Slovak Party's Ninth Congress, was substantially correct; in many respects it was not, however, properly substantiated and it was not justified in all details. (Novotný, *Works*, Vol. 3, pp. 231 and 236.)

The 'Barnabite Commission' had not really been expected to do more than confirm this view, but its inquiries led it to the conclusion that the charge of bourgeois nationalism had no justification. In September the Central Committee resolved to recall Široký from his post of Prime Minister and proposed Lenárt in his place.

With the cooperation of many experts, the 'Barnabite Commission' examined an enormous quantity of documentary material, court files, summaries of evidence and so on; it heard evidence or read statements from prominent politicians and State Security officers, and its findings – set forth in a thousand-page document – provided the basis for a report to the Central Committee in December 1963. The meeting adopted a resolution on the re-examination of the criticism of bourgeois nationalism, made at the Ninth Congress of the Slovak Party; the charges were described as unjustified, having been fabricated and based on invented charges and the tendentious exaggeration of mistakes. The Central Committee resolved to annul the decisions adopted by the Czechoslovak Central Committee and the Slovak Central Committee in 1950–51, whereby Comrades Husák, Novomeský and Clementis had been expelled from the Party and dismissed from Party and Government posts. The Czechoslovak Central Committee also stated that their terms of Party and public office had expired after the termination of the electoral period.

The case of the 'bourgeois nationalists' and their rehabili-

[1] *The name was taken from the St Barnabas Monastery in the Prague Castle district, now adapted as a luxurious State hotel where the Commission worked.*

tation was in many ways a classical example, although it had its specific features.

The search for bourgeois nationalists inside the Party, as well as the charge of bourgeois nationalism made at the Slovak Party's Ninth Congress, was a prologue and ideological groundwork for persecution and legal proceedings. In this respect, the case of the 'bourgeois nationalists' followed the typical procedure of the trials. Its particular features were the long intervals between the links in the mechanism (general accusations, definite charges, indictment, legal proceedings) and the fact that its repercussions affected the entire Slovak nation.

The rehabilitation of the 'bourgeois nationalists' proceeded in the reverse order. What had been the last link in the first mechanism (the legal proceedings) became the first link in the rehabilitation process. It was not until January 1968 that the Slovak Communists who had been the victims were accorded full and proper political and moral rehabilitation.

THREE

POLITICAL RESPONSIBILITY

THE apportioning of political responsibility, which forms the third part of the Report, derives from our examination of the sources of the illegal trials and of the failure to make a proper reassessment.

Two rehabilitation commissions appointed by the Party's Central Committee have already examined the matter. The basic failure of the 1955–7 Commission lay in its proven disregard for facts, while the 1962–3 Commission was inconsistent in its findings and neglected to make an overall analysis of the causes underlying the trials. In both cases the work and the findings were influenced also by political expediency, i.e. by the immediate interests of the Party leaders and of the policies they were pursuing from positions of power. Consequently the Report issued by the 1957 Commission placed the responsibility on Slánský and the other victims, with some on Čepička; while in 1963 the onus was put on Slánský, Čepička, Kopřiva, Barák, and to a lesser extent on Bacílek, Köhler and Bareš.

If we are not to be faced with renewed rehabilitation proceedings at some future date, consistent application of the following measures will be needed:

1. Complete rehabilitation in the political sense for all the Communists wrongly condemned in the political trials, expelled from the Party, from its Central Committee and other committees or institutions for crimes they never committed; the Party must provide them with the necessary material and moral support and suitably acknowledge their revolutionary services.

2. Definition of the political responsibility of the Party and Government bodies concerned in the trials and in the incomplete reassessments, together with the personal responsibility of the members of these bodies or members of the executive

apparatus who gravely violated the laws of the Republic, and their duty as members of the Communist Party.

Any attempt to apportion political responsibility must proceed from an analysis of the causes that produced the trials and of the mechanism that made them possible.

Uppermost in the initial phase were the external factors, if only because of the prevalent attitude to Czechoslovakia's place in the socialist camp. The trials took place at a time of keen conflict between socialism and imperialism, when war seemed imminent.

A consequence of regarding the Soviet system as the model for social change in Czechoslovakia was both an uncritical acceptance by the Czechoslovak leaders of Soviet experience in the ideological, economic and political spheres, and a readiness to respond to particular pressures emanating from the Soviet Union and from the People's Democracies. While the nature of these pressures varied with the concrete situation, it is true that when it came to reviewing the trials these external influences, especially with regard to any criticism of the evils of the past, played a much lesser role than in the days leading up to the trials. Since from the archive material so far available in Czechoslovakia it has been possible to discover only the nature of the external factors, but not their underlying causes, it remains for further historical research to tell us more.

While the part played by these external factors is significant insofar as it reinforces the internal factors, it in no way absolves the latter from responsibility, but merely adjusts the balance. The atmosphere of the time was one of class struggle and political tension, accompanied by anxiety about the future of socialism in the country and by fears that hostile forces were at work even in top places in the Party and Government. Hence the suspicion and mistrust that prevailed in public life. A feature of the Party's internal life was the prestige enjoyed by Gottwald and his leadership, which gradually developed into an attitude of uncritical faith and readiness to obey orders. Nor should one overlook the potentially strong sectarian trends in the Czechoslovak Party, which powerfully influenced its policies and tactical approach. The history of the Party after February 1948 was marked by over-simplified political attitudes, with the

theory of intensified class struggle reinforcing the sectarian
and dogmatic line of policy. This course led automatically
to the point where legality and Party principals were violated.

Foremost among the internal factors was the deformed
political system, which rapidly evolved into a centralized
bureaucracy and, ultimately, into one-man rule. The defects
of this system became evident when the very first moves
towards the trials were being made. The main defect was the
failure of the system to prevent political mistakes from being
exaggerated to the point where they became equated with
treason; indeed, the system actually facilitated this transition.

The main feature of the centralized bureaucratic system was
the concept of power as the prerogative of the Communist
Party, and the way this 'leading role' was exercised. All
political, economic and ideological power became concentrated
in the hands of an ever smaller group, thereby excluding any
division or control of that power. In assuming governmental
functions, the Communist Party usurped the sovereign status
of the organs of State. The more power is exercised independently of State and the Law, and the more another organ of
power assumes the role of government, especially in administering justice, the farther such a system has advanced on the
road to violation of the legal order and, ultimately, to disregard
for its own laws.

Those institutions that in the past were designed to, or
actually did, supervise the exercise of power, now became
levers obedient to the will of the ruling group. A political
system of this kind could not but breed disrespect for the law.
A select ruling group was then free to usurp power in defiance
of the Constitution and to pave the way for illegality. Paradoxically, this absolute concentration of power did not give
the ruling group a free hand, because it was restricted both by
the external circumstances and by the political system itself,
which by its very weakness and ineffectiveness made it impossible for the rulers to wield absolute power; the result was
that they themselves became prisoners of the system they had
created.

An exceptionally powerful influence in producing this
type of system was the state of affairs in the Communist Party,

where a tiny group began to arrogate powers denied to it by the Party rules. This situation and the attitude to Party discipline made it possible for all the other links in the Administration to be converted into the instruments of the Party's will. Unquestioning obedience to orders from the top was the condition for Party membership and for holding any office, and failure to carry out orders was qualified as a sign of incapability or even of hostile intent. Hence the test was compliance with the ruling group, rather than agreement with the Party's programme and aims, with which indeed official policies were often in conflict. In connection with the political trials and the responsibility for them, this fact is of vital importance.

Approval for most of the trials and for the arrests was given by a Party committee, by the top group by a commission to which it delegated its power – or by a single individual (usually Gottwald). These decisions were in the nature of Party resolutions, or were regarded as such, and everybody who carried them out believed he was fulfilling Party resolutions. The fact that most of those who obeyed such orders were not aware that they were wrong and acted in good faith cannot alter this.

The political system and the type of organization which existed in the Party completely disrupted the natural links of political responsibility. With power concentrated in a ruling group that controlled all appointments to top posts, the men who exercised executive power were answerable only to this top group and not to the offices where they worked or to the people who had elected them. This pattern of responsibility was vitally important in the matter of the trials. The decisions about the trials were made by the ruling group in defiance of the Constitution, and the people who carried out its orders were, directly or indirectly, responsible to it alone. There was, therefore, no question of holding responsibility, but simply of shifting it as required onto someone else's shoulders.

Moreover, this deformed political system created its own ideology to justify its existence and its practices. A long, hard road had to be travelled before the public consciousness awoke to the truth about a system that was defending itself with weapons of both ideology and power – coercion and censorship; indeed, the final awakening was not to come until twenty years later, in January 1968.

True, over the years the system established in the early 1950s changed its forms and its personnel, but its basic features – concentration of power in the hands of a small group with strong trends towards one-man rule – remained until 1968. From the moment the groundwork had been laid, the logic of things led to a situation in which no one was safe from the machine, with the result that many of those who had helped to build it later became its victims. On the whole, however, the leadership had been stabilized by 1955-6, by which time the main wave of trials had subsided, and the ruling group that emerged had been associated with those events. Similar changes took place in other parts of the mechanism that had produced the trials, and here, too, the personnel was by 1955-6 more or less stable. Most of the people concerned remained within the machine which, after its work of staging the trials, was integrated into the political system and assumed a new function – the making of decisions about reviews of the trials.

It is also necessary to differentiate between responsibility for the trials as such and for the procedures in reviewing them. The verdicts at the trials were unjust, yet the sham reassessments up to 1962 actually reaffirmed the guilt of many Communists, and did so at a time when the top leaders already knew the truth about the fabrications; once again, in short, they were resorting to illegal practices.

The Commission recommends that the following principle be established: that none of the Party leaders, Security officers or members of the legal profession who had any part in preparing and conducting the political trials, or in the so-called reassessments of 1955-7, shall ever again hold high Party or Government office or work in Security or in the legal profession.

RESPONSIBILITY OF PARTY AND
GOVERNMENT INSTITUTIONS

In the system of political offices, direct responsibility for the trials and the events associated with them rests primarily with the inner Political Secretariat (its members having been Gottwald, Slánský, Široký and Zápotocký), and from 6 September 1951 with the Political Secretariat (which consisted of Bacílek, Čepička, Dolanský, Gottwald, Slánský, Široký, Zápotocký and, from December 1951, Kopecký and Novotný). The responsibility of this Political Secretariat is chiefly that in contravention of the Constitution and the law it took power into its own hands and, in the last resort, approved the preparation, conduct and findings of the main political trials.

However, the supreme power group that had arrogated to itself the main voice in decision-making was often restricted to a few members of the above-mentioned bodies – a matter decided by the Chairman or the First Secretary of the Party Central Committee, who thereby ensured reliable support for the regime of personal power. The members of this select group, whom no one had elected, were the men who had usurped the function of decision-making and the authority of elected bodies (the Presidium and the Central Committee of the Party), and they bear the heaviest responsibility for the trials and for all that happened in the country in those days.

The members of the Presidium, however, do bear full responsibility for this state of affairs in that they supported and carried out this policy, which gravely violated socialist legality and the standards of Party life. The Presidium is also responsible for having discussed and endorsed the measures taken in the Olomouc, Karlový Vary and Brno cases, and the arrest of Slánský and other Communists. Its members knew about the wholesale arrests, yet no case is known of any one of them expressing doubts about what was happening, even though many of their fellow Presidium members were involved.[1]

---

[1] The members of the Presidium were: Bareš (dismissed in January 1952), Baštovanský (dismissed in January 1952), Václav David, Dolanský, Ďuriš, Erban (dismissed in January 1952), Fierlinger, Frank (arrested in

The top political bodies at the time of the trials also included the Secretariat[1] of the Central Committee and the Organizing Secretariat attached to it.[2] The responsibility of these bodies lies mainly in their having looked on passively while Party members were suffering unlawfully, and in their having grossly infringed the Party rules; they shared also in the handling of cases involving Party members, they acquiesced in the transfers to Security and took part in implementing measures directed against innocent victims and their families. Moreover, they conducted ideological and propaganda campaigns in connection with the trials.

A measure of political responsibility rests also with those Party committees and commissions which in one way or another helped to prepare and organize the trials, to victimize the families of the accused and to cause the long delays over the restoration of Party membership to the victims of persecution.

January 1952), Gottwald (died 14 March 1953), Jankovcová, John (dismissed in September 1953), Kliment (died 22 October 1953), Kopecký, Krosnář, Kopřiva, Nejedlý, Nosek, Slánský (arrested in December 1951), Smrkovský (arrested in April 1951), Široký, Švermová (arrested in February 1951), Zápotocký. Bacílek and Čepička were elected to the Presidium at a Central Committee meeting on 6 September 1951. At a Central Committee meeting on 6 December 1951 Novotný was elected; in January 1952 Harus was coopted by the Presidium; on 4 September 1953 Tesla was elected by the Central Committee.

[1] Members of the Secretariat of the Central Committee in 1949–51 were: Bareš, Baštovanský, Frank, Gottwald, Kopřiva, Slánský and Švermová; Köhler and Pastyřík cooperated *ex officio*, and in 1951 David. Following the Ninth Party Congress the Organizing Secretariat consisted of members of the Secretariat, together with Geminder, Sova, Kolský, Hejzlar, Novotný, Nový (arrested in November 1949), Procházka, Pavel (arrested in February 1951) and Kapoun, and from January 1951 Zupka, Köhler, Pastyřík, Hendrych, Papež, Kolář, Koucký, Hruška and Valouch.

[2] The Organizing Secretariat elected by the Central Committee on 6 September 1951 consisted of: Bareš, Baštovanský, David, Frank, Gottwald, Hendrych and Novotný, and from 23 January 1952 Tesla, Uher and Voda-Pexa. In January 1953 its members included the Central Committee secretaries Baramová, Hradec, Köhler, Krutina, Nečásek, Šalga (the last two until 4 September 1953), Tesla, Voda-Pexa and Gottwald – following Gottwald's death Novotný. On 4 September 1953 Novotný, Köhler, Krutina, Voda-Pexa, and on 14 September Bacílek, were elected secretaries of the Central Committee and as such formed the Organizing Secretariat.

The Security Commission of the Central Committee[1] played a big part in 1949–50 in preparing the trials and establishing the mechanism of judicial procedure behind closed doors. It not only discussed the measures preparatory to the main trials, but also the verdicts to be handed down. It bears a share of responsibility for the work of Security, including the departments immediately concerned with the trials.

The Party Control Commission was involved through certain aspects of its work. In handling matters of an internal nature, it frequently resorted to Security measures – measures incompatible with the standards of Party life. It transmitted information to Security, and suggested stronger action, including Security action, against some Party members – for example, during a check-up in the heavy engineering industry, action against officials in foreign trade, in Security etc. The net effect of all the Commission's work was to thicken the atmosphere of suspicion, fear and unlawfulness. The gravest responsibility is borne by its leading members – Kapoun, Taussigová, Bína, Hora – together with the staff and the Party men in charge of the Commission's work – first Kopřiva, later Köhler.

Some sections of the Party Central Office shared in preparing the trials. The Records Department, and later a section of the Department for State Administration, obtained information about Party members and communicated it to Security. Some of the staff attended interrogations of Communists, or helped in the preparatory work (this occurred in the initial stages, 1949–50). The Department was headed by Šváb, later replaced by Oldřich Papež and Květoslav Innemann.

The Personnel Department, too, supplied information to Security and, in turn, received information from it. Members of the Department took part in 'screenings' of Party members and in Party interrogations – for example, after Šling's arrest. The head of the Department was Kopřiva, and later Köhler.

Some of the staff in the Secretariat of the First Secretary of the Party selected material from the Central Committee archives for use by Security; these materials, intended as evi-

[1] Members in 1949–50 were: Slánský, Nosek, Veselý, Šváb, Závodský, Rais, Čepička, Reicin and Pavel.

dence against leading Party members, were supplied mainly for the trial of the 'Centre'. This work was performed in 1951 by Marie Kunštátová. Complaints about the trials reached the head of the First Secretary's Office, Jan Svoboda, but he failed to pass them to the appropriate committees.

There were also the commissions set up in connection with the different trials.

The Commission for the Field–Pavlík case, for example, conducted interrogations of a combined Party and Security nature. The following Party and Security men took part: Kopřiva, Šváb, Závodský, Veselý, Milén, Čech, Papež, Pechník, Žižka, Dolanská, Pimpara, Šmolka, Hruška, Hrbáček, Mikušík, Brumhofer and others.

Kopecký, Köhler and Bareš formed the Commission of Inquiry into the Šling–Švermová case; it obtained information through Party and Security investigation and interrogations. It submitted to the Central Committee an untruthful and subjective report, which had a damaging effect on the further investigation of the case, aggravated the already highly charged atmosphere of suspicion and confirmed the attitude taken by Security. After Šling's arrest, the staff of the Personnel and Records departments checked up on all Party officials who had known him and recommended their dismissal. This work was directed by Köhler and Mrs Baramová.

The Political Secretariat set up three commissions for the trial of the 'Centre'. One edited the indictment, although such procedure was illegal. Its members were Bacílek, Čepička, Kopecký and Rais. The Political Commission, which supervised the conduct of the trial, consisted of Bacílek, Čepička, Kopecký, Novotný and Rais. The Press Commission that operated during the trial had the following members: Köhler, Koucký, Prchal, Taufer, Klos and Doubek.

Similar work was performed by commissions of the Central Committee for preparing the trial of the 'bourgeois nationalists'. Members of the Commission for the Indictment were Bacílek, Rais, Benada and Gažík; of the Political Commission, Pavol David, Klokoč, Michalička, Melichar, Moučka and Gešo.

The main burden of responsibility for the outcome of the 1955–7 reassessment of the political trials falls, on the political side, on the group forming the Politburo. In 1954–8 its members were Bacílek, Barák, Čepička (to 20 April 1956), Dolanský, Kopecký, Fierlinger, Novotný, Široký, Zápotocký; candidate members, Jankovcová and Šimůnek. Their responsibility is shared also by the two 'Barák Commissions'. Commission 'A' consisted of Barák, Innemann, Košťál (to 15 August 1955), Švach, Kunštátová; Commission 'C' of Barák, Bakula, Hruška, Innemann, Mlýnek and Kunštátová. Their responsibility is the greater because by their decisions on the reassessment they, in effect, repeated the trials. On their initiative and in the light of their resolutions the victims were, for the most part, condemned anew; true, the sentences were lighter, but this was at a time when both the political leadership and the members of the commissions knew perfectly well that the trials had been fabricated. It is regrettable to note that, although aware of the facts, those politically responsible ranged themselves on the side of the perpetrators of illegality, and that while their attitude to the innocent victims was somewhat milder than before it was nevertheless still unjust and inhuman.

The Central Committee of the Communist Party of Czechoslovakia must, as a body, also be held responsible. In 1951, at its meetings in February and December, it endorsed the main trial. In 1957 it discussed the matter of reassessment and approved the Barák Commission's report, thereby reaffirming the condemnation of innocent people. In 1963 the Central Committee returned for the third time to the trials. True, the Committee was never fully and accurately informed on these matters; it, too, was an object of political manipulation by the top men. Only in this sense can it be said that the Central Committee bears no responsibility. Yet it does bear responsibility for never trying to assert itself as an institution of the Party. There is no case on record where a member questioned the correctness of a decision in relation to previous decisions. The members of all three Central Committees, of the Presidium, and of other leading bodies that decided about the trials, simply gave their assent to three different sets of decisions, demonstrating thereby that they lacked the qualities needed for high positions in the Party and Government; insofar as they still occupy such posts, they should be released from them. Political responsibility is held by members of the Central Committee elected at the Ninth, Tenth and Eleventh Congresses of the Party. It is necessary to take into account, however, that some of the members elected at the Ninth Congress were subsequently brought to trial, or resigned their membership. Of the ninety-seven members elected at the Ninth Congress, twenty-two had their membership terminated, of whom fifteen were arrested; a further seven resigned. Those arrested were Slánský, Clementis, Růžena Dubová, Josef Frank, Vítěslav Fuchs, Gustav Husák, Hanuš Lomský, Koloman Moškovič, Vilém Nový, Josef Pavel, Josef Smrkovský, Otto Šling, Marie Švermová, Jarmila Taussigová, František Vais; those who were recalled or resigned included Bareš, Baštovanský, Hejzlar, Homola, Kapoun, Procházka, Ludvík Svoboda, Šmidke, Babej, Erban, Gregor and Oldřich John.

Although the Central Committee of the Slovak Party and its executive bodies played no decisive part in framing the trials of the bourgeois nationalists, their compliance and the encouragement given to the campaign by many of their members make them responsible for violating the Party rules and socialist legality. This applies primarily to the Presidium in Slovakia. In this case, too, the principle should be applied that those who were members of leading committees in 1950–54 and who still hold such positions today should not be allowed to remain in top Party positions.

Besides the Party institutions, responsibility belongs to those State bodies that participated in staging the trials and later in reviewing them.

First place, carrying a grave burden of responsibility, is taken by those departments of State Security that were engaged in preparing and holding the trials and in reassessing them, and which also constituted important elements in the mechanism that produced the trials. This does not apply, however, to Security as a whole, nor to other departments of State Security.

The Security departments came to the fore when they had the accused in their power. They conducted the interrogations, wrote the reports and prepared the prisoners for trial. They used illegal methods, including physical and mental coercion, they falsified written evidence and extorted 'confessions'. The prime responsibility for these methods and for fabricating the trials lies with Security, and especially with its top officers. It is impossible even briefly to describe all the methods used, but they can be characterized generally as violations of the law.

Security officers 'accompanied' the accused right up to the moment when sentence was passed. They stage-managed the main trials and compelled the accused to memorize the parts allotted to them. Other Security departments were in charge of the convicted men even when they were serving their sentences.

Naturally these officials also shared in creating the atmosphere of suspicion and fear. The evidence they procured about their victims was circumstantial, based largely on the 'confessions' made under duress; these 'confessions' were then used as grounds for arresting other Party people, and it was on the basis of this information that the top officials made their decisions.

Chief responsibility in the Security sector is borne by the successive Ministers of the Interior, later of National Security. The measure of their responsibility stems not only from their official position, but also from the fact that they were well aware of the illegalities. Some of them were directly involved in these practices and, far from taking action to stop them, they sided with the perpetrators, never with the victims. None of the Ministers of the Interior or of National Security who held office up to January 1968 made the slightest effort to have charges brought against those Security officers whose illegal methods had resulted in the deaths of prisoners; on the contrary, they hindered the judiciary in dealing with such cases. At the time of the trials and their reassessment the successive Ministers were: Václav Nosek, Ladislav Kopřiva, Karol Bacílek and Rudolf Barák. It should be noted that no Minister of the Interior or Security over the years 1949–62 ever suggested a thorough review of the trials or advocated rehabilitation of the victims, although they were aware of the fabrications on which the whole affair had been based. Attempts made in this direction by Barák in 1954–5 were nullified by the work of his Commissions 'A' and 'C'.

All the Deputy Ministers of the Interior and Security played a leading part, especially those responsible for State Security and the command staff of that service. No member of Security who in any way shared in work connected with the trials can ever again be allowed to serve in Security units. This principle applies also to Security men who took part in the Barák and other commissions (those for instance, investigating the cases of Field–Pavlík and Šling–Švermová), and to Party representatives who held leading posts in State Security during the 'reassessment' of 1955–7.

In the case of the judiciary, too, responsibility for the trials belongs to the sections involved and not to the profession as a whole. Certain officials of the judicial system bear a major responsibility for the sham reassessment in 1955–7.

The trials saw the emergence of a system of administering justice behind closed doors. The guilt of the judiciary in this respect lies primarily in allowing itself to be used as an executive arm of the political system and of Security, thereby lending its decisions a semblance of legality and professionalism. Yet the members of the legal profession involved in the trials could not but know that they were violating the law. They contributed in no small measure to the concealment of the truth; in fact it fell to them to put the finishing touches to the work of Security and the politicians. By its conduct during the trials, the judiciary delivered a crushing blow to the authority of the law and to public confidence in the administration of justice; the onus lies with them for turning the court proceedings into a theatrical performance in which judges and prosecutors played undignified and irresponsible roles – the very opposite of their true calling. No excuse that they were misinformed can lighten this grave burden of responsibility; whatever substance there may be in that argument, it is the duty of the courts to ascertain the truth, and the very preparation and staging of these trials should not have failed to arouse doubts. Insofar as some prosecutors and judges advance the argument that the accused had, after all, confessed and there was no reason to disbelieve them, it should be borne in mind that some refused to 'confess', and of this the courts took no account; they handed down the sentences previously agreed in political quarters.

The judiciary bears an even greater responsibility in the matter of reassessing the trials. For here, too, they acted as usual behind closed doors, indeed in even greater measure than before. Even more serious is that, from 1955 on, officials at the highest level knew, or were in a position to know, how the trials had been staged, and who had taken part in these illegal proceedings; yet they did nothing to promote the truth, although this is their prime duty. Indeed, their attitude to the men guilty of unlawful actions made a mockery of the law. Another point is that the Prosecutor-General's Office and the Supreme Court had received dozens of complaints concerning the illegalities of the trials, together with demands that they be re-examined. Rarely, however, was there any response.

The Supreme Court acted as an instrument for relaying Party decisions. Where the political trials are concerned it made no independent effort to right the wrongs, although this was its duty under the law. On the contrary, during the reassessment it again made decisions, on Party instructions, that contravened the law. This applied primarily to the first phase of the reassessment in 1955 and in subsequent years.

The Prosecutor-General's Office and its conduct can be equated with that of the Supreme Court.

The responsibility for introducing the system of judicial procedure behind closed doors lies firstly with the constitutional officials – Ministers of Justice Čepička, Rais, Škoda, the President of the Supreme Court Urválek and the Prosecutor-General Bartuška. A heavy burden of responsibility rests also with the deputies of these officers of State for their share in all these practices. The same goes for the members of the commissions set up by the Ministry of Justice to prepare the trials, decide how they were to be staged and fix the sentences. Nor can we exclude the prosecutors, judges and defence counsel who officiated during the trials, contravened the law and prevented the truth from being established, or who, acquainted with the facts, failed to act in accordance with them. The responsibility is the greater in the case of those officials concerned with the review of 1955–7, for by that time they had abundant information about the illegalities and did nothing to redress them. If law and justice are to prevail it is essential that all members and officials of the judiciary who shared in any way in the trials and in the reassessment of 1955–7 should never again be employed in any positions connected with prosecution, the courts, lawyers' offices or in the Ministry of Justice, because they have by their past actions gravely injured the standing of law and justice.

For the trial of the 'Centre' the services of expert assessors were used. As directed by Security and by Minister Bacílek in person, these assessors produced reports backing up the faked charges of sabotage in industry and in the Armed Forces. One notes with surprise that the majority of these people failed to withdraw their false reports when the trials came under review in 1955–7 and, what is more, that a group in the Planning Office even recommended that the charges of 'sabotage' be extended to include Dolanský [then a leading Party spokesman on economic matters]. 'Experts' reports' were also used in the trial of the 'bourgeois nationalists' and of Army officers.

No less essential than the political rehabilitation of the Party is that of the State and its constitutional institutions.

The President of the Republic was responsible, in exercising his extensive powers, for appointing the Government, the Prosecutor-General and many officers of State. He was also in a position to influence effectively the general lines of work done in the Government, the National Assembly and the other constitutional bodies. Gottwald, Zápotocký and Novotný all held presidential office at the same time as they represented the Party. This combining of State and Party functions cannot, however, free the office-bearers from responsibility for the gross abuse of their position as Head of State in the matter of the trials and their reassessment, for they also had the power to commute sentences.

The Government – the supreme executive body – included the Ministers of the Interior (later National Security), National Defence and Justice. From 1952 to 1960 the Prosecutor-

General was responsible to the Government. Under the Constitution the Government as a whole and its individual Ministers are answerable to the National Assembly. Yet there is no known case of the Government having considered the trials and their reassessment with a view to examining the procedure and responsibility of the Prosecutor-General or of the Ministers concerned.

The National Assembly – the supreme legislative body – never called the Government or individual Ministers to account for the illegal acts brought to light when the trials were reviewed. From 1960 the Prosecutor-General was directly answerable to the National Assembly, while the President of the Supreme Court submitted reports on his work. The National Assembly never called to account those officers of the law who were directly involved in the trials and their reassessment, nor did it ever examine their conduct in this respect.

It is undeniable that the top men of the Party and the members of its Central Committee were simultaneously members of all constitutional bodies. All of them regarded their functions as Party tasks and were conscious that their first responsibility was to the Party and its leading committees. This, however, does not imply that in carrying out their Government functions they were not answerable to the people, whose representatives in the State they were. This should be given full weight when assessing individual responsibility.

In weighing the extent to which the various officers were responsible for the trials and the failure to reassess them properly, we are dealing with only one aspect of their roles. Yet since, in addition to violating both the law and Party standards, the trials introduced a state of lawlessness that affected the entire community and spread with the expansion of the centralized bureaucratic system to undermine the humane principles of socialism, an impartial assessment of political responsibility is an urgent, indeed the fundamental task of the present Commission.

PERSONAL RESPONSIBILITY OF
LEADING OFFICIALS

The political system and its built-in mechanism for holding political trials constituted a complex apparatus of Party and Government in which individuals and institutions were cogs obediently performing their set roles; these roles were allotted to them from the moment when they became links in the apparatus. The system functioned as a whole, the influence of its individual members varying with their posts; since reshuffles took place from time to time, the standing and consequently the responsibility of individuals might vary from one phase to another. [With this qualification, three degrees of responsibility can be established:]

1. Within the system there were posts that invested their holders with the role of pathfinders, initiators and leading ideologists. These men bear the greatest measure of responsibility.

2. Second place belongs to those who formulated the basic line, making suggestions to the creators of the system without being in a position to decide whether their ideas would be used in policy-making, but merely implementing those adopted; that is, they worked on the executive side of the Party and Government apparatus.

3. The third and largest class consisted of those who merely carried out orders. Here the range of responsibility is wide indeed, but broadly speaking the class can be divided into two groups:

(a) those who in working along the lines set by the system had sufficient information at their disposal to enable them to pin-point the abuses ['deformations'], and yet went meekly ahead; and

(b) those who lacked this information and carried out their instructions in good faith.

Assessing political responsibility for the trials does not imply judgement on political activity as a whole, but only on its negative aspects. Seen in this sense, the 'evaluation' is one-sided, because almost all those involved are men who have devoted their lives to Party work and have done much for the Party and for society. It is not the purpose of the Commission to advance a comprehensive evaluation of individual politicians; we are concerned solely with their relationship to the trials and to the reassessments.

In the matter of individuals we have confined ourselves to those members of political committees and institutions directly involved in the trials, i.e. members of the Political Secretariat and those members of the Politburo who in 1955–7 played a direct part in the trials or in their reassessment. In the case of people due for rehabilitation, and of those who occupied leading posts in the judiciary and in Security, a fuller evaluation of their responsibility is appended to this part of the Report[1] (Köhler, Bareš, Kopřiva, Rais, Bartuška, Škoda, Urválek, Taussigová, Reicin, Šling, Šváb).

As Chairman of the Communist Party and President of the Republic, Klement Gottwald occupied during the 1950s the highest posts in the Party and State. No major step either in the Party or in affairs of State was taken without his knowledge and consent. He was also aware of matters concerning the political trials. He gave his consent to the arrest of high-ranking officials and to the sentences passed on them. From this standpoint he bears full and major responsibility for the trials.

Gottwald's responsibility should be judged also from the standpoint that as President of the Republic and Party Chairman he had the fullest opportunity to discover the facts about methods of interrogation; he initiated and helped to construct the entire political system; he took part in concentrating power in the hands of a select group – to the point where that power could no longer be kept under control; he submitted completely to the view, current at the time, of the Party's leading role whereby it arrogated to itself direct control of functions that belonged to the Government and State bodies. The result was a system that inevitably bred illegal practices.

Although Gottwald's responsibility for the trials cannot be minimized, the above formulation of it is somewhat one-sided. For the trials were only a part of his work, and they are linked

[1] *This section is missing.*

with the last four years of his life. Certainly his personality cannot be judged wholly from this standpoint. It is a historical fact that Gottwald stood at the head of the Communist Party from the early 1930s, and one cannot conceive of the Party's growth, its successes and its difficulties alike, without him. Over the years he came increasingly to the fore as an outstanding personality in Czechoslovak politics and in the international Communist movement. The years 1944-8 marked the peak of his political achievement, his contribution to the victory of the working class and of the socialist course in Czechoslovakia. He proved himself in those days to be an experienced statesman, an organizer of the people's democratic power, a leader of the working people.

After February 1948 Gottwald continued to make sound decisions; but gradually these came to be outnumbered by negative actions, notably by his part in the trials. With hindsight one can see that Gottwald changed after those February days when his political acumen was so much in evidence. The growing isolation in which he found himself bore down upon him, his health declined and, losing the will to fight, he accommodated himself to his environment and to circumstances.

So it was with the trials. Gottwald was under pressure from without and at first he tried to resist, and to avert the looming tragedy. Yet he lacked perseverance and courage in the fight – though admittedly he had little reason to believe he could be successful. By degrees his initial resistance to pressure was replaced by retreat and passivity and, later, by his incomprehensible participation in the actual preparation of the trials. And it is here, in his attitude to the trials, and notably to the victims, that we have the clearest reflection of the duality in Gottwald's personality. On the one hand human feeling, on the other acquiescence in the inhuman treatment of his associates; on the one hand long years of friendship with many of the victims, on the other the incredible hostility he displayed even towards their children.

Gottwald was a politician of his day – a Czechoslovak Communist of the Stalin era. There were times when he was successful in recognizing Czechoslovak realities; yet he also revealed the Stalinist traits which, during the Cold War period, became so pronounced a feature of his make-up. At first he had tried to fight, to resist the pressures from within and without, but now he lacked the courage and, evidently, the strength to carry on. Having submitted, he was fated to witness, and indeed to make a substantial contribution to, the biggest political trials in post-war Europe. Yet he battled with himself and it would be difficult to guess the force or the nature of this struggle. What we do know for sure is that the trials were his tragedy too, casting a shadow over the last years of his political career. Still, while his career was stained towards the end by his major responsibility for the trials, deriving from his position at the head of the Party and of the State, this, as we have said, was just one part of his work; he remains an outstanding figure in Czechoslovak politics.

Antonín Zápotocký was an official of many years' standing in the working-class movement and in the Communist Party, a man whose whole life was devoted to the working-class struggle for power and socialism. Among the founders of the Communist Party, he was closely associated with all its work. He held many posts in Party and Government, rising from a humble office-holder to be President of the Republic. His political career and the evolution of his views were not without complications, and more than once he had been criticized for right-wing and opportunist deviations; these charges had left him with something of a 'complex' that continued to influence his political attitudes after February 1948 and during the trials.

Zápotocký's responsibility for the trials derives from his place in the top Party leadership, as Prime Minister and, later, as President of the Republic. This grave responsibility he shares with Gottwald, both for the trials and for the 're-assessment' of 1955–7. During the 1950s he was one of the three or four most powerful politicians – the men, that is, who had the final say about the arrests and the trials. He was relatively well-informed about what was happening, and all the basic political decisions made in those days, mainly by the Political Secretariat, came fully within the sphere of his responsibility. He was President when the 'subsequent' trials took place, including that of Osvald Závodský. No instance is known where his view differed from that of the others.

When holding the highest office, Zápotocký received from the innocent victims complaints about the methods of interrogation and extorting confessions. In some instances he informed the Political Secretariat about the complaints, but added that he rejected the statements.

While frequent requests for a review of the trials came to the President's Office during 1955–7, we have no evidence that Zápotocký disagreed with his colleagues on this matter. He was one of that select group of leaders who in 1955 were acquainted with Doubek's testimony, and therefore knew that the trials had been faked. Yet he supported and argued in favour of the theory that Slánský was the Czechoslovak Beria. In 1956, when the Twentieth Congress of the Soviet Communist Party was in session in Moscow, he supported the view that rehabilitation was not a matter for discussion. One of his arguments was that this was a closed chapter, that no one would benefit were the Party to launch out on a reassessment. He was anxious, too, about the possible economic effects of any move towards rehabilitation.

In 1953–4 he already knew something about the problems affecting Security personnel; he called attention to them, but of course no steps were taken. He advocated the reopening of particular cases and opposed some arrests (for example, of certain Social Democrats).

For Zápotocký, too, the trials and their reassessment were only a part of his life's work. Although his grave political responsibility cannot be minimized, this should not be the sole measure of his work. In his case, too, the personal tragedy is magnified by a lack of courage and strength to grapple with these matters when the facts became known. Although the whole chapter of the trials casts a shadow over his career, Zápotocký has earned a leading place in Czechoslovak political life and in the country's revolutionary movement.

The name of Antonín Novotný is associated with almost twenty years of the complicated post-war history of the top political and Government bodies. Novotný belongs to that small group of office-holders who played a part both in the trials and in the reassessments, and he therefore bears his share of responsibility for both, a responsibility deriving primarily from the posts he held – a secretary of the Central Committee, later its First Secretary, combined finally with the office of President of the Republic.

In September 1951 he was elected a Central Committee secretary, working in the Organizing Department; on 6 December of that year he was elected to the Presidium, with membership of the Political Secretariat. From then on he was one of the special group holding the monopoly of power and decision-making on all major issues.

Novotný's responsibility for the political trials, and for the handling and results of the subsequent reviews and of rehabilitation, derives particularly from the following circumstances.

He joined the Central Committee staff and became a member of the top Party committees in the autumn of 1951, when the machinery for fabricating the trials was in full operation. While not among the chief originators of the 'Centre' trial, he was, as a member of the Presidium and the Political Secretariat, soon involved in preparing the trials, and he knew all about them.

As a member of the Political Secretariat he was present at the meeting on 24 November 1951 that endorsed Slánský's arrest. His share in preparing the trial was that of a medium for passing on to Security information contained in the Central Committee archives and designed to secure conviction of the accused.

On 13 November 1952 he took part in discussing the draft indictment in the case of the 'Anti-State Conspiratorial Centre'; he was elected to the Political Commission set up by the Political Secretariat to supervise the trial.

Novotný was First Secretary of the Party when eight 'subsequent' trials were held. In 1953 and 1954 the general situation differed from that of 1950–52. Nevertheless, the trials in Czechoslovakia went on. In these circumstances the Party committees bear a still greater responsibility, and Novotný, as First Secretary, holds the largest share.

This was a time when the Political Secretariat had a mass of documents before it concerning the final handling of the 'subsequent' trials. Usually this information came from the departmental Minister, Barák, who was not then a member of the Secretariat; the documents were submitted to the meetings by Novotný in his capacity as First Secretary.

Novotný, clearly, was not one of the chief men concerned with preparing the 'Centre' trial, but he did take part in its final phase. Subsequently, in 1953–4, by right of his office as First Secretary, he was present at the discussions of almost all the 'subsequent' trials and was fully acquainted with the circumstances. There is no documentary evidence to suggest that his views differed in any way from those endorsed by the Political Secretariat.

Novotný bears a big share of responsibility for the conduct and results of the reassessment and rehabilitation. Although there are isolated cases where he tried to alleviate the sufferings of victims, he never advanced the demand for a thorough-going rehabilitation, and he was most vehement in his opposition to any rehabilitation of certain men with whom he had had disagreements in the past (Slánský, Šling, Landa).

The failure over the years to review the trials adequately owes much to his influence. While the proposal in January 1955 that the Politburo should set up the Barák Commission came from him, so did the proviso that the Commission should confine itself to examining the severity of the sentences. He submitted the proposals for the membership of both Barák Commissions, including men whose immediate concern was that rehabilitation should not take place and others who quite obviously were not equipped to go all out to correct the distortions. Several documents show that Barák consulted Novotný about the more important cases considered by both Commissions, before submitting them to the Politburo.

By the second half of 1955 at the very latest, Novotný knew perfectly well from Doubek's testimony how the trials had been staged. He therefore bears the major responsibility for the failure to rehabilitate innocent people in the years 1955–7. On 23 December 1955 he submitted the outlines of a report to the Central Committee reviewing some of the cases. Contrary to the already established facts, he gave a false account of the causes and nature of the trials, and even advanced new and unfounded charges against many of the victims. In speeches after the Twentieth Congress of the Soviet Party, Novotný came up with a revamped version of the indictment in the Slánský case, depicting him as the Czechoslovak Beria; he also made fresh charges against Smrkovský, Švermová and others. At a Central Committee meeting on 20 April 1956, when he announced that a new Commission, again headed by Barák, had been set up to re-examine the Slánský trial, he outlined its terms of reference with the remark: 'It is already clear that we shall not carry out any rehabilitation in the case of Slánský and others.' He agreed to the Politburo passing a resolution on 19 November 1956, whereby the release of people convicted in the trials was halted and rehabilitation was for all practical purposes brought to a standstill. There is not a single document from the time of the Barák Commission to indicate that Novotný ever criticized the unsatisfactory examination of the trials.

He suppressed the opposition of those who had criticized the failure to rehabilitate, and at a Central Committee meeting held on 2 October 1957, and again at a conference on 6–7 October, he denounced his critics as 'factionalists' and even took a hand in Party and other sanctions against some of them.

When some of the cases were reviewed in 1958–9, Novotný usually arranged that the Politburo should make the decisions, or at least be kept informed. The guiding principle in this reassessment was that the charges against people convicted in the 'subsequent' trials should be restated to enable the majority of prisoners to be released as having served their sentences. This was not rehabilitation – merely another illegal verdict of guilty.

Although the Political Secretariat decided that the Ministry of Security personnel who had committed illegal acts were to be called to account, the actual measures taken were paradoxical. True, the former chief of the interrogation department, Lieutenant-Colonel Doubek, was taken into custody on 12 July 1955 and held until 17 May 1957, before being sentenced to nine years' imprisonment (along with Captain Kohoutek). But by 17 December 1957 the Politburo was already discussing his case, with Novotný proposing that he be released as an act of clemency.

Novotný's responsibility for the perfunctory rehabilitation measures also derives from his office as President of the Republic. He withheld the large numbers of letters addressed to him between 1958 and 1962 by innocent victims and their families; only a few were shown to the Politburo, and these merely for information; he made no suggestions for re-examining cases, although the letters provided new evidence of illegalities and the fabrication of trials.

Novotný personally supervised the work of the Commission of Inquiry operating in those years; by a resolution of the Politburo, Dr Kolder was obliged to 'inform Comrade Novotný of the Commission's deliberations and to submit the conclusions regularly to the Politburo'. Thus, while not actually a member of the Commission, Novotný must be held responsible in large measure for the perfunctory nature of the rehabilitation and for the reluctance to assess the degree of personal responsibility for what had happened. From 1953 at the latest, he had at his disposal all the main documents of the trials, and subsequently those of the reviews of 1955–7 and 1962–3. By virtue of his office as First Secretary of the Party from 1953, and President of the Republic from 1957, he was at the helm of Party and State and was the best-informed man in the whole leadership.

Karol Bacílek was a member of the committees that decided about the trials and about rehabilitation. From September 1951 he functioned as a member of the Political Secretariat, from 1953 as First Secretary of the Slovak Party and from 1954 to 1963 as a member of the Politburo of the Czechoslovak Party.

In his office as Minister of National Security (January 1952–September 1953) and as First Secretary of the Slovak Party, Bacílek was deeply involved in the trials. A number of Party leaders (Josef Frank, the economists and others) were arrested in 1952, during Bacílek's period of office as Minister. He was particularly active in preparing the trial of the 'Centre'; he personally took part in interrogations, visiting the accused in their cells as a 'persuader'; it was Bacílek who submitted the draft of the indictment to the Political Secretariat, and it was he who instructed the expert assessors; he was Chairman of the Political Commission that handled the 'Centre' trial and a member of the commission for editing the indictment; it was Bacílek who supervised the conduct of the trial. He was to the fore also in managing the trial of the 'bourgeois nationalists', while his harsh treatment of those wrongly convicted extended to other trials as well.

When reassessments of the trials took place during Bacílek's term as First Secretary of the Slovak Party, he made no attempt to ensure a successful outcome of the inquiries or to obtain rehabilitations. True, he admitted at a Central Committee meeting in 1956 that physical force had been used by Security, but in later years he attempted to justify the trials of the 'bourgeois nationalists'. The leadership of the Slovak Party, which he headed, continued after 1956 to attack 'bourgeois nationalism', even to the extent of labelling as manifestations of nationalism criticism voiced by a number of Party members (Pavlík, Púll, Bráník and others). Nor did Bacílek make any contribution whatever to the 1962–3 rehabilitation.

Rudolf Barák headed the 1955–7 Commission for reviewing the trials. His recommendations conflicted with the facts that had been established by then. The 'subsequent' trials that took place in 1953–4 were also linked with his term as Minister.

At the time Barák became Minister of the Interior the Political Secretariat was receiving a steady flow of material concerning the findings of the 'subsequent' trials of the remaining 'enemies' in the Party.

The bulk of these reports was submitted by the departmental Minister, Barák, who, not being at the time a member of the Presidium or of the Political Secretariat, passed on the materials through the First Secretary, Novotný.

The 'Barak Commission' was not intended to approach the subject of rehabilitation through objective assessments of individual cases. Its function was merely to examine instances of over-severe sentences, avoiding any tampering with the main trial of Slánský and others. As chairman, Barák steered the Commission from two angles. First, he was the link with the

Politburo, making verbal reports on the latter's meetings and decisions. He consulted some of its members, notably Novotný and Zápotocký, and either passed on their views or implemented them in directing the work of the Commission; one result of this was that not a few of the draft documents were suitably amended.

Secondly, by virtue of his office as Minister of the Interior, he defended the Security sector at Commission meetings and transmitted the views of his advisers during the sessions of the Commission; as Minister he was in a position to obtain (and did obtain) more detailed information on particular cases; on his instructions a special group of Ministry officials was engaged in assembling this information and preparing briefs for the Commission.

The facts established during the re-examination of cases and during the investigation into the conduct of Doubek and Kohoutek were of such a nature that there could be no doubt that the 'Centre' trial was a monstrous fabrication.

Barák was also responsible for suppressing many of the correct conclusions arrived at by members of the two commissions that he headed. To secure acceptance for new interpretations of the victims' guilt he produced written statements procured from his Ministry. In the more important cases he personally amended and rewrote the draft findings. In both commissions, he often intervened to ensure that the original charges were extended in the reports, or at least maintained. On the other hand, there is no evidence that Barák ever made any effort towards the full rehabilitation of innocent people – on the contrary, in December 1955 the Commission recommended to the Politburo that consideration be given to arresting the two remaining Party members alleged to have been members of the 'Trotskyist Grand Council' who were still at liberty. In 1957 he wanted to penalize one of the interrogating judges who in 1949 had refused to obey instructions. His voice was raised solely on behalf of ex-employees of State Security, and in 1957 he declared that 'to bring Doubek and Kohoutek to trial would be tantamount to clearing Slánský, Taussigová and Šváb'.

Alexej Čepička, as one of the top men in the Party and

State, helped to prepare the trials. Within the ruling group Čepička occupied a special position: in July 1951 he deputized for Gottwald in talks with Stalin concerning Slánský; he was a member of the commission that drafted the indictment and of the Political Commission in charge of the trial of the 'Anti-State Conspiratorial Centre'. On many occasions at the time he bitterly attacked Slánský and his fellow accused.

Čepička's responsibility derives not only from senior positions which he held within the Party, but also from his office as Minister of Justice and, later, of National Defence.

During his term as Minister of Justice he initiated the practice of judicial procedure behind closed doors. As Minister it was he who, from December 1949, submitted to the Security Commission of the Party's Central Committee, of which he was a member, proposals for verdicts in the political trials. The Commission endorsed or amended these proposals, and the Minister saw to it that they were carried out – for which purpose the backroom judicial procedure was established.

Military matters figured largely in the trial of the 'Conspiratorial Centre' and were the main theme in the subsequent trials of generals and other officers of the Czechoslovak Armed Forces.

From 1950 accusations were levelled against the former Army Command, their volume keeping pace with the difficulties encountered in a hurried drive to build up the Forces; the climax came with the military experts' reports prepared for the 'Centre' trial and for the subsequent trials of former military men. The resultant report ('Final Report on Sabotage and Subversion in the Armed Forces'), was prepared by a commission headed by General Kratochvíl; the Commission took its instructions from Čepička, who was acting on a decision of the Political Secretariat. It should be added that the campaign against the former Army Command was launched by the top Party people in the Army long before Čepička took office.

Čepička was fully informed about the cases of former officers under arrest, and he cooperated with the Ministry of National Security. Nevertheless, the documents available to date show that the initiative in staging the political trials of military men came from the Security side. Some members of the Army staff, now rehabilitated, stated in interviews that they wrote to Čepička from prison declaring their innocence but received no answer. Čepička did do something to redress wrongs and gross infringement of the law when steps were taken to undo the work of Bedřich Reicin and his associates; this was in the first half of 1951, when the Mírov forced labour camp, the 'Cottage' and other places were closed. These fairly extensive measures were well received by the Army staff.

Pavol David, as a member of the top Party committees, also bears responsibility for the distortion of socialism during the 1950s. He was among those who took a hand personally in preparing the trials. As First Secretary, and later as a secretary of the Slovak Central Committee, he arranged, mainly in 1952-3 at the request of Novotný, to have documents extracted from Party and other archives in Slovakia for the purposes of the Slánský trial. For the trial of the 'Slovak bourgeois nationalists', David headed the group set up to ensure that the proceedings went smoothly, and he displayed no little zeal and initiative.

Even when, as a member of the Politburo and a secretary of the Slovak Central Committee, he must have known that the trials had been rigged, David did nothing to hasten the rehabilitation of the innocent victims.

Jaromír Dolanský – one of the leading figures in the Party – held top posts from 1945 to 1969, and from this derives his share in responsibility for the trials of the 1950s. The minutes of the top Party committees that handled these matters, and of which he was a member, reveal only occasional contributions by him, so that it is difficult to form any real opinion of his attitude. Insofar as there are records, they suggest that Dolanský's views did not substantially deviate from those current at the time.

Dolanský was not a member of any commission or other appointed body directly concerned with the trials. All in all, it can be said that his responsibility is identical with that of the committees on which he served. When reviews of the trials were discussed he always agreed with the reports submitted and never queried the statements of the 'guilt' of the victims.

What is more, he concurred with the conclusions of the 'reassessment' in the case of the economists, although he knew that in this case, as in that of the 'Centre', the charges of economic sabotage referred to measures which, being decided by Party institutions, could hardly be classed as 'sabotage' by individuals.

Whenever he spoke in Party committees on reassessments or rehabilitation, Dolanský was always in tune with the current official line. This was the case, for instance, at a meeting of the Politburo on 28 December 1955. At meetings of the Presidium and of the Central Committee towards the end of 1962 and at the beginning of 1963, he spoke at some length in the discussions and, as usual, concurred with the report and whatever proposals followed, maintaining, in common with the majority present, that he had had no idea of the appalling facts now disclosed.

At that time Dolanský also threw out the suggestion to the Presidium that, in view of his political responsibility for the events of the 1950s, he should be allowed to retire from his leading posts.

In sum, it should be said that, while he shared responsibility, as a member of the leadership, for initiating the trials, he in his turn had charges levelled against him; during the Slánský trial especially he was blamed, in letters addressed to Gottwald, for shortcomings and errors in economic policy, whereby, it was said, he had enabled 'Slánský's gang of traitors' to disrupt our economy.

Václav Kopecký was not only partly responsible for the mechanism of fabricating the Czech political trials, but was also one of the creators of the accompanying ideology, who helped to dot the i's and to concoct propaganda. In 1948 Kopecký had had a share in the 'case' of Professor Kolman, and he also played his part in launching the trials of non-Communists.

In October 1950, after Šling's arrest, a commission consisting of Kopecký, Bareš and Köhler was set up by the Presidium to elucidate Švermová's relationship to Šling and his activities. The Commission's approach was patently prejudiced, and in winding up the inquiry Kopecký presented the Central

Committee, meeting in February 1951, with a mass of fabrications, idle gossip and irresponsible dramatics about the 'Šling–Švermová case'.

In his Book *Třicet Let KSC* ['Thirty Years of the CPC'], published in 1951, Kopecký contributed to creating the atmosphere of the political trials, helped to shape the seeming logic of their ideological background, and, in large measure, launched the 'war against the enemies in the Party'. Kopecký's view of the Party's record as depicted in this book and in other memoirs from his pen is completely suspect, for facts of both Party and recent Czechoslovak history are falsified in them.

He did not confine himself to ideological excursions, however, for he played a prominent part in investigating Rudolf Slánský's case and securing his conviction. Kopecký was, moreover, one of the chief inspirers of what was in essence an antisemitic campaign against Zionism and cosmopolitanism; he also shared, towards the end of 1952, in organizing the Slánský trial. He was a member of the commission set up by the Political Secretariat, on 13 November 1952, to produce the final draft of the indictment in the case of Slánský and his fellow accused.

Kopecký's responsibility for the trials derives also from his status as a member of the top Party committees that endorsed them; furthermore, he was a member of the bodies that decided about the reviews of trials, and he identified himself completely with the negative standpoint of 1955–7.

Rudolf Slánský's whole life was associated with the Party, to which he was devoted. In common with the entire leadership of the day, he had a profound faith in the Soviet Union. He submitted wholly to the authority of the Comintern and, later, of the Cominform, and was among the interpreters of their policies in the Czechoslovak Communist Party. Nor was he merely a passive exponent; he elaborated certain ideas and directives, notably at the Cominform meetings in November 1949 and during the Moscow talks in January 1951.

As a top Party man, Slánský played a big part in shaping the overall political line, and from 1949 onward he advanced theoretical arguments to support the intensification of the class struggle and the search for the enemy inside the Party.

Up to September 1951 he belonged to the innermost group in the Party, which meant, after February 1948, in the country. Until September 1951 he took an active part in the top leadership, intervening in the Administration and taking harsh and unjustified measures against real and imaginary enemies; until 1950 he took part in the campaigns connected with 'seeking the enemy inside the Party'.

Slánský was actively involved, for instance, in the Kolman case, and in the Karlový Vary case, where he was a member of the three-man commission that prepared the final draft resolution for the Presidium. At the subsequent meeting of the Presidium on 2 May 1949 he called for severe punishment on the grounds that the affair should be treated as an 'exemplary' case. As General Secretary he also decided, on 22 June 1949, that Tannenbaum should be arrested and investigated by Security.

Although as a leading Communist he knew all about the harsh treatment to which Czechoslovak nationals had been subjected in Hungary in connection with the Rajk trial, he nevertheless intervened to the disadvantage of the accused in the Field–Pavlík case in Czechoslovakia.

At a joint meeting of the Czechoslovak and Slovak Party Presidiums in the spring of 1950, Slánský attacked Clementis for alleged bourgeois nationalism.

He also shared in assembling the machine that yielded the evil methods used both in the Party and in the Government.

On all basic issues Slánský consulted Gottwald and without the latter's agreement never ventured to assume responsibility.

The Party Control Commission and the Personnel Department, which carried out investigations along Party lines, were directly subordinated to Slánský as General Secretary.

Slánský intervened in the workings of Security when he became Chairman of the Security Commission and when, in the autumn of 1949, employees of the Party's Central Office were transferred to that sector. Things went so far that by mid-1949 Slánský had, in effect, assumed the direction of State Security, thereby contravening the Constitution and the legal regulations; he did so without the knowledge of the Minister of the Interior. Along with a select few of the topmost

Party officials, he was kept regularly informed about Security plans and gave his approval to them. He was also informed in detail about progress in interrogating prisoners, he gave his opinion on various projected measures and, with the other members of the Security Commission, he participated in the backroom practices of deciding verdicts before cases even came to court. He also knew about the illegal methods used by military counter-intelligence and by State Security, but did nothing to stop them.

Viliam Široký's services in the fight for working-class power and in building socialism are indisputable. Yet this cannot conceal or wipe out his share of responsibility for the political trials of the 1950s, or for the distortions of socialist life throughout the country, notably in Slovakia.

Široký, as one of the ruling group in Party and State, was a member of the bodies that decided on the trials and on rehabilitation; from 1951, as a member of the Political Secretariat, and from 1954 to 1963 of the Politburo, he endorsed the indictments and proposed verdicts in all the trials; he was a member of the Political Commission responsible for the trial of the 'Centre'. He joined in the campaign of seeking the enemy inside the Party which led up to the rigged trials, being most closely associated with the trial of the 'bourgeois nationalists'. In fact, Široký must be held jointly responsible for fabricating the 'Anti-Party Group of Bourgeois Nationalists' against which unfounded charges of treason were subsequently lodged. He exerted all the weight of his undoubted prestige to persuade the Party membership to accept the allegations about bourgeois nationalism; he helped draft the indictment in this case, some of his amendments being included in the final version.

As a leading figure in the Slovak Party, Široký helped to assemble the machine for the trials in Slovakia. All appointments and changes in the Security force and the administration of justice were made with his approval. The decisions to arrest Slovak functionaries were made in the inner leadership of the Czechoslovak Party (the 'five') with Široký's participation (for example, in the cases of Moško, Baláž, Clementis).

Yet Široký himself fell under suspicion in 1949, and in 1952

Party and Security officials were busily collecting compromising material about him.

By the time of the reassessments and rehabilitation, Široký was still among the ruling group that decided these matters. But never did he use his knowledge to further the cause of rehabilitation. On the contrary, at Party meetings, especially at meetings of the Slovak Party, he persisted in trying to prove that the trials were correct.

CONCLUSIONS

Examination of the Czechoslovak political trials and the history of their reassessment provides valuable lessons for the present and grave warnings for the future. In the Communist Party and among the public generally insistent demands are made for guarantees against any repetition of such events, be it in different or milder forms. The Party leadership and the Government in its programmes have more than once proclaimed that a return to similar conditions will never be permitted. Yet these honourable intentions cannot be dependent on the goodwill or the wishes of politicians – they require the backing of built-in guarantees in the political system, in the mechanism that initiates, exercises and controls policy, and in the mode of exercising the Party's leading role.

The Party sees the creation of a system of guarantees against any repetition of the political trials as an inseparable part of its post-January [1968] policy, and part of its endeavour to eliminate the bureaucratic distortions of the political system. This will be a long-term process, in which the experience of the trials will certainly play its part. Realization of the measures will be further proof of the Party's resolve to make a clean sweep of all previous distortions, to ensure security before the law for all citizens, and to restore the authority of the Constitution and of the law.

As part of this system of guarantees society must be provided with the antibodies that will render it immune to distortions. Hence the greatest value attaches to the provision of as much sober and factual information as possible concerning the political trials, their causes and consequences, and the subsequent reviews of them.

The really effective prevention must come from the political system itself, for the centralized bureaucratic distortion to which this system has been subjected, and which produced one-man rule, gravely weakened socialism and resulted in the Communist Party exercising its leading role in a corresponding manner.

The system of personal power, which provided the political basis for the trials and decided the manner of their reassessment, culminated in such an enormous concentration of power that any division or control of its application was out of the question. All the countervailing levers – essential to any political system – and all the natural chains of responsibility, had snapped. The authority concentrated, initially, in the hands of a select ruling group passed gradually into the hands of one man – the representative of the Party and State. Nor was it only at the top that power got out of control – it was the same in other areas of government and administration (for instance, in the Security forces and in organs of power at lower levels). And in this violation of the Constitution and of the law we find one of the chief sources of all the illegal practices.

It is essential to note, however, that the system of personal power operated through a highly intricate mechanism and is not to be equated with the absolute rule of one man. The topmost leader could assert his power only through the machinery of Party and Government institutions, which usually acted as his obedient instruments, regardless of law or the rules of the Party. Without this machine, clearly, the system of personal power could not function. The system, moreover, led to the same crushing of democracy in the top bodies of Party and Government as had taken place in society at large. True, some of the operators of this machinery did their jobs in the belief that they were serving the cause of socialism, that they were doing the right thing; others were more interested in maintaining their social status; others again lacked the courage to speak up or considered the time was not ripe to do so, even though they knew or sensed that many decisions were wrong.

At every step Party people, including some at the very top, were claimed as victims by the regime of personal power.

These circumstances sapped men's courage to proclaim the truth; political argument, honesty in politics, a sense of responsibility of officials to their leaders, control over decisions -- all these things ceased to exist. And, in advancing ideological backing for its decisions, the system always invoked Marxism-Leninism, appealed to the working class and so on – all without the slightest justification.

Over its twenty years of power, the system assumed in successive phases two forms, determined by many factors, of which the person of the leader was all-important, though the situation in the foreign and domestic political arenas was also relevant. The feature of the first phase, often referred to as the days of the personality cult, was the natural authority enjoyed by the Party leader, Klement Gottwald, the confidence he commanded and the widespread belief that all his decisions were correct ones. Yet it was at this very time that the big political trials took place. With 1955–6 we have the advent of a second phase, with the system of personal power dominated by a man who, lacking any natural authority, resorted to different means to underpin his leadership; deploying, for instance, his own men, demoting potential rivals, providing incentives for certain officials, and so on. While at this time the political trials were on the way out, they had not yet ended. Similarly, the mode of government was milder, 'more democratic', but the law was still being violated; for the system could operate only by suppressing democracy and by flying in the face of the Constitution and the legal code.

If a democratic political system is to function, and if the system – that is to say, our entire society and the Communist Party – is to have built-in safeguards against future distortions, all traces of one-man rule must be obliterated and its revival in any shape or form prevented. Certainly the experience of the Czechoslovak political trials, and of their reassessment, provides useful pointers towards realizing this vital purpose.

The political system of our country is based, and will continue to be based, on the principle that the leading role is exercised by the Communist Party. The Party, however, and especially its leadership, should proclaim and consistently observe the principle that its leading role cannot be asserted in violation of the Constitution and the law. The Party should give this intention the weight of incorporation in its programme and should apply it to the full in drafting proposals to be submitted to the next Congress.

The principle also extends to the rights and duties of each and every member of the Party. A Communist has the right, and also the duty, not to abide by any Party resolution that violates the Constitution and the law; it will also be his duty to inform the higher Party authorities in the likelihood of such a situation arising. This in turn implies the duty of taking the necessary disciplinary measures when a case of this nature has been duly investigated. The Central Committee of the Party should be guided by this principle until Congress meets and should define it precisely in the draft rules to be submitted to Congress.

The Party regards violation of the law as a grave infringement of its rules, and it will take disciplinary measures in such cases. It will be especially strict with those whose professions make them responsible for ensuring observance of the law – for instance, members of the judiciary and Security officers. A similar attitude will be adopted towards those who fail to act when violations of the law are brought to their notice, or who even try to prevent measures being taken.

One of the leading built-in features of any political system should be a division of power and a corresponding freedom for State bodies to fulfil the functions assigned to them under the Constitution. The Party Central Committee should declare it impermissible for the sovereignty of the Government in the performance of its functions to be restricted in any way, and for any sector or area of decision that comes within its competency to be taken from it and transferred to some other, non-competent body.

The same principle should apply to the legislative assembly. In this case, Communist deputies should have the right, without laying themselves open to Party disciplinary proceedings, not to vote for any measures which, in their view, conflict with the Constitution and the legal code. It would be the duty of the deputies concerned to justify their stand to the appropriate Party committee.

The experience of the trials and of their reassessment reaffirms the absolute justification for firmly establishing the independence of the courts. In this respect the renewal of the constitutional and administrative courts is a sound step. The Party holds that it is inadmissible for Party bodies to intervene in court proceedings, to decide about their conduct and findings, or to delegate such powers of decision, which are a matter for the courts alone, to any extra-judicial body whatsoever. Communists in the judiciary are under the solemn obligation, in the event of such cases arising, immediately to inform the appropriate Party committees, which should then take the necessary action. The same procedure should apply where a Party or other institution shelters offenders from warranted sanctions, even if the offences are committed in fulfilment of decisions made by these institutions.

The Security Service occupies a vital and influential position in the machinery of power; the relationship of the Communist Party and its leadership to this Service is a crucial one, a relationship particularly liable to distortion under a system of personal power. The Party considers it impermissible for its committees to use Security dossiers in forming opinions and making decisions about anyone holding an official post; it is equally a breach of the Party rules for Communists employed in Security to use their positions to collect information, for use by the Party, about functionaries. Since this has been common practice in the past, with Security dossiers on Party members and functionaries placed in Party files, with Security in its turn holding Party dossiers, it is essential that each of the two sides should hand back to the other the appropriate files.

In view of the tragic sequel to the practice of searching for and compiling information designed to incriminate Party and Government leaders, and because this proved to be one of the loopholes that enabled Security to evade control by the proper authorities, it is now essential to adhere firmly to the principle that any compiling of dossiers and checking on members of the Party's Central Committee, the Party Control Commission, the Government and Members of Parliament is permissible only with the consent of the Prosecutor-General and after consultation with the First Secretary of the Party (acting for the Central Committee and the Control Commission), with the Prime Minister (for the Government) and with the President of the National Assembly (for Members of Parliament). The responsibility for ensuring that this procedure is observed rests with the appropriate Ministry of the Interior [that is, of the Federal, Czech or Slovak Government]; failure to adhere to this procedure would be seen as a grave breach of Party discipline and of ministerial orders – or possibly a law should be drafted. This principle should apply to the corresponding Party and Government bodies in the Federation.

Abuse of the Party's leading role signified a resort to coercion as the chief means of maintaining its dominant status in society. Similarly, the top echelons of the Party, where power was concentrated, consisted of a small group who had their hands on the vital instruments. To end this state of affairs it is essential that we arrive at a really well-considered structure for the top committees and that we introduce a system of control. The personnel of these committees should be such as to ensure that they are not dominated by representatives from the seats of power in the Party and Government and from the staff of the political apparatus. Further, it should be considered impermissible for any Party or Government body to delegate its powers of decision on important political issues, or its right of appointment, to any subsidiary bodies without ensuring proper control over their work.

A rota system in filling official posts would be a valuable safeguard against the concentration of power. The rule of the few made no allowance for a 'natural selection' for offices, with the result that only minor changes were effected in the membership of the leading committees – and even these were usually occasioned either by the death of the incumbent or by the 'punishment' of individuals. This circumstance, too, was a retarding influence on the reviews of the trials and the rehabilitation of the victims. Consequently, it is essential that the revised Party rules should provide for alternation of office-holders at all levels.

Democratic election to Party and Government offices is a

vital factor in the control of power. No one can be allowed to override democratic procedure or in any way obstruct democratic elections conducted in accordance with the Party rules and the Constitution of the Republic. Moreover, observance of the law is the prime duty of every Party member and any neglect of that duty merits strict condemnation by the Party.

The public organizations and the National Front as a body also have a part to play in the control of power. If they are not to lose this function, they must not allow themselves to become mere transmission belts.

The mass media share in framing policy and in its realization, and also in controlling it. Consequently, any restriction of the media weakens their power of control.

Considerable power of control over the executive is possessed by Parliament. The experience of the trials and the history of their reassessment underline the urgent need for control over the Security force and over all departments of the administration of justice, for these are the foremost instruments of power.

The Party itself has to find ways and means of controlling power. A guiding principle should be that no member of the Central Committee or any other body can be expelled unless the matter is first discussed by the committee concerned *in his presence*. Equally it is absolutely binding for Party members not to make statements in public – or in the Party – accusing other members of maintaining contact with the intelligence service of a capitalist country, or linking his words or actions with actions, interests or ideas emanating from the imperialist world or from any representative of that world, unless the charge has been substantiated and considered by the appropriate Party or Government office. Having learnt the bitter lesson of the trials, and knowing how the arrest of leading Party officials was preceded or accompanied by public accusations of working for the imperialists, the Party condemns such practices and will take action against anyone who may resort to them.

A real contribution to control over power in the Party would be to provide an opportunity for members and officials to exercise their rights and fulfil their duties, and this could also act as a safeguard against any attempts to manipulate members of committees. Democratic centralism – the guiding principle in Party organization – should so operate that the ability to act rests on a consensus of opinion. Resolutions made must be carried out, with committees responsible for their actions and policies to their members and to committees at lower levels.

At the time of the trials, ideological unity in the Party was insisted on to a degree that turned it into blind, unquestioning obedience to the directives and decisions issued by the leadership. To hold divergent views was classified as a hostile act incompatible with Party membership. Expulsion followed, and sometimes criminal proceedings. The trials contributed to this state of affairs, and this, in turn, generated more trials. The Party earnestly proclaims that no one shall be prosecuted for his political views or subjected to surveillance by the Security Service. Charges may be made only when there is evidence of an offence. Non-observance of this principle will be classified as a breach of Party conduct.

As interpreted in the 1950s, ideological unity ossified Marxist thinking and led to a severe restriction of the Party's functions, reducing it to an instrument for carrying out the orders of the group at the top, without any share in framing policy. Ideological unity, if it is not to become a tool for manipulating committees and members, or a mere means for getting orders obeyed, must be the product of conflicting opinions and of divergent views; unity has its place mainly in respect of the Party's basic aims as expressed in its programme or in the course agreed by its leading committees. But the members, or the committee, have the right to maintain a critical attitude even to a resolution that has been adopted; implemented it must be, and criticism may still be voiced only within the Party. After the past bitter experience the Party will never allow the demand for unity to be used as an instrument for realizing the anti-Party and anti-socialist measures embodied in the political trials. We can take warning from the fact that in the name of this unity, and in the effort to achieve it, many of the great values of our national history were trampled underfoot – values that could have provided a natural foundation for socialist reconstruction. Attempts were made to deny such values as the national liberation struggle, with its highlights in the Slovak National Uprising and the Prague Uprising, not to mention the humanistic content of socialism and other Marxist values. The counterpart to these attempts was the endeavour to unite the Party around views utterly alien to Marxism, involving such complete negations of socialism as antisemitism, the witch-hunt against 'bourgeois nationalism', the inhuman treatment of innocent victims and the declarations of 'hatred unto the grave', the glorification of lies, and the voices screaming for death sentences.

The drive to brainwash and to 'unify' was pursued through the mass media, backed up by Party propaganda until it overflowed into a mass psychosis directed against innocent Party and non-Party people alike. This mania helped enormously to create an atmosphere of suspicion in which the innocent were condemned on all sides. In these circumstances the ability to form reasonable opinions atrophied, facts were ignored, the victims had no opportunity to defend themselves – they were condemned in advance, against an ever-growing demand for maximum penalties. With this experience behind us, it is necessary to proclaim that the Party will do all in its power to prevent conflict of opinions and political struggle from reaching the point where they induce a mass psychosis fed by unjust or unproven charges against men in official positions.

Indeed, the entire experience of the trials and their aftermath indicates the need, in selecting functionaries and in all personnel work, to be guided by the qualities essential to a representative of the Communist Party. The trials and the system of personal power perverted the relationships among Party functionaries. Men who had been comrades for years and who had worked together became enemies overnight, hurling charges at each other, even to the point of imprisonment and execution. The men who were denounced or arrested were isolated, no one came to their help, although there were many who must have known that the charges were false; and they maintained this attitude even when they knew quite definitely that the trials had been rigged. Those who knew this were men who had lost their courage, their sense of truth, justice, and of human relationships. Under the system of personal rule, when men were selected for the highest posts they were required to obey without question, to serve the ideas and pursue the aims of the men who wielded power. When we speak of the prime responsibility resting with the system of personal power, we should bear in mind that the system was the work of the men – especially those at the top of the ladder – who turned it into flesh and blood and maintained it in being. When we choose administrators, therefore, we must, while requiring special skills and a devotion to socialism, give equal weight to such personal qualities as courage in upholding the truth and defending one's views, an aptitude for independent political thinking, and everything that shows a truly comradely attitude to one's fellows, friends and colleagues – a readiness to trust them, respect for human life and so on.

The Central Committee will apply the findings concerning the political trials and the history of their reassessment in preparing documents for the coming Congress, especially in its proposals for re-structuring the political system and for new Party rules. With the tragedies of the 1950s ever in mind, the Party will strive to establish a system of management in society that will bear the stamp of security before the law and strict observance of socialist legality. This will be the best proof that the political trials and all that they signified belong to the past, that such things are alien to socialism and to the policies of the Communist Party.

APPENDIX

DRAFT RESOLUTION ON THE COMPLETION
OF PARTY REHABILITATION, FOR SUBMISSION
TO THE CENTRAL COMMITTEE OF THE
COMMUNIST PARTY OF CZECHOSLOVAKIA

Over the past twenty-four years the foundations of socialism have been laid in Czechoslovakia. The results achieved during this phase of history are the product of the dedicated labour of millions of our people who of their own free wills, drawing on past experience and acting in the profound conviction that the way indicated by the Communist Party was the right one, chose socialism. The Czechoslovak Socialist Republic qualified for a leading position in the socialist camp and in the international working-class movement.

The time was a complex one, which involved pioneering in new lines of social development, and drawing on the first-hand experience and practice of other socialist countries, and of the Soviet Union in particular. Together with the progress recorded in those days there were also mistakes and shortcomings, so serious that they led to grave distortions in the structure and work of the Party, in the political system and in the system of law; included in these distortions were the political trials of the 1950s, the consequences of which have yet to be fully overcome. Only now has an atmosphere been created that enables this plenary meeting of the Central Committee to re-examine with the utmost objectivity, and in the light of the information now available, the political background to the trials that took place in the first half of the 1950s, to analyse their causes, conduct, consequences and impact on Party policy, and, as far as possible, to redress the wrongs inflicted on the victims.

For this purpose the Central Committee, meeting in April

1968, appointed a Commission to complete the process of political rehabilitation and instructed it to prepare the necessary documents and suggestions.

I

The Central Committee of the Communist Party of Czechoslovakia regards the political trials as the most grave distortion that took place during the building of socialism in the 1950s. This distortion of the Party, of the political system and of the legal structure had its source in the conditions accompanying the political struggle then taking place in the country, with working-class power emerging in the shape of the socialist State and with the laying of the foundations of socialism.

Czechoslovakia, a small country in the middle of Europe, has always been exposed to external influences. Her first steps towards socialism, especially after February 1948, coincided with the disintegration of the anti-fascist coalition and the accompanying formation of military blocs, that is, when the Cold War was at its height. The response of the newly emerging socialist camp to the moves of the imperialist countries towards military and economic integration, to the danger of war and to atomic blackmail, was to set about closing its own ranks, reinforcing its military potential and securing a reliable hinterland for defence in the event of a conflict.

Things were complicated by the developments taking place in the international working-class movement, where the promising unity born of the war-time anti-fascist struggle was now disturbed by the revival of the Socialist International with its hostile attitude to the working-class movement in the socialist countries.

Confusion was sown in the movement by Cominform policy in relation to Yugoslavia and its mistaken decisions concerning the Communist and Workers' parties.

Internal developments after February 1948 were characterized by the consolidation of working-class power, and by a policy of restricting and excluding capitalists from the seats of power, and completing the transfer of the means of production to socialist ownership. Reactionaries within and without did not relinquish their positions voluntarily; they resorted to sabotage, espionage, and even to acts of terrorism. As part of its defence the new working-class power hastened to build up its machinery of State – in the Administration, including Security, and in the nationalized economy. As a result of these revolutionary changes many young people, dedicated to socialism but most of them inexperienced, were given jobs in the Administration and in the economy. The endeavour to consolidate and extend the newly-won positions encouraged the centralistic trends in the Administration and in industrial management; soon a new integrated and highly centralized political system was established, a system suited, according to the ideas of the day, to fulfilling the function of the dictatorship of the proletariat.

The measurable political, economic, social and cultural success achieved during the first phase of the socialist reconstruction, actively supported by the majority of the working people, provided ample evidence of the remarkable viability of the socialist system; for the political leadership, moreover, it was proof that they were using the right methods. The steady concentration of power – Party, political and governmental – in the hands of a select group led, gradually, to a situation that precluded the exercise of any external or internal control over that power, and culminated in the demand for a blind faith in the political leaders. By degrees the Party committees assumed functions of State, thereby undermining the sovereignty of the State bodies they had themselves created. With the growing trend towards the exercise of power independently of the State and of the law, and with Party bodies assuming State functions, including the making and administering of the law (which when made and administered by any other authority than the State ceases to be law and becomes unlawful practice), the fateful step was taken that resulted in breaches of socialist legality and discredited the law of the revolution itself.

It was in this situation that Stalin's arbitrary theory about the advance towards socialism being accompanied by a corresponding intensification of the class struggle, and the theory of a single and unique road to socialism (all other roads being condemned), spread to those Communist Parties then controlled by the Cominform. According to the first theory, the most dangerous enemies would infiltrate the leading positions in the Parties, where, provided with excellent cover, they could do most harm. With the emergence of the community of socialist nations, enemy action came to be seen as an interlinked, complex affair extending to the leaderships of all the Communist and Workers' parties in power, as a permanent plot by the imperialist countries and their agencies. These agencies, according to the theory, existed in every Party; if they had not been discovered, the sole reason was that those whose duty it was to discover them were inexperienced and lacked the necessary vigilance.

In this atmosphere any official or employee who came under criticism for, or admitted, a political error was readily suspected of being involved in anti-Party and anti-State plots organized from abroad. The people most vulnerable to suspicion were those who for one reason or another had at one time resided in capitalist countries for long periods, those who had survived the Hitler death-camps and prisons, those who had served in the International Brigade in Spain and on foreign fronts during World War II, and those who had relatives abroad. After the second Cominform resolution on the Communist Party of Yugoslavia, anyone who had had official dealings with the Yugoslavs was strongly suspect. From the moment that, in pursuit of these ideas, political trials got under way in Poland, Hungary and other socialist countries, it was inevitable that our Party and our socialist State should likewise be drawn into this process of seeking, convicting and liquidating the 'enemies' inside the Party.

The political trials were a heavy blow to our socialist reconstruction. While it is true that these distortions of socialism were never the main feature of the social process, in time their impact began to be felt everywhere. The trials detracted from the success of socialism in Czechoslovakia, retarded it, damaged it in the eyes of its convinced supporters at home and abroad, and discredited the endeavours of the people. For long they frustrated every attempt to get to grips with the real causes of the political and economic difficulties facing our country; they sapped the will of Communists and the public generally to seek a more effective way of organizing the life of the community under socialism.

Later, when the fabrication of the trials had been incontrovertibly proved, the procrastination in reviewing them and the perfunctory rehabilitation of the victims had a similar effect. All who bear the political and moral responsibility for these trials, or for their belated and reluctant reassessment during 1955–68, have, objectively, caused grave injury to socialism, whatever their personal intentions may have been. This incompatibility between the whole business of the trials, including the failure properly to reassess them, and the ideal, cherished by the Party and the majority of the working people, of socialism as a humane system, constantly threatened to erupt in a social crisis; only by resorting to extreme measures did the leadership succeed in warding off this crisis. If socialism is really to advance, this chronic source of political tension must be removed by completing the process of Party rehabilitation and by providing, in the Party and in society generally, absolute guarantees against a recurrence in any form whatsoever.

II

The political system and the type of organization which existed in the Party resulted, in the atmosphere of the 1950s, and subsequently, in complete disruption of the links of political responsibility. With power concentrated in a top group that controlled all appointments to top posts, the men who exercised executive power were answerable only to this top group and not to the offices in which they worked or to their electors. This pattern of responsibility was vitally important in the matter of the trials.

Approval for most of the trials and for the arrests was granted by a Party committee, by the top group or by the appropriate commission. Their decisions took the form of Party resolutions which were binding, or regarded as such. All who carried out these decisions believed that they were fulfilling Party resolutions. Had they refused, they would have risked losing social and political status. The fact that most of those who obeyed such orders were not aware that they were wrong and acted in good faith does not alter this. The decisions about the trials were made by the ruling group in contravention of the Constitution and the legal code, and those who carried out its orders were, directly or indirectly, responsible to it alone. There was, therefore, no question of the responsibility deriving from the properly defined links, but simply of switching it to other shoulders as political expediency might require.

The ruling group consisted of the members of the top Party committees; that is, immediately after February 1948, the Presidium of the Central Committee, especially its inner Presidium, and the Organizing Secretariat, later the Political Secretariat (Gottwald, Zápotocký, Široký, Kopecký, Novotný, Slánský, Bacílek, Dolanský, Čepička), later replaced by the Political Bureau (Novotný, Zápotocký, Kopecký, Čepička, Bacílek, Fierlinger, Dolanský, Široký, Barák).

While it is true that over the years the system established in the early 1950s changed its forms and its personnel, its basic feature – concentration of power in the hands of a tiny group with pronounced trends towards one-man rule – remained until 1968. From the moment the groundwork had been laid, the logic of things led to a situation in which no one was safe from the machine, with the result that many who had helped to assemble it later became its victims. On the whole, however, the leadership had been stabilized by 1955-6, by which time the main wave of trials had subsided, and the ruling group that emerged had been associated with the trials. Some of them had consolidated their positions in the leadership as a result of the gaps caused by the trials; others got their posts for the same reasons. Similar changes took place in other parts of the mechanism that had produced the trials, and here too the personnel had become more or less stable by 1955-6. Most of the people concerned remained within the machine which, after its function of staging the trials, became integrated into the political system and assumed a new function – the making of decisions about reviews of the trials.

The Political Secretariat, established in 1951 as an inner committee of the Presidium of the Central Committee, assumed much of the authority previously reposed in the Presidium. However, the supreme power group was often restricted to a few members of these bodies – a matter decided by the Chairman or the First Secretary who thereby ensured reliable support for themselves. The members of this select group, whom no one had elected, were the men who usurped the function of decision-making which by right belonged to the elected bodies (the Presidium and the Central Committee), and with them rests the immediate and heaviest responsibility for the trials and for all that happened in the country in those days.

The Presidium members, however, bear full responsibility for this state of affairs since they agreed with and carried out this policy, which gravely violated socialist legality and the standards of Party life. Political responsibility for the trials and for the perfunctory nature of the rehabilitation process rests with the members of the Presidium and the Politburo at the time of the Ninth, Tenth, Eleventh and Twelfth Party Congresses.

A measure of political responsibility rests also with the Party committees and commissions which in one way or another helped to prepare and organize the trials, and to victimize the families of the accused. The bodies primarily concerned here were the Secretariat of the Central Committee, the Organizing Secretariat, the Security Commission, the Party Control Commission and some of the staff in the office of the First Secretary, and in the Records, Personnel and Security departments of the Party Central Office. Although from the complaints reaching them and from their interviews with individuals they must have known that the indictments had been fabricated, they never protested and never told the Party what they had learnt; these officials therefore bear a share of political and moral responsibility. The Central Committee accordingly resolves that those of the staff in the Central Party Office who between 1949 and 1952 had access to this information be removed from their posts – wherever this has not already been done – not only in the Party Central Office, but also in the corresponding departments of State, and for the same reasons as in the case of Security and judiciary officials.

Responsibility for the trials rests also with the members of the commissions that were empowered by the Central Committee to prepare documents and reports. This concerns the members of the commissions on the Field–Pavlík and Šling–Švermová cases, and those who took part in screening the people 'placed by Šling in various posts'.

A share of responsibility is borne by the members of the commission which edited the indictment in the case of the 'Anti-State Conspiratorial Centre', by the political and press commissions which functioned in this case and by similar bodies in the case of the 'bourgeois nationalists'.

A semblance of credibility was lent to the trials by the reports submitted by the assessors who handled economic, foreign trade and military matters. The responsibility of most of these men is the greater because, when the reassessment had established the falsity of all the charges, they did not come forward to withdraw their reports.

Political responsibility rests with all those committees and commissions that in 1955–62 were concerned with reassessing the trials, especially for their part in delaying the reinstatement in the Party of unjustly condemned Communists. This concerns the members of the Politburo in those years, members of the Barák Commission and of the Party Control Commission.

The first genuine and extensive rehabilitation was made by the Central Committee after hearing the Report of the 1962–3 Kolder Commission. But this Commission, too, failed to draw general conclusions and, being hampered both by the regime of personal power and by the limited information at its disposal, made no real effort to apportion political responsibility with any consistency. This Commission was supervised not only by Novotný but also by the Presidium, which twice had the matter on its agenda. The members of the Kolder Commission bear political responsibility for the inconsistency of their conclusions, which left some of the victims saddled with Party penalties for acts they had never committed. The members of the Presidium and the leadership of the Party Control Commission are responsible for failing to apply in full the resolution adopted by the plenary meeting of the Central Committee on 3 and 4 April 1963, and also for the action taken by the Presidium in implementing the resolution.

The Central Committee, too, bears responsibility as the

supreme authority in the Party between Congresses. (True, the Central Committee was never fully or accurately informed about the trials or the circumstances surrounding them; in this sense it, too, was an object of political manipulation. Its responsibility consists in its failure to assume its proper role in the matter of the trials as the supreme authority between Congresses – a role accorded to it by the Party regime – and in merely endorsing the line laid down by the inner caucus.) In 1951 the Central Committee twice, at its meetings in February and December, approved the holding of the main trial. In 1957 it discussed the reassessment of the trials and approved the Barák Commission's reports, thereby endorsing the renewed condemnation of the innocent. In 1963 it returned for the third time to the trials when it discussed the report of the Kolder Commission.

There is no case on record of a member questioning at these meetings the correctness of a decision in relation to previous decisions. The members of all three Central Committees, elected at the Ninth, Tenth and Eleventh Congresses, who decided about the trials, giving their assent to different decisions each time, have demonstrated that they lack the qualities needed for high positions in the Party and Government, and insofar as they still occupy these posts they should not be nominated for re-election to the Central Committee. Political responsibility rests with the members of the Central Committee as constituted by the Ninth, Tenth and Eleventh Congresses, and (in respect of rehabilitation) with the members elected at the Twelfth Congress.

Although the Central Committee of the Slovak Party and its executive bodies played no decisive part in framing the trials of the 'bourgeois nationalists', their compliance and the encouragement given to the campaign by many of their members make them responsible for violating the Party rules and socialist legality. This applies primarily to the Presidium of the Slovak Party in 1949–62 and also to members of its Central Committee. In this case, too, the principle should be applied that those who were members of leading committees in 1950–54 and who still hold such positions today should not be allowed to remain in top Party positions.

A considerable measure of responsibility rests also with the organs of State that shared in staging the trials and later in reviewing them.

The President of the Republic was responsible, in exercising his extensive powers, for appointing the Government, the Prosecutor-General and many officers of State. He was also in a position to influence effectively the general lines of work done in the Government, the National Assembly and the other constitutional bodies. Gottwald, Zápotocký and Novotný all held presidential office, while in addition Gottwald and Novotný served simultaneously as representatives to the Party. This combining of State and Party functions cannot, however, free the office-bearers from responsibility for the abuse of their positions as Head of State in the manner of the trials and their reassessment; moreover, they possessed powers to commute sentences and to proclaim amnesties.

The Government, as the supreme executive body, included in its membership the Ministers of the Interior (later of National Security), National Defence and Justice. From 1952 to 1960 the Prosecutor-General was responsible to the Government.

III

Having studied the Final Report of the Commission for Completing Party Rehabilitation, the Central Committee resolves:

1. To rescind the resolution of the plenary meeting of the Central Committee held on 3 and 4 April 1963 which re-affirmed the expulsion from the Party of Comrades Rudolf Slánský, Otto Šling, Bedřich Reicin, Karel Šváb, Eduard Outrata, Otto Fischl, Matyáš Lewinter and, of those still alive, Mikuláš Landa and Jarmila Taussigová, and to proclaim full Party rehabilitation of these comrades.

2. To annul the Party penalty of expulsion from the Central Committee and dismissal from official posts during the term of office concerned in the cases of Rudolf Slánský, Otto Šling, Bedřich Reicin and, of those still alive, Marie Švermová, Josef Smrkovský, Hanuš Lomský, Koloman Moškovič,

Vítězslav Fuchs, Růžena Dubová, and of dismissal in the cases of Bedřich Geminder and Jarmila Taussigová.

3. To instruct the Presidium to prepare for the information of the Party and the public a final report on completing the rehabilitation of those who suffered from the violation of socialist legality and of Party standards in the main trials. The report should indicate in what manner the decisions clearing those wrongly condemned, including Party rehabilitation, shall be made in public.

The Central Committee is guided in these decisions by the following principles:

(a) The comrades named were condemned in the political trials and, in consequence of the verdicts, expelled from the Party and deprived of their Party posts for acts that they never committed, as is irrefutably demonstrated by the reassessment of the trials.

(b) The reasons given for the Party penalties that were imposed at a later date, or for those reaffirmed by the Central Committee resolution of April 1963, related to acts that had no connection with those in respect of which the original sentences were passed. In all cases these were penalties based on charges that could not be linked in any way with the fabricated offences against the State for which the comrades had been tried.

(c) In most cases the Party penalties were imposed on these comrades at a time when they were unable to defend themselves. Party penalties cannot be imposed on men who, being dead, cannot defend themselves against charges subsequently levelled against them. Insofar as the Report now before the Central Committee has revealed that these comrades played an active part in the distortion of our political life, their share has been justly assessed by the Commission when discussing the responsibility of the other comrades concerned.

(d) The selection of the accused for the trials was an arbitrary operation, and anyone in public life could have become a victim. The resolution concerning full rehabilitation is therefore to be seen as the final refutation of the false charges produced at the trials.

IV

1. The degree of political responsibility and the role of the different institutions and their members in the mechanism that fabricated the trials of 1949–54 and the reassessments of 1955–62 show some differences. Some members of these bodies later became victims, that is, they were arrested or removed from their posts. Some who subsequently realized the causes and the consequences of the trials tried hard to put things right, speaking out for full rehabilitation of the victims and against the power system. Nevertheless, the principle that those who played a part in the trials of 1949–54 and in their reassessments of 1955–62 cannot be allowed to hold leading Party posts applies to the members of these bodies and their commissions (with the exception of those who were victims of the trials or were removed from their posts in 1949–53).

2. The members of different bodies bear varying degrees of responsibility. This could be expressed by the Party taking disciplinary measures in the case of those who bear the greatest responsibility for the violations of socialist legality.

The Central Committee decided at its plenary meeting in May 1968 to suspend the membership of Novotný, Bacílek, Pavol David, Köhler, Rais and Urválek – men whose share in the trials was indisputable, or who were concerned in the protracted and inconsistent reviews. The information available at the time about their actual share in and responsibility for these events did not allow of any clear definition of their guilt, nor was it possible to draw any definite conclusions. Now the Commission for Party Rehabilitation has assembled sufficient facts to enable the role of these men to be assessed from all aspects, and in the light of this assessment to decide the degree of responsibility from the Party standpoint.

For the purpose of determining the responsibility as Party members of those who have been suspended, the Central Committee hereby appoints a Disciplinary Commission consisting of the following members:

Chairman . . . . [left blank]

Members . . . . [left blank]

Within one month from the conclusion of the present meeting, this Disciplinary Commission shall submit to the next Central Committee meeting its proposals regarding the Party membership of the above-named comrades.

3. The Central Committee agrees that the members of those committees and commissions that actively participated in fabricating the political trials, and in the reassessments of 1955–62, and who are still in responsible Party and Government posts, shall be recalled from those posts.

4. The Central Committee resolves that at the coming Congress of the Czechoslovak Communist Party and at the Congress of Communists in the Czech Lands it will not recommend or nominate as members or candidate-members of the Central Committee or as members of the Party Control Commission anyone who has been, uninterruptedly since the Ninth Party Congress, a member of the Central Committee or of the Control Commission.

5. The Central Committee instructs its Presidium:

(a) to ensure through Party members working in the judiciary, the Prosecutor's Office and in State Security that any official in these sectors who shared in fabricating the political trials and in their perfunctory reassessment in 1955–62 shall never again be employed in the Law Courts, in Prosecution, in lawyers' offices, in State Security or in the departmental ministries;

(b) in the light of the principles set out in this resolution, to submit to the next plenary meeting a list of those presently employed in Party and governmental institutions who demonstrably took part in fabricating the trials or who are to blame for the delays in reviewing them, and to arrange that these people shall not in future hold important posts in the Party or Government;

(c) to ensure that the principles concerning Party and political responsibility set out in this resolution are implemented in the Party and the Administration with the help of Communists employed in the respective institutions;

(d) to arrange that the families of the victims, especially their children, be invited to discuss the Central Committee's findings, thereby closing in a dignified way this sad chapter in their lives.

V

In the interests of continued progress in building a socialist society it is the duty of our Party to draw the historical lessons from the political trials and from the delay in reassessing them – lessons concerning the Party's own mode of work and its organization, concerning the institutional organization of the socialist State and society and the framing of the legal code, so that a system capable of repeating the trials in any form shall never again be established.

The Central Committee sees the creation of a system of guarantees against any repetition of the trials as an inseparable part of its post-January policy and a part of its endeavour to eliminate the bureaucratic centralistic distortions of the political system. This is seen as a long-term process in which measures stemming from the experience of the trial reassessments will undoubtedly play an important part.

Conclusions concerning Party work to be drawn from the re-examination of the trials are:

1. The political basis for the trials and for the delay in reassessing them was provided by the regime of personal power, which was a product of the centralism and bureaucracy that deformed the political system. One feature was the immense concentration of political and economic power, together with an almost total lack of responsibility on the part of those who wielded that power and the impossibility of controlling them. This situation can be overcome and the danger of any return to that system eliminated solely on the basis of full democracy inside the Party, with the entire political system operating in a democratic way, and only if the Party exercises its leading role correctly in relation to the State and the community.

2. The key to eliminating the centralized bureaucratic concentration of power in the Party is to give greater weight to the whole range of its institutions (from branch meetings to the Central Committee), enabling them to decide at the appropriate levels on all fundamental issues and, simultaneously,

to control the work in practice. Insofar as it proves essential for these bodies to delegate decision-making on important matters of policy and personnel to any smaller Party bodies, they must without fail ensure proper control of decisions and maintain their responsibility for the measures taken.

3. A valuable guarantee against any repetition of the system of personal power can be provided by filling leading positions on a rota system; given the rotation of top personnel, a long-term, well-considered policy for appointments will gain in importance, and when a prominent man vacates his post this will no longer be seen as a punishment involving loss of political prestige and social status.

4. In electing or setting up collective bodies it will be necessary to ensure that professional functionaries and employees of the Party machine, and representatives of the Administration, do not form the majority in Party committees. This is the only way to prevent a return to the power structure of Party organization which, as a rule, brings together representatives of the chief instruments of power, whereas the Party should, on the contrary, control the work of these instruments by political means and with the utmost objectivity.

5. The Party cannot assert its leading role by violating the Constitution and the law. Deliberate violation of or disregard for the law must be considered as a gross breach of the Party rules. An especially strict view will be taken in the cases of those whose professions place them in authority over law observance; for instance, members of the judiciary and Security officers. The same view will be taken of those Party members who fail to act when cases of violation of law are brought to their notice, or who even try to prevent measures being taken. This principle means that a Communist has the right, and also the duty, not to abide by any Party resolution running counter to the Constitution and the law, and it will be his duty to inform the higher Party authorities in the event of such a situation arising.

6. A vital principle in Party work is to safeguard the rights of members and functionaries. Any important discussion concerning a question of membership shall take place in the presence of the member concerned. It is forbidden for Party

members to make statements in public – or in the Party – accusing any member of anti-State or any other dishonourable conduct without this conduct being first discussed and substantiated before the appropriate Party or Government body.

7. A real contribution to creating a democratic climate in the Party would be to provide opportunity for members and officials to exercise their rights and fulfil their duties. Democratic centralism – the guiding principle in Party organization – should operate so that the ability to act rests on carrying out resolutions in unity, and that committees are responsible for their decisions and policies to members and committees at lower levels.

8. At the time of the trials, ideological unity in the Party was insisted on to a degree that turned it into blind, unquestioning obedience to the directives and decisions issued by the leadership. To hold divergent views was classified as a hostile act incompatible with Party membership. Expulsion followed and sometimes even criminal proceedings. The trials contributed to this state of affairs, and this in turn generated more trials. The Central Committee proclaims that no one shall be prosecuted for his political views or subjected to surveillance by the Security services. Charges may be made only when there is evidence of an offence. Non-observance of this principle, in addition to being a breach of the law, will be classified as an offence against the standards of Party conduct.

As interpreted in the 1950s, 'ideological unity of the Party' ossified Marxist thinking: it severely restricted the Party's function, reducing it to an instrument for carrying out the orders of the group at the top without any share in framing policy. Ideological unity, if it is not to become a tool for manipulating committees and members, or a means of getting orders obeyed, must be the product of conflicting opinions and divergent views; unity has its main place in respect of the Party's basic aims as expressed in its programme or in the course agreed by its leading committees. But the members, or the committee, have the right to maintain a critical attitude even to a resolution that has been adopted – implemented it must be, and criticism may be voiced only within the Party.

After the past bitter experience the Party will never allow the demand for unity of views to be used again as an instrument for realizing the anti-Party and anti-socialist measures embodied in the political trials.

9. The experience of the reassessments indicates the need, in selecting functionaries and in all personnel work, to be guided by the qualities essential to a representative of the Communist Party. The trials and the system of personal power perverted the relationships among functionaries. Men who had been comrades for years and who had worked together became enemies overnight, hurling charges at each other, even to the point of imprisonment and execution. The men who were denounced or arrested were isolated, no one came to their help, although there were many who must have known that the charges were false; and they maintained this attitude even when they knew quite definitely that the trials had been rigged. Those who knew this were men who had lost their courage, their sense of truth, and justice, and of human relationships. Under the system of personal rule, when men were selected for the highest posts they were required to obey without question, to serve the ideas and pursue the aims of the men who wielded power. When we speak of the prime responsibility resting with the system of personal power, we should bear in mind that the system was the work of the top men in the Party, who applied it, shaped it and maintained it. When we choose administrators, therefore, we must, while requiring special skills and a devotion to socialism, give equal weight to such personal qualities as courage in upholding the truth and defending one's views, an aptitude for independent thinking, and a truly comradely attitude to one's fellows, to friends and colleagues.

10. A vital feature of a democratic political system is a precise definition of the authority assigned to the constitutional bodies, based on a socialist division of work, accompanied by strict respect for the independence of these bodies in fulfilling their State functions. This also applies to the relationships between the Party and the organs of State under the federal system of government. It is impermissible to restrict the Government and the other organs of State in the performance of their functions and to exclude them from exercising their

authority or taking decisions in any area where they alone are competent.

Similarly, the legislative assembly must be able to play its special role within the political system. Communist deputies are entitled when debating measures to state their views in the form of amendments, and if they find any measure to be in conflict with the Constitution and the legal code they should have the right, without laying themselves open to Party discipline, to abstain from voting. It would, however, be the duty of the deputies concerned to justify their stand to the appropriate Party committee.

11. The experience of the trials and of their reassessment reaffirms the absolute justification for firmly establishing the independence of the courts and for appointing independent examining magistrates. In this respect the renewal of the constitutional and administrative courts is a sound step. The Party holds that it is inadmissible for Party bodies to intervene in court proceedings, to decide about their conduct and findings, or to delegate such powers of decision, which are a matter for the courts alone, to any extra-judicial body whatsoever. Communists in the judiciary are under the solemn obligation, in the event of such cases arising, immediately to inform the appropriate Party Committee, which should then take the necessary action. The same procedure should apply where a Party or other institution shelters offenders from warranted sanctions, even if the offences are committed in fulfilment of decisions made by these institutions.

The Security Service occupies a vital and influential position in the machinery of power; the relationship of the Communist Party and its leadership to this Service is a crucial one, a relationship particularly liable to distortion under a system of personal power. The Central Committee considers it impermissible for Party institutions to use Security dossiers in forming opinions and making decisions about anyone holding an official post; it is equally a breach of the Party rules for Communists employed in Security to use their positions to collect information about functionaries for use by the Party. Since this has been common practice in the past, with Security dossiers on Party members and functionaries placed in Party files, with Security in its turn holding Party dossiers, it is essential that – insofar as it has not yet been done – each of the two sides should hand back to each other the appropriate files.

To give citizens greater security before the law, particularly those engaged in public life, it is essential that the duties of Police and State Security officers be redefined in the penal code, or in some other statutory measure, to exclude any abuse of technical equipment and operative methods and to provide the necessary legal safeguards.

VI

By preparing documentary evidence and by submitting and debating the Report on Completing Party Rehabilitation, and by adopting this Resolution, the Central Committee of the Communist Party of Czechoslovakia considers the work of the Commission to be completed.

VII

Truth and justice have been served by the debate which has taken place on this Report and by the adoption of its findings. This act has cleared the names and restored the honour of those Communists who, after many years of selfless work in the Party and in public life, became the innocent victims of the political trials. Honour has been restored also to their families.

With its assessment of the political responsibility resting on all the Party members who had anything to do with the trials, with preparing and conducting them, and subsequently with reviewing them, the Party has closed a chapter in its history. The Central Committee and other Party institutions will draw the necessary conclusions for their future work. The thorough and frank consideration of the causes and mechanism of the trials by the Central Committee is indicative of the Party's sincere desire to learn the lesson of this troubled period of its history.

The trials were not organized by the Party as a whole, and essentially they have always been alien to it. The Central Committee therefore decided, in the name of the entire Party and for the further progress of socialism, to re-examine with the utmost responsibility and objectivity the steps so far taken in reviewing the trials; in this resolution it has adopted measures to eliminate the distortions that Party and Government policy have suffered in the past and to create a system of institutional safeguards that will fully restore public confidence in the Party, the socialist State, its institutions and legal order.

POSTSCRIPT

WITH the knowledge gleaned from this Report, the reader may well ask if there is a danger of the trials being repeated. One would gladly answer, No! The Report rightly states that any return to the political trials of the 1950s would have catastrophic consequences for the Communist Party and for socialism.

True, there are many reasons for believing that Czechoslovakia may be spared that tragedy. For one thing, history knows of no mechanical repetitions. Although one could compare the situation since August 1968 with the years 1949–54, much has changed since then; the world, and specifically the socialist part of it – including Czechoslovakia – has experienced twenty years of dramatic events, full of hopes and disappointments, including relapses into the old maladies and errors; but lessons have been learnt and we have advanced somewhat.

The Czechoslovak public, Communist and non-Communist, can no longer be manipulated as in the 1950s. Although the full truth about the trials has been hidden away, as we have seen, in the safes, people have learnt quite a lot from the facts published via the press, radio and television between January and August 1968. The mass media in these months performed a magnificent service (despite some inaccurate and biassed reporting) in helping the public to understand what had gone wrong – the first barrier to any repetition. This, indeed, is one of the reasons why we can say that the eight months of the Prague Spring have not been lost. They can never be erased from the hearts and minds of the people, for they knew they were being told the *truth*, however unpleasant. That, of course, is why the mass media in Czechoslovakia have been so bitterly attacked by dogmatists at home and abroad.

The present leadership has, therefore, to reckon with public revulsion at any sign of disregard for legality. That is why

Dr Husák and President Svoboda have given repeated assurances that a return to the methods of the 1950s is impossible.
That is why a new tactic has had to be adopted: any decision
contrary to the Constitution and the law – and their number is
growing – must at least be 'legalized' after the event, if only by
emergency powers. Any disagreement with the leadership can
then be declared 'infringement of the law' and punished as such.
For instance, on 24 February 1970 Husák announced:

We have said many times, and we repeat today, that we shall not
permit any fabrications, imaginary offences or breaches of the law.
But that is only one side of the matter. In order that there shall be
no misunderstanding, we say with equal clarity that we shall use
all legal means to protect working-class power, the socialist order
and the international interests of the Czechoslovak State.

In other words, you will not be punished for your political views
if you hold your tongue and toe the line; indeed, we are so
magnanimous that we are willing to see that you are not put in
prison, but woe betide you should you dare to voice your
views in public.

Political opponents are, in the meantime, being 'politically'
exposed, isolated, stripped of all public positions and silenced.
These 'opponents' include Dubček and most of the Party
leadership of 1968 (many of whom, being victims of the trials,
could return to public life only after January of that year),
and with them the majority of the nation. That, according to
the present leadership, is where the matter is to rest. But, once
put in motion, the practices acquire an inexorable logic – either
the accusations levelled against the men of the 'post-January'
policy are justified, in which case punishment must be meted
out, or there will be no punishment, with the result that sooner
or later it will be seen that the whole business was simply a
smoke-screen with no substance behind it.

The difference this time is that the accused, the supporters of
Czechoslovak socialism with a human face, refuse to admit
'mistakes' and to beat their breasts to satisfy their judges and
redeem themselves. Dubček, Smrkovský, Kriegel, Vodsloň,
Miková, Slavík, Černý, Kosík and others not only refused to
indulge in self-criticism at the Central Committee meetings in

April and September 1969, they also made grave accusations against the present leadership; we, the 'accused', they said, are muzzled, while facts are being distorted, and those sitting in judgement on us have themselves, as members of the 'post-January' leadership, voted for all decisions, including the Action Programme and the calling of the Fourteenth Party Congress, and have condemned the Soviet invasion during the night of 21 August 1968! And so the 'accused' of today may easily become the judges of tomorrow, for today they are not alone, as Slánský, Clementis, Švermová and the others were alone; they know that the majority of the nation, including the Communists, are behind them; on all sides they feel this solidarity, often expressed in moving and utterly spontaneous ways.

Nor can one overlook the fact that today the judges, prosecutors, defence counsel and some Security officials are no longer willing to play their parts in blind obedience to the ruling group. They now consider the 'evidence' and hesitate; for they, too, were shaken by 1968 – some by the truth revealed, some quite simply by the realization that if the old system, seemingly entrenched for generations, had proved susceptible to change, the day might come when they would be called upon to answer for their deeds. Significantly, Dr Němec, Minister of Justice in the Czech Republic, complaining about the 're-luctance' and the 'softness' of the judiciary, found it necessary to call for a 'class approach' in administering the law.

We should not, however, have any illusion but that obedient instruments for perpetrating illegalities will be found. In the judiciary, for instance, many are compromised by their part in the major or minor trials of the past and would be only too willing to comply once more. This goes especially for some groups in Security, where many officers who were deeply involved in the brutalities of the 1950s have for this reason thrown in their lot with the occupation regime.

Lastly, the international situation suggests that a repetition is unlikely. Nowadays the quarrel with Yugoslavia has been replaced by the quarrel with China, and it would be difficult to accuse the advocates of socialism with a human face, label-led persistently as 'revisionists' and 'right-wing opportunists', of cooperating with the Chinese. (Though even this is possible: after August 1968, some Soviet newspapers accused both the 'Chinese adventurers' and the 'Yugoslav revisionists' of jointly, from different positions, aiding world imperialism.) But while propaganda at this level may or may not be swallowed by present-day Soviet readers it is altogether too transparent for Czechoslovakia. Moreover, the conflict with China drives the Soviet leaders to seek agreement with the USA, West Germany, France and other Western governments. For this they need the 'Czechoslovak affair' to be conveniently forgotten, so that they can pose as 'defenders of European civilization on the Ussuri River'. That being so, it would be inadvisable to shock public opinion in the West by resorting to political trials. There would be repercussions not only among the general public, but also among those Communist Parties that have reconciled themselves to the Soviet occupation of Czechoslovakia as a 'reality', but who could hardly swallow such a bitter pill as political trials. To do so would gravely endanger their precarious unity and their influence, especially among intellectuals, students and young people generally.

However, all these arguments need qualification. In the first place, there is danger, paradoxically, in the very fact that the people of Czechoslovakia – a large body of Communists and the overwhelming majority of the population – refuse to renounce the vision of socialism with a human face, to support the new leadership, or to regard the entry of the Warsaw Pact troops as anything but armed occupation. So the men in the Kremlin are dissatisfied with the present Czechoslovak leadership, and exert relentless pressure, through a small group entrenched in Security, in the Army, in the Party and in the Administration. This group of 'collaborators' lives in fear and trembling of an end to the military occupation, or indeed of any political change that might expose them to the wrath of the people.

For these reasons we are witnessing much that is all too reminiscent of the atmosphere that prevailed at the time of the political trials in the 1950s.

There is every reason to believe that the mechanism of persecution has been set in motion, and the lesson of the past is that a point is reached at which even the very best of intentions are powerless to apply the brakes. Admittedly, Husák and his colleagues are probably not subjected to the same exceptional external pressures as those brought to bear on Gottwald in his day. But they are definitely under pressure from the 'collaborators' at home, as being the only group on which they can rely in pursuing their highly unpopular policy.

With Soviet backing, this group is conducting a vendetta of lies and slander against the men and policies of 1968. Leaders who won popularity and the confidence of the people – a serious failing in the eyes of Brezhnev, Zhivkov, Ulbricht and Husák, who evidently think that a good Communist must necessarily be unpopular – are charged with undermining the Party's dominant position, and this despite the fact that few political parties have enjoyed such support as did the Czechoslovak Communist Party under Dubček's leadership. They are alleged to have trampled on friendship with the Soviet Union when in fact they were trying to put that friendship on a healthier footing, to have allied themselves with West German revanchists and American imperialists (with whom Brezhnev then negotiates), to have sought to restore capitalism (although Czechoslovakia, in contrast to East Germany, Poland and Hungary, has no private sector in trade, in the services or in agriculture), to have undermined economic management (when they were trying to rid it of bureaucratic ballast), to have thrown open the mass media to 'right-wing forces' (when they simply abolished censorship and put the media at the service of the public) – in short, they are accused of offences which, measured against the Soviet concept of socialism, merit the most severe punishment, and assailed with all the old weapons of the 1950s, including character assassination.

It is worth re-reading the notorious *White Book*, put out by the Soviet Press Agency in 1968, in order to compare this farrago of lies and half-truths with the current propaganda of the official Czechoslovak press and radio services, and the pretexts used to get rid of the men of 1968. We find the script prepared in Moscow is now being followed with a remarkable consistency. Facts have no meaning for men who can allow their imagination to run riot in this way. When, for instance, Tass named the former Minister of Foreign Affairs, Dr Jiří Hájek, as a 'Gestapo agent, formerly known as Karpeles' (a delicate way of suggesting – quite inaccurately – that he was a Jew), this Minister of an allied Government took the liberty of stating that he could not have been a Gestapo agent, since he had spent the entire war in a Hitler concentration camp as an anti-fascist, and that his name from birth was Hájek. Tass omitted to publish this statement, and Dr Hájek resigned his post shortly after – there can be no straying from the script.

Tass put out a similar item on 31 August 1968 about the author of this essay. The report, printed in *Pravda* on 1 September 1968, said that a Lebanese newspaper, *Al Chalder*, published an interview between Jiří Pelikán and a US Congressman, John Culver. I am quoted in *Pravda* as saying:

The leadership of the country must come into the hands of people who will be able to get Czechoslovakia politically and economically out of the clutches of Red ideology and turn her in a direction corresponding with Western traditions.

At the time I was Chairman of the Foreign Affairs Committee of Parliament, so I made a strong protest through the Ministry of Foreign Affairs of my country, stating that I had never given such an interview and asking for an explanation from the Lebanese paper. Whereupon the Czechoslovak Embassy in Beirut informed us that there was no periodical of that name in the Lebanon and that the Tass correspondent, not knowing Arabic, could offer no explanation – they should have verified the report in Moscow; meanwhile, Tass, *Pravda* and the Soviet Foreign Ministry continued to ignore my protest. Within a few weeks I was dismissed from my post as Director of Czechoslovak Television – and the interview that never took place was repeated almost daily by the 'Vltava' radio station, then broadcasting in Czech and Slovak under Soviet military control; months later, in April 1969, the Czechoslovak media again quoted the interview that never was.

When, in the autumn of 1968, the Bulgarian Government newspaper made the sensational disclosure that pornographic material and a portrait of Hitler had been found in my office, there was a burst of laughter in the studio as the item was transmitted by Czechoslovak television. Yet within a year a Brno magazine 'revealed' under the dateline 20 November 1969 that Jiří Pelikán must be 'a Gestapo agent', for he had 'managed' to survive imprisonment by the Gestapo during the Hitler occupation and during three years in the underground had evaded arrest and execution!

It would be ridiculous, if it were not so reminiscent of the accusations in the Report now before us, for instance in the case of Josef Smrkovský, and in the indictment at the Slánský trial, where almost all the accused were labelled as Gestapo agents and spies.

These slanders are reproduced through the mass media and at public meetings, while the victims are denied the opportunity of refuting them. Indeed, their statements are suppressed, their speeches at meetings of the Party Central Committee are kept from the public, the slanders are circulated and anonymous letters demanding exemplary punishment are given wide publicity. Note, too, that attacks of this kind are circulated by the official media even against men still in high posts, while the authorities pretend they know nothing, that it is the work of 'extremists'.

The leadership maintains that the purpose is to defeat the men of 1968 by 'political means'; to suggest that the campaign is a prologue to trials is to echo 'bourgeois propaganda'. But already voices are heard from below insisting that, if all that is said is true, then such grave offences cannot remain unpunished, while the newspapers are printing accusations which often read like formal indictments.

By way of illustration I quote from the article, 'Where Are the Roots of the Treason?', written by a group of Security officials and published in *Rovnost*, organ of the Party Regional Committee in Brno, dated 20 November 1969:

Pelikán was one of those concealed enemies who, operating on a long-term plan, seized and consolidated positions in order at a certain stage in political development to be sacrificed [*sic*]. We know, of course, how he organized and publicly appeared in campaigns that were in sharp conflict with the vital interests of the Party and State at home and abroad. On the strength of his position he sowed confusion directly or indirectly in important offices of State, he worked in a socially dangerous manner so that these offices could not fulfil their functions, facilitated their disintegration, and made it possible to disrupt the system of unified State power, including important international, economic and military interests of the Republic. In effect his actions were aimed in the most dangerous manner against the alliance with the Soviet Union and the other countries of the socialist world system, as embodied in the Constitution (Article 1, paragraph 3, and Article 14, paragraph 2).

This would be laughable, were not its very wording reminiscent of the indictment in the case of Rudolf Slánský and the 'Anti-State Conspiratorial Centre' in 1952.

The Czechoslovak Party leadership is known to have been divided about whether or not to bring some of the men of 1968 to trial. Should the men in the Kremlin insist on exemplary punishment, Husák, though reluctant, would be powerless to prevent it. Such is the logic of things once the need for Soviet intervention is seen as the sole defence against counter-revolution'. For, if they 'had' to intervene, then 'counter-revolution there must have been. And since there was 'counter-revolution' there must be counter-revolutionaries. And if there are counter-revolutionaries among us then they must be punished, for not to punish them would be to shield them.

Once the Soviet leadership and their Warsaw Pact allies had 'discovered' counter-revolution in Czechoslovakia they had to find proof of its existence, and willing helpers were available among those with experience of the years 1949-54. Evidence of their work is to be found in many speeches and articles; to quote but one, Pezlár, a Slovak Party official, writing in the Bratislava Party paper *Pravda* of 10 March 1970, while blandly admitting that there was still no complete analysis of events in 1968-70, asserted that he knew that

some groups investigating partial aspects have already arrived at notable conclusions. Even at the present stage of the analysis it can be confidently stated that in 1968 there was a concerted attempt by right-wing and anti-socialist forces to stage a counter-revolution.

Pezlár maintained with equal confidence that 'those at home and abroad who were organizing the counter-revolution drew on the Hungarian experience of 1956, but their aim was ideological destruction rather than armed terror'.

Again, in the journal *Život Strany* of 3 March 1970, we find an article on 'The Specific Face of the Czechoslovak Counter-Revolution', whose author, Václav Král, reveals 'three stages of counter-revolution':

> The first stage was to have ended with the Extraordinary Party Congress which would have elected a new Central Committee with a membership to suit the right-wing opportunists. The second stage was to decide the question of political power. Elections . . . at all levels of government were to be conducted according to the so-called plurality system. . . . The third stage was to see the all-out social-democratization of Czechoslovakia.

Horrified by this 'counter-revolutionary' prospect of a Congress and democratic elections, the author breathed a sigh of relief: 'Thanks to the military intervention by the Warsaw Pact armies not even the first stage could be completed.'

Nor does the argument that the Soviet leadership does not want trials really hold water. The hard fact is that Brezhnev went further with Czechoslovakia in 1968 than Stalin did with Yugoslavia in 1948. And, while the split with China calls for agreement with the West, it also demands 'iron discipline' among the European socialist countries, for in the event of a conflict the Soviet Union will need a reliable hinterland. Nor should it be forgotten that long after the wave of trials had ended, even after the Twentieth Congress of the Soviet Party, we had the secret trial and execution of a Communist, Nagy, and some of his colleagues in Hungary. And did not Kádár say in a broadcast just after the 1956 uprising: 'We have pledged that no judicial proceedings will be taken against Nagy and his friends'? Did he not say at a Central Committee meeting in March 1957: 'At the time when it might have been appropriate to try Nagy we were not strong enough. Today, when we are strong enough, there is no point in holding a trial'? And when Gomulka visited Budapest in May 1958 did not Kádár assure him that 'the problem of Nagy will be solved without bloodshed'? (See Peter Gosztony in *Schweizer Monatshefte*, 2 May 1958.) And yet, not long after, Nagy and his colleagues were convicted at a secret trial and Nagy was executed. The public, both in Hungary and abroad, heard the news after the execution had taken place. One doubts if this was the personal wish of Kádár, once Nagy's comrade; it is more likely that he gave in to the external pressure demanding that someone must pay for the counter-revolution. One is forced to ask, will someone have to pay for the Czechoslovak 'counter-revolution'? Who will be the 'Czechoslovak Nagy'?

Something like a blueprint for a future trial, or at least for a political onslaught, has been emerging more clearly in recent times. There is no longer talk of aggressive designs by West Germany or the United States, there is less of an outcry about the 'Two Thousand Words' and other matters used to justify the invasion. Today the spotlight is on the 'second centre' in the Party, alleged by Dr Husák in a speech to the Central Committee in September 1969 to have been 'organized before January 1968(!) . . . After January it pursued its own aims as a second centre' – naturally, anti-Party, anti-Soviet, out to seize power in the Party. The claim is that the 'centre' consisted of some members of the Dubček leadership (Kriegel, Smrkovský, Špaček, Slavík, Mlynář), the former City Committee of the Party in Prague together with the 'Prague intellectuals' (historians, lawyers, sociologists, political scientists, artists and others), also referred to as 'the brains trust of the counter-revolution', and last, but certainly not least, 'the mass media'. Articles in the Soviet and Czechoslovak press (East German and Bulgarian papers, too, have been quite zealous) suggest that the 'centre' had links with imperialist intelligence services in West Germany and the USA, who were evidently the main instigators of the events after January 1968, with the strategic aim of breaking Czechoslovakia's alliance with the USSR, and securing successively her departure from the Warsaw Pact, her neutrality, and finally her accession to Nato with the idea of building a bridgehead in Czechoslovakia for an aggressive war against the Soviet Union and the other socialist countries!

A grave accusation indeed! The very label is a warning, for Stalin's opponents in the Soviet trials were dubbed 'the parallel centre', Slánský and his comrades were condemned to death for their part in an 'anti-State conspiratorial' – or 'second' – centre. The authors are certainly consistent; or are they just incapable of inventing anything new?

The tactics of the plan outlined above are as follows: to discredit the leading men of the centre (that means the men of 1968), to accuse them of being careerists and adventurers, of maintaining 'contact with the West', to force them to indulge in self-criticism, or to muzzle them and banish them from all public posts, deprive them of parliamentary immunity or anything that might protect them. Then they must be isolated (by exile from the capital, posting abroad or arrest) and separated from the 'misled', that is those who are willing to admit their errors and are given the opportunity to make amends by supporting the leadership and acclaiming the occupation, whereby they are discredited, demoralized and so tied hand and foot to the ruling group. Stupendous efforts are made to convince the public that it was misused for dubious ends; but Husák and his associates have no illusions that they are succeeding. That, clearly, is why they have decided to postpone the Party Congress, to postpone a general election, to 'nominate' Members of Parliament and members of Party committees (thereby ignoring the Party rules, which require a Congress to be held in 1970, and the Constitution, which has no provision for bypassing elections).

Meanwhile, since the public cannot be won over by persuasion, it is hoped that resistance can be curbed by creating an atmosphere of fear. Thousands, tens of thousands, indeed hundreds of thousands of Party and non-Party 'right-wing opportunists' are being thrown out of their positions in public life, or made to resign 'voluntarily'; they are dismissed from their jobs, entire organizations are dissolved (the Students', Journalists', Film and Television Workers' Unions, the Coordinating Committee of Art Unions) and their funds impounded; scholars of international repute are expelled from the universities and the Academy of Sciences, hundreds of journalists are out of work or are forced to seek employment in agriculture or other manual labour, regardless of their state of health. Despite occasional assurances by the leadership that there is no question of revenge, in reality an avalanche has been set in motion. And all this regardless of the catastrophic effects on the economy, science and culture.

Observers in other countries tend to think that, since as yet no arrests have been made, things cannot be so bad. They overlook, however, the fact that since 1969, when Husák replaced Dubček and the public made its attitude clear on the occasion of the first anniversary of the Soviet occupation, hundreds of people have been arrested, for 'offences' which are named – and in reality as acts of outright political persecution. Thus hundreds have been sentenced on charges of 'disseminating illegal leaflets' simply because they distributed texts of speeches, for instance, by Dr Kriegel (while still a Member of Parliament) to the Party Central Committee, and by the journalist Karel Kyncl to a meeting of the Prague City Committee of the Party. Hundreds convicted of 'offending an ally' had simply declared aloud their disagreement with the Soviet occupation. The writer Škutina and the chess master Pachman were arrested for 'offending a public official', because they had dared to criticize Dr Husák, First Secretary of the Party – while simultaneously the State Radio was daily offending another public official, Alexander Dubček, then President of the National Assembly. The historian Tesář and the sociologist Battěk were in prison for months merely because they took the liberty of presenting a petition to official quarters criticizing present policies. True, none of the top men has yet been arrested, but does not the experience of 1949–54 show that minor violations of the law come first – as precursors of the big events?

There are other aspects of policy dangerously reminiscent of the past. To enumerate a few, very briefly: Professor Šik, author of the economic reform that never came to life, is made the scapegoat for economic breakdowns; censorship has been restored and has been even more rigid than under Novotný; intellectuals are accused of obstruction, workers of idleness; there is interference with writers, artists and scholars, restriction of travel abroad; highly qualified people are replaced by incompetent yes-men, snooping and informing are encouraged (for example, by the Minister of Education, Hrbek) – in short, there has been a return to the state of affairs existing

long before 1968, the full consequences of which will be felt
in the days to come.

Comparing, then, the arguments for and against the likelihood of a repetition of the political trials, one can perhaps
conclude that the situation is not auspicious for a repeat of
the show trials of the 1950s. There will evidently be trials, but
they may not be so ostentatious, nor are they likely to be held
in public or to result in sentences calculated to put the men of
1968 out of the way for a long time and thus scare those who
might want to support them.

Yet the biggest show trial of the century is already under
way, with all the people of Czechoslovakia and hundreds of
thousands of Communists in the dock, charged with aspiring
to build a just and free socialist society. Though physical
death may not be the penalty in this trial of a nation, its toll in
human demoralization may well be enormous, for the faith in
socialism and the prestige of the Communist Party are likely
to be shattered for years to come; the cream of the nation will
be cast out into the wilderness. The people will be condemned
to live in an atmosphere of fear and conspiracy, unable to seek
a way out of the crisis, waiting until the accumulated tensions
burst out in an explosion far louder than that of January 1968.

Some of our friends may object that we are over-concerned
with the problem of trials in the socialist countries, when
similar injustices take place every day in the capitalist world.
Of course, we are not such egoists as not to feel that suppression
of freedom anywhere is our concern. When from January to
August 1968 we tried to rid socialism in Czechoslovakia of its
inhumanity, we believed we would thus gain the moral right
to condemn injustice wherever it occurred; one cannot condemn political trials in Greece, for example, and suffer them
in one's own country – to do so would be hypocrisy, not
solidarity.

The question remains whether the trials and the illegalities
that have disfigured socialism can be described, as they are
in the socialist world and by the authors of the Report (who,
of course, could not know at the time of writing that the
tragedy would recur so soon), as *deformace* – 'deformations' or
distortions. That term implies something alien, not typical.

Unfortunately, however, these evils occurred to a greater or lesser extent in all the socialist countries. Again, it may be objected that other revolutions, too, have 'devoured their children'; yet the socialist revolution was to have been distinguished from all others by a new quality of freedom. The question, especially for Communists and Socialists, should surely be: what is the fundamental fault in the one system of socialism realized so far that leads it, almost automatically, to injustice and persecution?

The documents now before us are confined to examining the consequences of Stalinism in Czechoslovakia; the Commission did not probe – nor was it empowered to do so – the roots of these evils in the first socialist country, the USSR. For one cannot take seriously the official Soviet contention that the 'cult of the personality' was a mere aberration, the work of Stalin in his latter years. The true causes call for a profound study by those who see socialism as the only alternative for modern society.

The main question, then, remains unanswered – were these 'deformations' the inevitable accompaniment of the attempt to build the new socialist system, or were they an accidental occurrence that could have been avoided?

The reader may well put another question to us: 'Is it possible, after all that has happened, to retain a belief in socialism?' It is not easy to give a truthful answer. The more sincere and noble the hopes reposed in socialism, the greater the disappointment is liable to be. Yet, paradoxical as it may seem, the document before us now attests the strength of socialist society which, having the courage to diagnose its own disease, seeks to achieve its own renaissance. And the proof of this was the 'Czechoslovak Spring', when from January to August 1968 Czechoslovakia was, in the words of the Austrian Marxist Ernst Fischer, 'the freest land ever known'.

The sceptical reader may object: 'True, but the attempt failed!' That would be a mistake – the Czechoslovak attempt to build socialism with a human face did not fail; on the contrary, in a very short time it won over the overwhelming majority of the people and it worked miracles. Just because of its remarkable success, and of the wide international support that it enjoyed, it could not be crushed by any ordinary kind of putsch, and an army, half a million strong, had to be brought in to do the job. In the 1950s it was enough to destroy a few score men in order to silence the entire nation; today that is no longer possible. The nation has seen that socialism can be different, and that is where its sympathies lie. In defeat, therefore, there is the germ of victory.

We Czechoslovak Communists, especially those of my generation who have grown up under socialism and devoted the best years of our lives to it, are painfully aware of our responsibility – if only through ignorance – for what happened. We welcomed 1968 with enthusiasm, seeing it as the last chance to restore the socialism of which we had dreamed. For the present we have failed; and it will only be possible to go forward once more on the new foundations that will be laid by the present spontaneous movement of resistance to the occupation and oppression.

The new feature is that some Communists – and all patriots – refuse to wait passively; they reject the false unity and discipline that would make them accomplices in a new tragedy. The trials have taught them that it is their duty to reject Party decisions that run counter to the law, decisions that conflict with the Party's aims and with their own conscience. There is, as yet, no organized action, but growing numbers of Communists at home and abroad are realizing that something has to be done. A situation entirely unique for a socialist country has developed – discontent is gradually finding expression in underground resistance, while those who are, for the present, in exile can be the voice of the movement abroad. They can expound and evolve the post-January policy, prepare ideas for the future when – perhaps in a different form – it will be possible to continue in the endeavour to revive socialism. They can contribute by their experience to the socialist and progressive movement throughout the world, of which they are a part. For a truly humane and just socialism new paths are needed, paths indicated by the Communists, non-Communist Marxists and Socialists who, in many countries, are thinking and acting in a new way.

The Prague Spring was a courageous attempt to step out

along one of the possible paths. What we see on trial this time is not just a group of political leaders, but the entire people of Czechoslovakia, who wholeheartedly supported the concept of socialism with a human face. They have been put on trial by those who place their own power above the interests of socialism. But no matter what sentence is imposed, no matter what they may have to endure, this people, too, will live to experience rehabilitation.

Jiří Pelikán

INDEX OF NAMES
WITH BIOGRAPHICAL NOTES

Abbreviations

CC	Central Committee
CP	Communist Party
CPC	Communist Party of Czechoslovakia
CPS	Communist Party of Slovakia
CPSU	Communist Party of the Soviet Union
CSSR	Czechoslovak Socialist Republic
n	footnote
Parl.	Parliament (i.e. National or Federal Assembly), Parliamentary
SDP	Social Democratic Party

A single date following particulars of an appointment, membership of a committee, etc., normally refers to commencement – the date of termination being unknown, or unimportant, or stated or implied later in the entry.

Abakumov, Viktor Semyonovich, Beria's Deputy Minister of State Security; conviction and execution announced Dec. 1954 – p. 22

Aleš, Václav, prosecutor in Slánský trial 1952; Deputy Prosecutor-General 1952–3 and 1956–9, Prosecutor-General 1953–6, Director of Law Institute of Ministry of Justice from 1959 – pp. 125–7, 149, 184–98 *passim*, 212

Andropov, Yuri Vladimirovich (b. 1914), head of Fourth European Department of Soviet Foreign Ministry 1953, Counsellor at Soviet Embassy in Budapest 1953–4, Ambassador 1954–7. Now Minister of Security and member of Politburo – p. 219

Arazin, Security interrogator – pp. 83, 102, 135

Babej, Petr, farmer, member of Parl. from 1945, of CC CPS 1945–52, of CC CPC 1949–52. Head of regional agricultural committee of CPS in Prešov, Chairman of Ukrainian National Council in Czechoslovakia; accused of 'Ukrainian nationalism' and relieved of all offices Dec. 1952 – p. 254

Bacílek, Karol (b. 2.10.96 near Poděbrady in Bohemia), went to Slovakia 1919, joined CPC 1921, Party official in Slovakia from 1924. Lenin School in Moscow 1930–31; emigrated to Moscow 1939. Took part in Slovak National Uprising 1944. A secretary of Slovak Party Secretariat 1945, Chairman of Slovak National Council 1950–51, Minister of State Control 8.9.51 to 22.1.52, of National Security 23.1.52 to 14.9.53, Deputy Prime

of CP of Eastern Slovakia was responsible for terrorist campaign to abolish Greek Catholic Church (merging it with Orthodox Church) and suppress Ruthenian minority (his own), declaring them to be of Ukrainian nationality; these measures, designed to subordinate population to USSR, exacted a heavy toll of lives, and earned him membership of CC CPC June 1954, of Presidium Nov. 1954. Commissioner for Education and Culture in Slovakia Dec. 1958. Member of Parl. 1960, CC secretary 1962, Deputy Chairman of Slovak National Council 1960–63, member of Parl. Presidium 1964. Succeeded Dubček as First Secretary of CPS 1968. Failed to win election to any post at Slovak Party Congress Aug. 1968. Was in secret touch with Soviet leaders, and on returning from Moscow after Soviet occupation was reinstated in Party Presidium, in charge of international relations – pp. 30, 185, 241

Bína, A., employed in Personnel Department of CC CPC – pp. 67, 84, 96, 134, 251

Boček, B., general, Chief of Staff of Czechoslovak Army – p. 176

Boyarsky, Vladimir, Soviet security adviser in Prague. According to Agence France Presse and United Press International (20.1.70), returned to Czechoslovakia for 'consultations' – pp. 80, 93, 103

Bránik, Július (b. 1.9.08), related to Široký. Pre-war lawyer in Levoča, 1939–45 in Moscow, working for radio and Comintern press. Member of Central Planning Commission 1945, also of CC CPS and Economic Commission. Deputy Chairman of Slovak Planning Office in Bratislava March 1948, member of CC CPC 1949–54, of Presidium of CC CPS 1953, Chairman of Slovak Planning Office 1953, later accused of 'nationalism'. Head of a research institute of Ministry of Finance 1956 – pp. 74, 269

Brezhnev, Leonid I. (b. 19.12.06), graduated from technical school for soil improvement 1927, then studied metallurgy. Regional secretary of CPSU 1938, a political commissar, then major-general during war. Member of CC CPSU 1952, then of Presidium and a secretary of CC. Chairman of Presidium of Supreme Soviet 1960–64, succeeded Khrushchev as First Secretary of CC CPSU 14.10.64 – pp. 311, 315

Brichta, V., historian – pp. 67 n, 102 n, 108 n

Brieger, arrested in Field case – p. 77

Brumhofer, Security officer – p. 252

Bulander, R., general in Czechoslovak Army; Military Attaché in Paris 1944–6, head of Military Department of President's Office 1948–51, imprisoned 1951, died after rehabilitation – pp. 47, 96, 185, 211, 228

Čech, Josef, high-ranking Security officer in 1940s and 1950s, later served in Bulgarian Security. With other Security officers, accused of murder 1968; trial later adjourned *sine die* – p. 252

Čepička, Alexej (b. 18.8.10), joined CPC 1929, imprisoned during Nazi occupation. Minister of Internal Trade, then Justice, then National Defence; Deputy Prime Minister 1950–56. Married Gottwald's daughter. Member of Presidium and Political Secretariat of CC CPC 1951; of Politburo 1954.

Relieved of offices for 'deficiencies and mistakes in the execution of his duties' April 1956; expelled from Party for 'major part in organizing political trials against Communists in the personality cult period' April 1963 – pp. 21, 103, 106, 111–12, 117, 130–31, 138, 170, 172, 189, 192, 202, 209, 230–31, 233, 235–6, 244, 249–53, 257, 270–72, 292

Čermák, Ladislav, Security interrogator; later arrested, sentenced, rehabilitated, emigrated to Israel – p. 102

Černý, Alfred, chief secretary of South Moravian region, expelled from Party after making critical speech at CC session of May 1969 – pp. 308–9

Černý, Karel, head of organizational and personnel sectors of Security, sentenced at trial of 'anti-State group in Security' Dec. 1953; later released and rehabilitated – pp. 70, 95, 122

Černý, Oldřich, sentenced in trial of 'Trotskyist Grand Council' Feb. 1954. Died through denial of medical treatment in prison – p. 122

Chernov, J., one of Soviet advisers sent to Prague to organize Slánský trial – p. 109

Chlebec, Emil, deputy to Slovak Commissioner for Agriculture 1954, candidate member of CC CPC 1950, chairman of regional committee of National Front in Košice 1960; member of Parl., chief secretary of West Slovak regional committee of CPS – p. 236

Clementis, Vladimír (20.9.02 to 3.12.52), lawyer in Bratislava, defended Communists in pre-war trials, joined CPC 1924, member of Parl. 1935–8 and 1945–51; war years in West; having criticized Soviet-German Pact of 1939, expelled from Party, reinstated 1945. Leading Slovak politician: State Secretary 1945, Minister of Foreign Affairs 1948. Member of CC CPC 1949. Expelled from Party 1951, executed with Slánský 1952. Rehabilitated and Party membership posthumously restored 1963 – pp. 15, 18, 48 n, 70, 74–5, 87–90, 98, 113, 128, 167, 193–4, 225, 234, 236, 254, 275–6, 309

Colotka, Petr (b. 1920), Associate Professor of Civil Law and Vice-Rector of Bratislava University; Professor 1960. Member of Bureau of Bratislava committee of CPS 1962. Member of International Court at The Hague 1962. Commissioner of Slovak Board of Justice 1963–8, member of Ideological Commission of CC CPC from 1963, of its Legal Commission from 1964. Deputy Prime Minister April 1968, elected to Party Presidium Aug. 1968. Chairman of Federal Assembly from 1969, Prime Minister of Slovak Socialist Republic from May 1969 – p. 241

Culver, John, member of US Congress – p. 312

Cvik, Rudolf (b. 21.7.23), joined CPS 1945. Chief secretary of regional Party committee in Bratislava 1953–6. Member of Parl. from 1954, studied at Party School in Prague 1956–9. Chief secretary of regional Party committees 1959–68. Candidate member of CC CPC 1962–6, full member 1966. Worked in Second Department of Foreign Ministry from April 1968 – p. 241

David, Jaroslav, Deputy Prosecutor-General 1953, First Deputy Prosecutor-General 1956 – p. 225

occupation, in Mauthausen concentration camp 1941–5. Member of CC Secretariat from 1945, of CC from 1946, of Parl. from 1948; secretary to CC CPC 1951. Secretary of regional committee in České Budějovice 1952–3, of Politburo 1958, of Presidium 1962. Chairman of Ideological Commission of CC 1965–8. In spring 1968 relieved of offices because of his violent criticism of Writers' Union; since Soviet occupation has published pseudonymous attacks on progressives – pp. 108, 186, 216–17, 219, 222, 230, 234–6, 238, 250 n

Hladký, Milan (b. 7.11.25), joined CPC 1951, lecturer in town planning at Bratislava Technical College 1952–6. President of Union of Slovak Architects 1959–64, chief architect of Bratislava 1962–4. Member of Parl. from 1964. Chairman of municipal national committee 1964–9. Member of CC CPC from 1966. Minister of Building and Technology of Slovak Socialist Republic Jan. 1969 – p. 35 n

Hlína, Jan (b. 14.5.10), joined CPC 1945, leading secretary of regional committee of CPC in Plzeň 1953–62. Candidate member of Politburo 1958–62, member of Parl. from 1960. Vice-Chairman of Party Control Commission of CC 1962–8, member of Defence and Security Committee of Parl. April to Dec. 1968, of Federal Parl. from Jan. 1969 – p. 222

Hloušek, E., employee of judiciary – p. 240

Hložková, Vera, imprisoned and forced to act as main witness in trial of 'bourgeois nationalists' and to witness against Šváb in Slánský trial – p. 194

Hodinová-Spurná, Anežka (12.1.95 to 1.4.63), joined CPC 1921, various Party and public functions 1921–9. Member of Parl. 1929–39. In leadership of Czechoslovak Communists in Britain and member of State Council 1939–45. Member of CC CPC 1945–54, of Parl. and its Presidium 1945–63. Candidate member of CC CPC 1954–8, full member from 1958. For many years chairman of Committee of Czechoslovak Women, vice-chairman of International Federation of Democratic Women, and of Czechoslovak Committee of Defenders of Peace – pp. 73–4

Hofman, Leopold (b. 16.11.13), joined CPC 1932, fought in Spanish Civil War, political commissar of Dimitrov battalion 1937–9, interned in France 1939–40, joined Czechoslovak Army abroad 1940, returned Prague 1941, instructor in illegal CPC 1941–2, in Mauthausen concentration camp 1942–5. Security officer 1945–8, personal Security officer to Gottwald 1948–51; commander of head office of police force 1951; arrested 1951, imprisoned till 1953. Worked in industrial cooperative for nine years, chairman of regional committee of South Bohemian industrial cooperatives 1962–8, member of South Bohemian regional committee of CPC from 1964, of Parl. from 1964, of Party Control Commission from 1966. Member of Presidium and chairman of Defence and Security Committee of Parl. April to Dec. 1968; member of Rehabilitation Commission of CC April 1968, of Presidium of Federal Parl. and chairman of Defence and Security Committee Jan. to Oct. 1969, when removed from all posts – pp. 12, 35 n, 120

Holátko, Bohumír – pp. 122, 162

Hruška, Čeněk (17.1.89 to 1969), joined SDP 1912, Red Army after Revolution. Member and official of district and regional committees of CPC 1921-4, member of Politburo 1924, of Parl. 1925. Imprisoned for political work and deprived of seat 1933. Sent to USSR, worked in executive of Comintern. Joined Czechoslovak unit in USSR 1943, as political worker in tank brigade; returned Czechoslovakia 1945. Member of CC 1945. Chairman of Union for Cooperation with Army 1951-61 – pp. 172-5, 177, 179, 185, 250 n, 252-3

Husák, Gustav (b. 10.1.13), joined CPC 1933, secretary of Society for Cultural and Economic Relations with USSR 1937 till war, then worked illegally. Member of illegal leadership of CPS 1943. During and after Slovak National Uprising Vice-Chairman of Slovak National Council and Commissioner for Interior. Vice-Chairman of CPS Sept. 1944, Commissioner for Transport and Public Works Sept. 1945, Chairman of Board of Commissioners Aug. 1946. Member of Presidium of CC CPS, and of CC CPC, 1949. Member of Parl. 1945-51. Expelled from CPC and arrested Feb. 1951, sentenced to life imprisonment 1954. Released 1960, rehabilitated and reinstated in Party 1963. Worked on building sites 1960-63, on research staff of Institute of State and Law, Slovak Academy of Sciences, 1963-8. Deputy Prime Minister April to Dec. 1968. First Secretary of CC CPS and member of its Presidium Aug. 1968 to April 1969; coopted to CC CPC and Presidium Aug. 1968, also member of Executive Committee of Presidium; chairman of Council for Defence of the State Nov. 1968 to April 1969. First Secretary of CC CPC and member of Secretariat from 17.4.69; Commander of People's Militia from May 1969. Member of Presidium of Federal Assembly from Jan. 1969. Order of Klement Gottwald 1968, Soviet Order of Lenin and title 'Hero of the CSSR' 1969 – pp. 12, 23, 74, 89-90, 119, 125-6, 128, 155-6, 193, 206, 213-14, 226, 234, 236, 242, 254, 308, 311, 314, 316-18

Infner, Štefan – p. 35 n

Innemann, Květoslav (b. 29.6.10), joined CPC 1928, arrested by Gestapo 1939, spent war in Dachau and Buchenwald. After war chief secretary of regional Party committees in Ústí nad Labem and Ostrava. Employed at Party Central Office 1953-9. Member of Parl. 1948-54; Director of Publishing House of Political Literature 1959-68. Member of CC CPC 1945-62, candidate member 1962 – pp. 149, 152, 159, 172, 180, 182, 226, 237, 251, 253

Jančík, Vojtěch, pre-war Party member, in Britain during war, economist, imprisoned and released 1958 – pp. 123, 155, 212, 226

Jankovcová, Ludmila (b. 8.8.97), joined SDP 1922. Member of Parl. from 1946, Minister of Industry 1947, member of CPC from 1948. Minister of Food 1948-54, Deputy Prime Minister 1954-63, candidate member of Politburo from 1954 and of Presidium of CC CPC 1962-3. Expelled from Party 1970 – pp. 222, 234, 236, 250 n, 253

war. Director of Czechoslovak Radio 1945-8. Member of CC 1946-52, Ambassador in Moscow 1948-9, Deputy Minister of National Defence 1950-52, candidate member of CC, head of International Department of CC 1961-4, full member of CC since 1962, member of Parl. since 1964 and Chairman until 1968. Member of Presidium of CC March 1966 to April 1968. (In a note to Novotný the Spanish War veterans, demanding an end to discrimination, expressed lack of confidence in Laštovička.) Chairman of Parl. Committee for Foreign Affairs and member of Presidium of Parl. from 1969 – pp. 28-9, 74, 223, 227-8, 241

Laušman, Bohumil (30.8.03 to 9.5.63), Social Democratic member of Parl. 1935-8, spent war in London as member of State Council. Social Democratic member of Parl. 1945-8, Minister of Industry 1945-7. Chairman of SDP 1947, removed from leadership 1948. Went abroad 1949, kidnapped and brought back to Czechoslovakia 1953. After ten years in jail, died in Ruzyň prison under suspicious circumstances – pp. 197-200

Leflerová, Helena, from Lidice, Czechoslovak village destroyed by Germans, sent with other Lidice women to concentration camp 1942. Elected to Parl. 1948, member of CC CPC 1958, chief secretary of CC of National Front and member of Presidium and chairman of Parl. Committee for Foreign Affairs 1960; lost these posts after Novotný left office – pp. 223-4

Lenárt, Jozef (b. 3.4.23), joined illegal CPC 1943, worked in Slovak Party apparatus 1948-50, member of CC CPS 1950-53. Deputy Minister of Light Industry 1951-3, attended Higher Party School in Moscow 1953-6. Member of CC CPS 1957-66 and of its Secretariat 1958-62, of CC CPC from 1958, of Parl. from 1960. Member of Presidium of National Front and of CPS, later of CPC. Prime Minister Sept. 1963 to April 1968. Candidate member of Presidium of CC CPC from April 1968, full member from Jan. 1970; member of Secretariat from 1968. First Secretary of CPS from Jan. 1970 – pp. 223, 235-6, 241-2

Lenert, official of Ministry of Justice – p. 124

Lettrich, Josef, member of Slovak Democratic Party, emigrated 1948, died beginning of 1970 – p. 156

Lewinter, Matyáš, imprisoned economist – pp. 126, 296

Lichnovský, M., historian – p. 82 n

Likhachev, Soviet adviser, high-ranking officer in Soviet Security Service, conviction and execution announced in *Pravda* Dec. 1954 – pp. 22, 76, 80-81, 93

Linhart, Security interrogator – p. 83

Litera, Josef, First Deputy Minister of Justice 1955, Deputy Minister of Justice from 1960 – pp. 149, 160, 182

Löbl, Evžen (b. 14.5.07), studied economics at School for World Trade in Vienna, joined CPC 1934, spent war in England, economic adviser to Jan Masaryk (Foreign Minister in Government in exile). Departmental head at Ministry of Foreign Trade and member of Presidium of Economic Commission of CC CPC 1945. Deputy Minister of Foreign Trade 1948; sentenced to life imprisonment in Slánský trial 1952. Released 1960,

Associate Professor of General Theory of the State 1964. Secretary of Legal Commission of Party Central Committee 1964-8, member of Secretariat 1968. Served as Secretary to CC June to Nov. 1968, member of Presidium Sept. to Nov. 1968 when he resigned all offices. Now working in entomological department of National Museum in Prague – p. 316

Mlýnek, see Mlejnek

Molotov, Vyacheslav Mikhailovich (b. 1890), held high Soviet Party and Government posts until 1957, when expelled from CC CPSU as member of dogmatic group engaged in Stalinist activities – p. 216

Moravec, employed in Personnel Department of CC CPC 1950 – p. 96

Morozov, G., one of Soviet advisers sent to Prague to organize Slánský trial – p. 109

Moškovič (also referred to as Moško), Koloman (b. 2.9.06), joined CPC 1925, member of CC 1934-6, spent war in Britain. High posts in Slovak Party 1945-50. Expelled from CPC and imprisoned 1952, rehabilitated and reinstated in CPC 1963 – pp. 74, 83, 116, 123, 155, 226, 236, 254, 276, 296

Moučka, M., Lt-Col. in Security 1953, awarded Order of Labour for part in organizing Slánský trial; in charge of investigation of Švermová case, and member of political commission that fabricated trial of 'bourgeois nationalists' 1954 – pp. 114, 123, 126, 161, 182, 252

Mudra, Security officer – p. 135

Müller, M., member of Kolder Rehabilitation Commission 1963 – p. 233

Musil, Security officer, awarded Order of the Republic for part in organizing Slánský trial – p. 114

Nagy, Imre (1896 to June 1958), fought in Red Army 1918-19, in Hungary for duration of Hungarian Republic. Returned to Hungary with Red Army 1944. Member of Politburo and a Minister, Prime Minister and representative of the 'new course' July 1953 to April 1955. Forced out of political life by Rákosi at end of 1955, but was again Prime Minister Oct. 1956. During revolt was given asylum in Yugoslav Embassy. When Kádár guaranteed his safety, left building but was handed over to Soviet authorities and interned in Romania. Later brought back to Hungary, sentenced to death and executed. On tenth anniversary of his death, long obituary published in *Literární Listy,* weekly paper of Union of Czechoslovak Writers (no. 16 of 13.6.68) – pp. 315–16

Nebesář, Social Democrat, chairman of board of National Bank 1945, later sentenced and imprisoned – p. 200

Nečásek, František, head of Cultural Department of President's Office 1948-53, chairman of OIR (international radio organization) 1955, Director of Czechoslovak Radio and Television 1956, chairman of State Committee for Radio and Television 1957, Director of State Publishing House of Literature, Music and Art 1960 – p. 250 n

Nechanský, major in Czechoslovak Army, executed 1949 – p. 198 n

Nejedlý, Zdeněk (10.2.78 to 9.3.62), Professor of Musical Theory at Prague University 1908, joined CPC 1929, spent war in Moscow, Minister of

Education and member of Parl. 1945, member of CC CPC 1946. Minister of Labour and Social Security 1946–8, of Education, Science and Art 1948–53, chairman of Czechoslovak Academy of Sciences 1952, Minister without Portfolio 1953 – p. 250 n

Nekvasil, M., Security interrogator – p. 135

Němec, Jan (b. 1914), member of Parl. for SDP (from which later expelled) 1946, for CPC from 1948, secretary of CC of Union of Czechoslovak-Soviet Friendship from 1950. Minister of Justice in Czech Socialist Republic from 1969 – p. 309

Neurath, Alois (b. 29.8.86 in Vienna), foundation member of CPC (German section), a secretary of CC until 1926, dismissed for 'factional activity'. Expelled from CPC 1929 – p. 175

Nikliček, L., historian – p. 87 n

Nosek, Václav (26.9.92 to 22.7.55), founding member of CPC, secretary of a section of International Trade Union Association. Member of CC CPC from 1929. Arrested and imprisoned 1939, then emigrated to Britain, member of State Council in London 1941, of Presidium of CC 1945–54, Minister of Interior 1945–53, of Labour 1953–5 – pp. 15, 74–5, 82, 250 n, 251 n, 255

Nová, wife of Vilém Nový, arrested 1949, released 1951 – p. 77

Novák, František, sentenced as member of 'Trotskyist Grand Council' – p. 122

Novák, Jaroslav, chairman of senate of State Court in Prague which tried Slánský 1952 – p. 110

Novák, Zdeněk, general, Commander of Third Military Region, imprisoned 1951 – pp. 47, 96, 185

Novomeský, Ladislav (b. 27.12.04), joined CPC 1926, poet, editor of Communist newspapers and journals, member of CC CPS 1944, Commissioner for Education 1945–50, member of Parl. 1949–51, expelled from CPC and imprisoned March 1951, sentenced to 10 years as 'Slovak bourgeois nationalist' April 1954. Released Dec. 1955, on staff of *Kulturný Život* 1963–8, rehabilitated May 1963, member of Ideological Commission of CC CPC from Sept. 1963. Elected to CC Aug. 1968, coopted to CC at session of 31 Aug. Member of Presidium of CC CPS from Aug. 1968, of Presidium of Slovak National Council from Jan. 1969 – pp. 89–90, 125–6, 156, 193–4, 236, 242

Novotný, Antonín (b. 10.12.04), joined CPC 1921, member of regional committee of CPC in Prague 1935, arrested by Gestapo 1941, in Mauthausen concentration camp until 1945. Chief secretary of Prague region 1945, member of CC CPC from 1946, of Parl. from 1948. A secretary of CC and member of Political Secretariat 1951. Deputy Prime Minister Jan. 1953. After death of Gottwald, First Secretary of CC CPC. Elected President of the Republic 19.11.57. Lost post as First Secretary Jan. 1968, resigned as President and from Presidium 22.3.68. Party membership suspended at CC session May 1968, but Soviet occupation interrupted investigations into guilt in connection with political trials and execution of innocent Commun-

joined CPC 1945, served on a Party district committee and in local government. Deputy Commissioner for Building 1951–4, member of CC CPS and its Bureau from 1953, Vice-Chairman of Board of Commissioners, member of Parl., director of Hydroprojekt in Bratislava. Minister of Transport and Communications of Slovak Socialist Republic since Jan. 1969 – p. 205

Sedláková, Mária (b. 6.8.22), joined CPC 1945, on editorial staff of Slovak Party paper *Pravda* 1949–68, studied at Slovak Party Political School, member of West Slovakian regional Party committee 1960–66. Elected to CC CPC 1966, coopted to CC CPS April 1968, member of CC Commission for Completing Party Rehabilitation from April 1968. Editor of *Pravda* May 1968 to Jan. 1969. Elected to CC CPS Aug. 1968. Minister of Labour and Social Welfare of Slovak Socialist Republic from 1969 – p. 35 n

Sedmík, V., CP member, unjustly imprisoned – p. 212

Šik, Ota (b. 11.9.19), in Mauthausen concentration camp 1940–45, joined CPC 1945, worked in regional Party committee in Prague and studied at university 1945–50, followed by a year at Party Political School. Head of Department of Economics at Higher Party School. Professor of Economics from 1953. Candidate member of CC CPC 1958–62, Director of Institute of Economics of Academy of Sciences 1962–9, chairman of Czechoslovak Economics Society 1962–8, member of CC CPC 1962–9. Deputy Prime Minister April to Sept. 1968, responsible for implementation of economic theories, member of Economic Council. Elected to CC and Presidium Aug. 1968. In Yugoslavia Aug. to Dec. 1968, now in Switzerland – p. 318

Šimek, J. – p. 241

Simone, André (27.5.95 to 3.12.52), joined German CP 1922, CPC 1946. Journalist and head of German publishing house, International Aid to Workers, 1922–32. In USSR 1932–3, Paris 1933–41, later London. Served in Czechoslovak Army in France, then went to Mexico. Returned Czechoslovakia 1946; appointed commentator on foreign affairs to *Rudé Právo*. Unjustly imprisoned and executed with Slánský; rehabilitated 1963 – pp. 48 n, 70, 108, 113, 128, 236

Šimůnek, Otakar (b. 23.10.08), joined CPC 1934, deputy director of consumer cooperatives 1948. Deputy Minister of Food 1949–51, Minister of Chemical Industry 1951–4. Member of Parl. and of CC CPC from 1954, chairman of State Planning Office 1954–8. Candidate member of Politburo 1954–8, full member and chairman of State Planning Commission 1958–62. Deputy Prime Minister 1959 to April 1968. Czechoslovak representative at Council for Mutual Economic Assistance, member of Party Presidium 1962–8 – pp. 217, 253

Široký, Viliam (b. 31.5.02), joined CPC 1921, secretary of various regional committees, member of CC 1930–8, of Parl. from 1935, candidate member of Executive Committee of Comintern 1935, chairman of regional committee in Bratislava 1938. When Party dissolved, emigrated to France, then to Moscow and worked for Comintern; returned Slovakia, arrested by Gestapo 1941; escaped to Moscow Jan. 1945. Deputy Prime Minister 1945–53,

member of Parl. from 1960. Minister of Interior 1961–5, member of Party Secretariat 1965–8, chairman of CC commissions 1965–9, Deputy Prime Minister and Chairman of Economic Council April to Dec. 1968. Member of Executive Committee of Presidium Nov. 1968 to April 1969, Presidium member, CC secretary, and chairman of Bureau for Directing Party Work in Czech Lands from Nov. 1968, deputy to First Secretary of CPC June 1969, chairman of State Council for Defence of Czech Socialist Republic from April 1969, Commander of People's Militia in Bohemia and Moravia from July 1969. Chairman of Federal Government from Jan. 1970 – pp. 223, 227

Stýblo, František, judge of State Court, member of bench in Slánský trial – pp. 110, 225

Šubrt, Security interrogator – p. 83

Šváb, Karel (13.5.04 to 3.12.52), brother of Marie Švermová. Pre-war Party member, sent to Sachsenhausen concentration camp by Nazis. Head of security sector of Party Secretariat from 1945, then head of Security and Deputy Minister of Interior. Imprisoned and executed with Slánský – pp. 48 n, 57, 67, 72, 74–7, 80, 82–4, 89–90, 93, 97, 102, 104, 113, 129, 131, 134–5, 163, 178–9, 182, 224, 230, 251–2, 261, 270, 296

Švach, E., Deputy Prosecutor-General – pp. 124, 149, 152, 160, 181, 182, 207, 225, 240, 253

Švermová, Marie (b. 17.8.02), wife of National Hero Jan Šverma, killed in Slovak National Uprising 1944, sister of Karel Šváb. CP member from 1921. Party official until 1926 when she went to USSR to study at Lenin Academy in Moscow for two years. Member of CC from 1929, directed work among women. In USSR 1939–45. Member of Parl. 1945–51, head of Organizing Department at Party Central Office from 1945, Presidium member from 1946, one of the deputies of the Party General Secretary from 1949. Expelled from Party Feb. 1951. Imprisoned; sentenced for life 1954. Released 1956, worked at Museum of Czechoslovak Literature 1958–62. Legally rehabilitated 1963 but not fully reinstated politically. Member of CC of Union of Czechoslovak Women April 1968 to Jan. 1969. Awarded Order of the Republic 1968 – pp. 65, 68, 90, 95, 97–9, 101, 120, 123–4, 128, 131, 149, 151–3, 158, 171, 180, 195, 209, 212, 225–6, 236, 250 n, 252, 254, 267, 273–4, 294, 296, 309

Svoboda, A., political commissar in International Brigade. After war, headed Military Section of Central Party Office in Prague, Lt-Col. in Czechoslovak Army, unjustly imprisoned – p. 185

Svoboda, Jan, head of Novotný's secretariat, then head of a department of CC CPC – pp. 159, 252

Svoboda, Ludvík (b. 25.11.95), lecturer at Military Academy in Hranice 1931–4, Commander of Czechoslovak Army Corps in USSR during war, promoted to general 1945. Minister of National Defence 1945–50, Deputy Prime Minister 1950–51, member of CC 1949–52 and of Presidium to 1951. Stripped of all posts after Slánský trial and investigated by Security. Accountant to a collective farm 1953–5, member of Presidium of Parl. and of Parl. Agricultural Committee, head of Klement Gottwald Military Academy 1955–8. Member of Presidium of CC of Union of Czechoslovak-Soviet Friendship 1957, retired 1959; later member of commission for electing judges to Supreme Court and military courts. President of the Republic since 30.3.68, coopted to CC CPC Aug. 1968, member of Executive Committee of Presidium Nov. 1968 to April 1969. Awarded the title Hero of the Soviet Union, and the Gold Star of a Hero of the Soviet Union, also Order of Lenin and Order of Suvorov – pp. 20, 22, 47, 117, 176, 254, 308

Swiatlo, officer of Polish State Security – p. 76

Synková, H., employed in Records Department of CC CPC 1950 – pp. 82, 96

Syrovátková-Palečková, Marie, member of Parl. for Brno – p. 92

Szönyi, Tibor, sentenced to death with Rajk in Budapest – p. 73

Szücs, colonel in Hungarian State Security – pp. 73, 75

Tannenbaum, A., regional Security secretary in Karlový Vary until 1949 – pp. 67–8, 275

Taufer, Jiří (b. 5.7.11), joined CPC 1930, translated books from Russian. Emigrated to USSR 1939, employed at Publishing House of Foreign Literature and Moscow Radio. Member of Party CC 1946–9, Ambassador to Yugoslavia 1948–9, candidate member of CC 1949–52. Deputy Foreign Minister 1949–50, Deputy Minister of Information 1950–53. Member of CC Press Commission connected with preparations for Slánský trial. A Deputy Minister of Culture 1953, First Deputy 1954. Now Cultural Attaché at Embassy in Moscow – p. 252

Taussigová-Potůčkova, Jarmila, pre-war Party member, sent to Ravensbrück by Nazis. After war worked for Party Control Commission and was member of CC. Imprisoned 1951 – pp. 67–8, 84, 94–5, 99, 108, 119, 124, 128, 182, 213, 236, 251, 254, 261, 270, 296–7

Tesář, historian – p. 318

Tesla, Josef (22.2.05 to 29.4.63), joined CPC 1921, Party official 1922–38, in Buchenwald 1939–45. Secretary of Party regional committee in Hradec Králové 1945–7, CC official 1947, candidate member and secretary of CC CPC 1952, member of Presidium 1953–4. Minister of Labour 1955–7, member of Party Control Commission from 1960. Member of Parl. from 1945 – p. 250 n

Thoř, military expert, wrote an untruthful report for 1952 trial – p. 185

Tito (Josipz Bro) (b. 1892), President of Yugoslavia – pp. 19, 52

Togliatti, Palmiro (1893–1964), General Secretary of Italian CP – p. 10

Tonhauser, Pavol (b. 27.1.09), head of Control Commission of Slovak Trade Union Council 1950–53, member of CC CPS 1954, chief secretary of regional Party committee in Banská Bystrica 1955–9, candidate member of CC CPC 1958, member of Parl. from 1958, chairman of regional national committee in Central Slovakia 1960. Order of Labour 1959 – p. 185

Trudák, Karel, Chairman of bench of State Court that passed death sentence on Horáková, Buchal, Pecl and Kalandra 1950 – p. 110